A-Z OF CARS
OF THE
1980s

A-Z OF CARS OF THE 1980s

Martin Lewis

BAY VIEW BOOKS

Published 1994 by
Bay View Books Ltd
The Red House, 25-26 Bridgeland Street
Bideford, Devon EX39 2PZ

Edited by Mark Hughes and Edward Herridge
Typesetting and computer make-up by Chris Fayers

ISBN 1 870979 54 0

Printed in Great Britain by
Butler & Tanner Ltd, Frome, Somerset

Jacket pictures: David Hodges, Neill Bruce

INTRODUCTORY NOTE

In common with its sister volumes, this book describes all cars that were on sale in the UK during the 1980s, but not overseas-built cars - including many US models - that were never offered here. In entries covering more than one model, the performance figures quoted are those of the fastest model for which independently verified magazine statistics are available. Our thanks are due to the editors of *Autocar* (to September 1988), *Autocar & Motor* (from September 1988) and *What Car?* for permission to publish these figures. The author, Martin Lewis, participated in road-testing by all three of these magazines during the decade.

KEY

Information in each entry is given in the following order:

MODEL NAME. Years of manufacture (production figures). Body styles available. Engine position/driven wheels, cubic capacity (engine configuration, number of cylinders, valve gear).

Abbreviations

F/F	–	front engine, front-wheel drive
F/R	–	front engine, rear-wheel drive
F/4×4	–	front engine, four-wheel drive
R/R	–	rear engine, rear-wheel drive
R/4×4	–	rear engine, four-wheel drive
M/R	–	mid engine, rear-wheel drive
M/4×4	–	mid engine, four-wheel drive
S	–	in-line engine
V	–	vee engine
HO	–	horizontally opposed engine
OHV	–	overhead valves
OC	–	single overhead camshaft
DOC	–	double overhead camshaft

AC (GB)

Britain's oldest car maker came to real fame in the 1960s with the Carroll Shelby-inspired Ford V8-powered Cobra. But its successor, the Frua-bodied 428, lacked the same brutal flair, finally fading from the scene in 1973. The Hurlock family, owners of AC Cars since the 1930s, continued development of the 3000ME, which after seemingly endless motor show appearances finally struggled into limited production, which ended in 1984. Autokraft and Ford eventually became equal partners in AC Cars, owning between them the initials AC and the Cobra name.

3000ME. 1979-84 (prod: 82). 2-door 2-seater coupé. M/R, 2994cc (V6 OHV). Max speed 125mph, 0-60mph 8.5sec. AC bought the Maxi-powered Diablo prototype in 1973, suggesting that within a year the 3000ME would be on sale. Five years later it was. With a transverse, mid-mounted Ford 3.0 V6 engine driving the rear wheels, but with only 138bhp, the 3000ME was short on the sort of performance its looks suggested. The monocoque chassis, with wishbone suspension front and rear, was clad with glass-fibre bodywork. Handling also left something to be desired, despite assistance from the aerodynamically-deployed under-bumper spoiler at the front.

ALFA ROMEO (I)

Determined to keep the name Italian, Fiat acquired Alfa Romeo from a state-controlled finance organisation, which had owned it since the mid-1930s, to prevent it falling into Ford's hands. The larger cars were built at the Alfa Nord plant in Milan, while the smaller ones came from the Alfa Sud factory near Naples. During the 1980s, the complex range of saloons and coupés was pruned back drastically as major efforts were made to improve build quality.

SPIDER 2.0. 1970-93 (prod 82,500). 2-door 2-seater convertible. F/R, 1962cc (S4 DOC). Max speed 121mph, 0-60mph 8.9sec. A real throwback to the days of kaftans and flower power. It started as the pretty Pininfarina Duetto, but with advancing years suffered from middle-aged spread. Safety requirements meant changes front and rear, with heavy bumpers. Built as LHD only, but one dealer (Bell & Colvill) and later importers offered an RHD conversion in the UK. The 2.0 twin-cam engine gave 120mph performance, but neither handling nor ride managed to progress much further than the late-1960s.

ALFASUD. 1972-83 (prod 567,093 all models). 2/3/4/5-door 4-seater saloon/hatchback. F/F, 1286/1351/1490cc (HO4 OC). Max speed 101mph, 0-60mph 11.8sec. Alfa went downmarket, looking for volume sales with the flat-four engined, front-drive Sud. A factory was built at Poligliano d'Arco, near Naples, to relieve unemployment in the area. Four-door fastback saloon body lacked looks, while base models with four-speed gearbox and rubber mats were built down to a price. But it did not take long for people to discover two things: the amazingly sure-footed handling and the meaning of instant rust. And many never did discover that the heater fan was worked by rotating the windscreen wiper stalk...

ALFASUD TI. 1974-81 (prod 156,000). 2-door 4-seater saloon. F/F, 1351/1490cc (HO4 OC). Max speed 118mph, 0-60mph 9.8sec. One thing was obvious with the 'ordinary' Suds – the chassis could handle more power with ease. And the two-door-only TIs proved this, with the flat-four engine breathing through a single twin-choke carburettor, but with more ambitious camshaft timing. The 1.3 gave 86bhp, while the 1.5 put out 105bhp. A wider track and alloy wheels made handling even better, while looks were improved with a four-headlamp grille, a boot lid spoiler and black wheelarch flares. Before anyone had thought about 'hot hatchbacks', this Sud signposted a 1980s phenomenon.

ALFASUD SPRINT. 1976-90 (prod 96,450). 2-door 4-seater coupé. F/F, 1286/1351/1490/1712cc (HO4 OC). Max speed 115mph, 0-60mph 9.1sec. Underneath this attractive shape lay a more or less standard Sud floorpan and suspension. As well as the 1.3 and 1.5 engines, the 118bhp 1.7 version of the flat-four finally proved that the chassis really was as good as everyone thought. And in place of the plain saloon body was an elegant coupé design from Giugiaro's ItalDesign studios. Clean-lined early cars looked the best, a 1983 facelift bringing a chunkier nose, heavier bumpers, unsubtle side rubbing strips and loads of matt black trim. As with so many Alfas, the driving position was uniquely Italian and most foreigners found it difficult to adapt.

33. 1983-94 (prod 196,300). 5-door 5-seater hatchbacks. F/F, 1350/1712cc (HO4 OC). Max speed 117mph, 0-60mph 9.1sec. It was Fiat in Turin rather than Alfa Romeo in Milan which decided that the replacement for the Alfasud should be brought back closer to the Alfa image. Although the 33 was only a couple of inches longer than the Sud, it ran on a 10in longer wheelbase to become a family-sized, four-door hatchback. The same flat-four 'boxer' engines were used, but while the handling was still good, it had lost that magic edge which had distinguished the Sud. Softened responses and the Italian notoriety for rust contributed to poor sales compared with the Sud, even though the 33 became a much sharper driver's car into old age.

33 SPORTWAGON. 1985-90 (prod 64,120). 5-door 5-seater estate. F/F or F/4×4, 1490/1712cc (HO4 OC). Max speed 120mph, 0-60mph 8.9sec. Considering Alfa's pedigree, the move into estate cars might have seemed odd. But the market was booming, and the front-drive 33 was the right platform. The simple 4wd system on the 1.5 was designed for snow and ice driving rather than performance, a feature that made this car all the more strange at a time when other manufacturers were selling 4wd to sporting drivers. Even the front-drive models had the anything-but-level load platform, needed to accommodate the rear diff on 4wd models.

ARNA. 1984-86 (prod 61,750). 4-door 5-seater hatchback. F/F, 1186/1490cc, (HO4 OC). Max speed 108mph, 0-60mph 10.2sec. An ill-matched marriage between Alfa Romeo and Nissan which ended in thankful and mutual divorce. The idea was for Nissan to establish a foothold in Europe, with Alfa Romeo putting its flat-four engines into Cherry bodyshells. The result was a car which people regarded with a good deal of justifiable doubt. Alfa dealers sold it as the Arna, Nissan dealers as the Cherry Europe – but it offered neither Alfa flair nor Nissan build quality. It was an episode that both firms will wish to forget – and that you had probably forgotten already.

ALFETTA. 1972-84 (prod 424,739). 4-door 5-seater saloon. F/R, 1962cc (S4 DOC). Max speed 111mph, 0-60mph 9.8sec. Don't be deceived by those rather conservative looks, because there was plenty of new engineering under the skin. The twin-cam 2.0 engine, at first with twin Dell'Orto carbs but later with fuel injection, developed 130bhp, enough to give this bulky saloon a top speed of 110mph plus. The gearbox was now in unit with the final drive to give better weight distribution, but the gearchange could be frustratingly awkward because of its long linkage. De Dion suspension geometry was used at the rear. Even now, Alfa's build quality was still suspect.

GIULIETTA. 1977-85 (prod 255,762). 4-door 5-seater saloon. F/R, 1570/1779/1962cc (S4 DOC) Max speed 107mph, 0-60mph 10.6sec. At least Alfa Romeo had the good grace to call this the Nuova Giulietta, because to a degree it was trading on past reputation. The rakish, angular bodywork concealed the fact that this was nothing more than an Alfetta underneath. The engine range, however, was wider, with 109bhp 1.6 and 122bhp 1.8 versions in addition to the 130bhp 2.0. Although never sold in the UK, Alfa's first diesel-engined car was a Giulietta...

GTV. 1976-87 (prod 196,724). 2-door 4-seater coupé. F/R, 1962cc (S4 DOC). Max speed 118mph, 0-60mph 9.8sec. To many the epitome of what an Alfa Romeo should look like. The ItalDesign body had all the right elements, with the traditional Alfa grille a prominent feature. But once more the Alfetta supplied the basis for the GTV, using a slightly shortened wheelbase. The lighter, smaller body, with the rear-mounted gearbox, meant that the handling felt superbly balanced – provided you could come to terms with curiosities like the driving position and the speedometer's location in the centre of the facia on early cars. A proper tailgate was a useful feature, but luggage space was pitifully small. Only a 2.0 version was available from 1980 (there were 1.6 and 1.8 models earlier), the year of an exterior facelift.

GTV6. 1981-87 (prod 83,097). 2-door 4-seater coupe. F/R, 2492cc (V6 OC). Max speed 127mph, 0-60mph 8.6sec. Just when it seemed that the Alfetta ideas bin must be all but empty, Alfa gave the GTV the shot of sporting adrenalin it needed. The new V6 was everything an Alfa engine needed to be: smooth, lusty, musical and great to look at. With Bosch L-Jetronic injection, it gave 160bhp, enough to give a top speed close to 130mph. Pirelli P6 tyres and a limited slip diff helped the handling, but even so this was never a car to be treated lightly – but it could be hugely rewarding to drive. Humped bonnet with plastic insert distinguishes it from the four-cylinder GTV.

75. 1986-92 (prod 187,300). 4-door 5-seater saloon. F/R, 1779/1962cc (S4 DOC), 2492/2959cc (V6 OC). Max speed 134mph, 0-60mph 7.9sec. At-a-stroke replacement for the Alfetta and Giulietta, with purposeful, quirky looks. Engines spanned descriptions from the ordinary to outstanding. New was the 2.0 Twin Spark with variable valve-timing, while the familiar 2.5 V6 was joined by a 188bhp 3.0 version. The rear-mounted gearbox was retained, with the change as baulky as ever. Near ideal weight distribution gave well-balanced handling. The interior 'design' bordered on the chaotic, with window switches on the roof, an awkward U-shaped handbrake and an anatomically impossible driving position.

ALFA 6. 1980-85 (prod 81,750). 4-door 5-seater saloon. F/R, 2492cc (V6 OC). Max speed 121mph, 0-60mph 11.4 sec. In the Alfa Romeo tradition, this was a car which simply did not seem to fit in. Big and looking slightly dated, it did have the splendid 2.5 V6 engine in the UK, but mated to a three-speed ZF automatic. The engine started life with three twin-choke carburettors, but switched to injection in 1985, by which time it could reach 120mph with 158bhp and low gearing. This cumbersome machine did nothing to alter Italy's reputation for building naff executive cars.

164. 1988 to date (prod 127,700). 4-door 5-seater saloon. F/F, 1962cc (S4 DOC), 2959cc (V6 OC). Max speed 138mph, 0-60mph 7.5sec. Out of the window went practically every one of Alfa's traditional ideas. The result was what has to be the greatest Alfa model for years. The sleek Pininfarina saloon body looked exactly right, while the transversely-mounted Twin Spark 2.0 and superb 3.0 V6 provided the performance – and with front-drive too. The handling felt as good as the car looked, although torque steer on early V6 models could catch the unwary. The interior design was a little unusual. And amazingly, this is an Alfa which seems to last...and last. The last of the quartet of cars to appear using the Type Four platform (the others were Fiat Croma, Lancia Thema and Saab 9000), it was also undoubtedly the best. A landmark in Alfa's regeneration?

ALPINA (D)

Starting in the mid-1960s with a mildly-tuned BMW 1600, Burkhard Bovenseipen established Alpina (the name came from the make of the typewriters his father repaired) as a marque in its own right. His other business is as a wine wholesaler. Connections with BMW are very close, with just enough distance being maintained to allow Alpina to develop specialist models in small numbers which would be impossible for the Munich factory.

C2. 1987-91 (prod 1500). 2-door 5-seater saloon. F/R, 2693cc (S6 OC). Max speed 142mph, 0-60mph 6.3sec. Forget any idea that the C2 is just a tuned BMW 325. Out goes the standard 2.5 engine, replaced by a long-stroke 2.7 developing 210bhp. Add to this Alpina's own very special suspension changes, with Bilstein dampers, 16in alloy wheels and limited slip diff, plus a purposeful-looking body kit and you have a car which new cost more than a Porsche 944. But at least it still carried the full BMW warranty.

B10/B12. 1987-92 (prod 1200). 4-door 5-seater saloon. F/R, 3430cc (S6 OC), 4899cc (V12 DOC). Max speed 171mph, 0-60mph 6.8sec. BMW felt that an M7 version of its 7 series saloon would not be in line with the company's image so Alpina was able to step in with the B12. Freed from the German industry's 155mph 'agreement' on top speed, the B12 rocketed to 171mph. The standard 535i-based B10 was not that far behind – and Alpina also experimented with a twin-turbocharged 400bhp version.

AMERICAN MOTORS (USA)

Founded 40 years ago with the merger of Nash-Kelvinator and Hudson, although the initials AMC were not used until 1968 on the Rambler range. The company bought Jeep in early 1970, and in 1979 it signed a deal to build and distribute the Renault Encore in North America. Acquired by Chrysler in 1985, with the Jeep now the only former AMC model still in production, and very successfully.

PACER. 1975-80 (prod: n/a). 3-door 4-seater hatchback/estate. F/R, 3799/4235cc (S6 OHV), 4979cc (V8 OHV). Max speed 96mph, 0-60mph 11.2sec. Nightmare creation which was meant to rival the Ford Pinto and a growing number of Japanese imports. Weird styling had right-hand door longer than left-hand one (the idea was to allow easier pavement-side exit for passengers in the US), and did nothing for UK sales, which were even more minimal than hoped for. Blundering engines provided gutless performance, while both ride and handling were best described as awful. *Motor* magazine was forthright in its condemnation and ut a memorable headline on one 1976 cover: 'We test the Pacer (and wish we hadn't)'.

ARO (ROM)

Very much a state-owned operation, which also produced the Renault 12-based Dacia passenger cars. Versions of the uncompromisingly basic four-wheel drive utilities were built in Portugal - hence the name Portaro - using Daihatsu diesel engines.

240. 1982-86 (prod n/a). 4-door 5-seater estates. F/4×4, 2660cc (S4 OHV). Max speed 71mph, 0-60mph n/a. It was only in the closing days of the decade that we realised just what had been going on politically in Romania. The ARO was very much a military vehicle dressed up with a different paint job for the export market. Big thumping diesel gave just 70bhp, so on-road performance was hardly impressive. Independent front suspension seemed overly-complex for such a vehicle. The main attraction, if it could be called that, was the low price.

ASTON MARTIN (GB)

Founded in 1913 by Bamford and Martin, the company name inspired by Lionel Martin's many successes in his Singer specials at the Aston Clinton hillclimb. DB range started with industrialist David Brown buying the company in 1947. Fortunes fluctuated until liquidation in 1975. In 1980, the company was bought by CH Industrials and Pace Petroleum, with Victor Gauntlett as executive chairman. Three years later a majority shareholding was taken by US distributors, but Ford's acquisition of a 75 per cent stake in 1987 has at last resulted in a secure future.

V8. 1972-90 (prod 2000 approx). 2-door 4-seater saloon. F/R, 5340cc (V8 DOC). Max speed 145mph, 0-60mph 6.6sec. Apparently ignoring all the financial crises about it, the V8, which Aston Martin insisted on calling a saloon, went about its majestic if increasingly anachronistic way. When the power of the hand-built all-alloy V8 engine was finally disclosed, it turned out to be a mere 305bhp – or just 18bhp more than Jaguar's V12. Automatic transmission became virtually standard, although there was a five-speed manual for muscular heroes. Considering its sheer size, the V8 had confident, if not exactly nimble, handling. By the time it gave way to the Virage in 1990, the basic design was 25 years old.

V8 VANTAGE. 1977-89 (prod 313 saloons, 116 convertibles). 2-door 4-seater saloon/convertible. F/R, 5340cc (V8 DOC). Max speed 168mph, 0-60mph 5.9sec. The V8 engine had piled up enough competition miles for the experience to be put into what was then Aston's most powerful and quickest production model ever. Engine tweaks included revised camshafts, manifolds and inlet valves, giving a claimed power increase of 40 per cent. The sound and sight as 432bhp (the ultimate power output available from 1986) hurled this huge car to 60mph in under 6sec was an experience indeed. The Volante convertible joined the saloon in 1986, both versions being recognisable by a blanked-off front grille and deep spoiler.

VOLANTE. 1978-90 (prod 810). 2-door 4-seater convertible. F/R, 5340cc (V8 DOC). Max speed 130mph, 0-60mph 7.0sec. With all its coachbuilding experience, Aston Martin did not have to turn to any outside help to develop the Volante convertible, based on the 305bhp V8. Extra body stiffening and a power hood system increased the weight, which, with the less efficient aerodynamics, made the car rather slower. But with most production going to the USA and the Middle East, that hardly mattered. The Volante was all about image...

ZAGATO. 1986-87 (prod 75). 2-door 2-seater sports coupé/convertible. F/R, 5340cc (V8 DOC). Max speed n/a, 0-60mph n/a. In the early 1960s, just 19 examples of the Zagato-bodied Aston Martin DB4GT were built, and those that remain are now worth a fortune. While the spiritual successor of the 1980s, produced by Zagato on the Vantage chassis, may have cost a fortune, few people would now put money on it ever achieving much more than curiosity value, thanks to its bulk and instantly dated looks. A top speed of nearly 190mph was touted, but never independently verified. Nevertheless, the limited run of Zagatos – 50 coupés and 25 convertibles – was snapped up in a market of investment hysteria, giving Aston Martin a lifeline during one of its most shaky periods.

VIRAGE. 1990 to date (prod 370). 2-door 4-seater coupé. F/R, 5340cc (V8 DOC). Max speed 155mph, 0-60mph 6.5sec. Against the mighty V8, the Virage has smooth, elegantly understated looks, penned by John Heffernan. With the aluminium bodywork a tribute to the panelbeater's art and skills, and a hand-assembled engine (look for the builder's name on the side), the six-figure price should come as no surprise. With new four-valve cylinder heads (developed by Callaway Engineering in the USA) and a catalytic converter, power was declared at 310bhp, backed with a huge 340lb ft torque. Although physically bigger than the V8, the car actually looks smaller – and certainly feels so to drive with its poised handling and ride.

Lagonda. Above: pre-1987 facelift. Below: post-facelift

LAGONDA. 1976-90 (prod 610). 4-door 4-seater saloon. F/R, 5340cc (V8 DOC). Max speed 135mph, 0-60mph 8.3sec. Proximity switches, high-tech electronics, 'TV' screen instrument displays and 101 other innovations went into this William Towns-designed razor-edged saloon. But most went by the board in favour of more conventional equipment after endless development problems. Quite unmistakable styling, initially futuristic but quickly becoming dated, even after the 1987 revamp. The Lagonda's problem was that it never quite seemed to know its object in motoring life, but its rather tasteless opulence – white upholstery was common – found favour in Middle East markets.

AUDI (D)

One of the more complex histories attaches to the Audi name, which first appeared on a Horch-designed car in 1909 - Horch translates into 'hark' in English and 'Audi' is the Latin equivalent. During 1932, Audi became part of the Auto Union, with Horch, Wanderer and DKW. After World War II, the Zwickau plant, by then in East Germany, was taken over to produce the Trabant. The Audi name and the four interlinked Auto Union rings were revived by DKW at its Ingolstadt factory in 1965, with Volkswagen becoming the parent company. Audi's place in the market is now as the upmarket alternative to the VW range.

80. 1978-86 (prod 3.1 million). 4-door 5-seater saloon. F/F or F/4×4, 1588/1781cc (S4 OC), 1921/2144cc (S5 OC). Max speed 120mph, 0-60mph 8.8sec. This was the 80 which managed to break away from immediate Volkswagen influence, no longer being Passat-based but the north-south engine layout remained. Among major changes seen in 1983 were the arrival of the 2.0 five-cylinder engine in the CD, plus the high-performance but short-lived 2.1 136bhp quattro version. This was replaced by a slower four-cylinder 1.8 version using the same 112bhp engine as the sport in the autumn of 1984, ahead of the introduction of the 90 range.

90. 1984-86 (prod 97,302). 4-door 5-seater saloon. F/F or F/4×4, 1994/2226cc (S5 OC). Max speed 118mph, 0-60mph 9.0sec. Audi decided to give its five-cylinder engined 80s a new image, with the new 90 title and higher specification, although the same bodyshell was kept. There were just two models, with the two-wheel drive using the VW Passat's new north-south 2.0/115bhp engine, and the four-wheel drive quattro, launched a few months later, having a larger, 2.2/136bhp version. The two versions were like chalk and cheese: the front-drive car was very stodgy, but the quattro had fine performance, impeccable handling and exquisite steering.

100. 1976-83 (prod 1,609,829). 4-door 5-seater saloon. F/F, 2144cc (S5 OC). Max speed 119mph, 0-60mph 11.1sec. Anxious not to lose any hard-fought market share to BMW or Mercedes-Benz, Audi dropped its new five-cylinder engine into the existing 100. Why five cylinders? It was a matter of space, a six being too long to fit. Audi's claims that the five was as smooth as a six were never quite born out, but the result was a quick, comfortable and spacious saloon. Equipment levels were high, with power steering standard.

100 AVANT. 1977-82 (prod 132,333). 5-door 5-seater hatchback. F/F, 1588/1994cc (S4 OC), 2144cc (S5 OC), 1986cc diesel (S5 OC). Max speed 108mph, 0-60mph 10.7sec. If the 100 saloon played it straight down the line with just one engine, the Avant had a far wider range for buyers to pick from. Using experience gained with the Golf diesel, the new five-cylinder engine, in slightly smaller guise, was given compression ignition. The fastback styling was a break for Audi, which, with the exception of the rare 100S coupé, had stayed with the saloon-only theme for many years. Looking back, it was an early clue to the new vibrancy that would characterise Audi in the 1980s.

200 TURBO/200. 1980-84 (prod 73,571) 4-door 5-seater saloon. F/F, 2144cc (S5 OC). Max speed 139mph, 0-60mph 7.5sec. Working on the success of the 100, Audi was tempted to move further upmarket with the luxury 200 Turbo and, from 1981, its normally-aspirated sister model. But as had happened so often before, the buying public seemed to know better than the marketing men. The 200 offered no more space than the 100, while the lusty performance of the turbocharged 170bhp engine was compromised by front-drive limitations. Body trim details and meatier nose styling were the only visual clues that this wasn't a 100 – which was perhaps part of the 200's problem.

80. 1986 to date (prod: 1,681,859). 4-door 4-seater saloon. F/F or F/4×4, 1595/1781/1984cc (S4 OC), 1588cc turbo diesel (S4 OC). Max speed 129mph, 0-60mph 8.4sec. Smoother, more rounded shape – but the engine stayed north-south. Capacity of smaller engine went up to 1.6/75bhp, but turbo diesel stayed unchanged at 80bhp. A year later the 1.6 was dropped for the larger-capacity 1.8, which gave 75bhp in carburettor form, 90bhp with injection. The final development, in 1989, was the 2.0 engine, with 113bhp. Quickest of the 80s, and rather treading on the heels of the 90, was the Sport 16V with 137bhp. Both 2.0 engines appeared in quattro versions. Small boot was a minus point, fully-galvanised bodyshell a major plus.

90. 1986-91 (prod: 153,937). 4-door 4-seater saloon. F/F or F/4×4, 1994/2226/2309cc (S5 OC). Max speed 138mph, 0-60mph 7.8sec. The 90 designation continued to indicate five-cylinder engines, but now there was a new performance image. The smaller 2.0/115bhp 90 was joined by a larger 2.2/136bhp version, with the same engine being used in the quattro. This went to 2.3/136bhp in mid-1989, with extra capacity making up for power loss caused by standard catalytic converter. At the same time Sport versions of the two- and four-wheel drive 90s were added, the 20-valve versions of the 2.3 engine pumping out 170bhp, with lowered suspension and fatter tyres to handle very quick performance. When Audi facelifted its 80/90 model in late 1991, the 90 title was dropped, with models being indicated simply by their engine size.

100. 1983-91 (prod 1,071,729). 5-door 5-seater saloon. F/F or F/4×4, 1781cc (S4 OC), 1994/2226cc (S5 OC), 1986cc turbo diesel (S5 OC). Max speed 134 mph, 0-60mph 7.5sec. Almost overnight the initials Cd took on a new significance – and it was all due to Audi's new 100. The slippery body, its wind tunnel design featuring flush side windows, had a Cd of 0.30, these figures appearing in the rear quarter windows of cars sold in the UK because a drag factor this low was, at the time, amazing. The four-cylinder version was dropped in 1988, replaced by the 2.0 five-cylinder. With new-found confidence, Audi added a 165bhp 2.2 turbo in front-drive and four-wheel drive quattro forms.

100 AVANT. 1983-91 (prod 308,385). 5-seater 5-door estate. F/F or F/4×4, 1781cc (S4 OC), 1994/2226cc (S5 OC), 1986cc turbo diesel (S5 OC). Max speed 132mph, 0-60mph 7.7sec. If the new Avant could not quite match its saloon sister in aerodynamic efficiency, it more than made up for it in carrying capacity. This was despite having a steeply raked tailgate, with distinct upper and lower windows. The engine range was similar to that in the saloons, and again there were quattro versions. But despite the advanced aerodynamics and sophistication of four-wheel drive, the 100s still suffered from dull three-speed automatics and barely perceptible fresh air 'ram' ventilation.

200. 1984-89 (prod 77,571). 4/5-door 5 seater saloon and estate. F/F or F/4×4, 2144/2226cc (S5 OC). Max speed 144mph, 0-60mph 7.5sec. Audi had got the high-tech bit between its teeth here, with five-cylinder engines all round and turbo versions producing 182bhp at first, later 200bhp, in saloon and Avant estate bodies. And were we impressed? The answer was not very. Prices put the 200s out of contention for many would-be buyers, despite the performance potential. As sales faded, the 200 was quietly shelved in 1989.

QUATTRO. 1983-89 (prod 11,452). 2-door 4-seater coupé. F/4×4, 2144/2309cc (S5 OC). Max speed 135mph, 0-60mph 6.3sec. With the exception of the Jensen FF, four-wheel drive had been the preserve of the off-roaders. Then came the quattro initially in LHD only, with a turbocharged 2.1 engine and an all-wheel drive system which rewrote the book of handling, once you had come to terms with the massive turbo lag and heavy front-bias braking. Anti-lock cured the braking deficiency a year after launch, when the awful digital/talking instrument panel was introduced. Later models, with a larger engine, shattering acceleration and massive grip, brought the magic back into what had already become a legend in its own lifetime.

QUATTRO 20V. 1989-91 (prod: see above). 2-door 4-seater coupé. F/4×4, 2226cc (S5 DOC). Max speed 142mph, 0-60mph 5.9sec. The last and greatest of the real quattros. With four valves per cylinder, twin overhead camshafts and clever electronics, power was boosted to 220bhp, while the huge torque curve peaked with 228lb ft at just 1950rpm. The Torsen diff looked after front-to-rear power distribution – and the result was a car blessed with fearsome but well-mannered acceleration. No matter that the boot was too small and the interior looked dated – it was the very feel of the quattro which mattered. For some pundits this was the greatest car of the decade.

COUPE. 1980-88 (prod 173,747). 2-door 4-seater coupé. F/F or F/4×4, 1781cc (S4 OC), 1921/2144/2226cc (S5 OC). Max speed 121mph, 0-60mph 8.7sec. Something of a Plain Jane as far as looks were concerned, but nevertheless an eminently practical car, with room for five at a pinch. Performance with either the original 1.8 90bhp or 1.9 115bhp engines was hardly thrilling, but the coupé came to life with the 2.1 and 2.2 136bhp engines. The Quattro had the same four-wheel drive system as its lusty turbocharged big brother, but with only a fraction of the performance. Like all Audis of this period, build quality felt rock solid. A mild facelift, with a slight softening of the lines, came in 1984.

COUPE. 1988 to date (prod XXX,XXX). 2-door 4-seater coupé. F/F or F/4×4, 1984cc (S4 OC), 2226/2309cc (S5 OC). Max speed 137mph, 0-60mph 7.5sec. Based on the larger 80/90 models, with a good-looking and reasonably spacious two-door body. But early models had ill-sorted suspension, which upset handling and ride, a problem not even the quattro version could address. With the 20-valve 2.3 engine packing 170bhp came the revised suspension, and the coupé finally got the handling it deserved. The quattro was too expensive for its performance, while the S2 replacement for the real quattro lacked the same brutal appeal.

AUSTIN-MORRIS (GB)

After a period of what seemed like mutual industrial self-destruction as British Leyland, where the standard of industrial relations seemed to reflect the standard of most of the cars being built, things started to sort themselves out when the Morris name was shelved in 1984, following the formation of the Austin Rover Group (ARG) in 1981. The Austin name joined Morris in the graveyard in 1988, with Rover Cars coming into being the following year.

MINI. 1959 to date (prod 5.3 million all models). 2-door 4-seater saloon. F/F, 998/1098cc (S4 OHV). Max speed 87mph, 0-60mph 13.4sec. Others were making cars which were faster and more comfortable, but none could match the Mini for sheer driving fun. Room for four, with the same upright driving position that Alec Issigonis dictated from the beginning. Its size, still a quarter of an inch over 10ft, makes it so easy to park, while the indestructible A-series engine gives adequate performance. Twenty-fifth anniversary edition in 1984, with 1098cc engine, was one of the best.

1275GT. 1969-80 (prod 117,949). 2-door 4-seater saloon. F/F, 1275cc (S4 OHV). Max speed 85mph, 0-60mph 14.6sec. The figures 1275 for Mini enthusiasts should be followed by the initial S. But the 1275GT was a rather forlorn attempt to cash in on the heroic days of the genuine 1275cc version of the Mini Cooper S. A solitary SU carburettor and kids-to-school camshaft gave totally unexciting performance, while the long-nosed bonnet sat unhappily on the classic Mini body. Notable as one of the two cars on which Dunlop's run-flat Denovo tyres were briefly fitted as standard – the other was the Fiat 126.

CLUBMAN. 1969-80 (prod 331,675). 2/3-door 4-seater saloon/estate. F/F, 1098cc (S4 OHV). Max speed 82 mph, 0-60mph 17.9sec. The finger has to point to the marketing department for this Mini aberration. The only apparent advantage of the extended snout was that access to the distributor became easier. Inside there was no more room than in the 'real' Mini. The estate had a longer wheelbase than the saloon, the extra space all behind the rear seats. A revised facia meant that switches could now be reached and the instruments were located where the driver could see them, directly ahead – but the driving position remained as uncompromisingly upright as ever.

METRO. 1980-90 (prod 758,218). 3/5-door 4-seater hatchback. F/F, 998/1275cc (S4 OHV). Max speed 93mph, 0-60mph 14.5sec. Twenty-one years after the Mini came BL's first supermini. Lack of capital meant that they had to stay with the ageing A-plus engine and four-speed gearbox in the face of far more advanced mechanicals in rival cars. But finally BL managed to put a car into production without leaving the customers to complete its development. Hydragas suspension resulted in great handling and reasonable ride. Another plus point was the amount of room contained in the compact size, but the Issigonis philosophy lingered on with that sit-up-and-beg driving position.

METRO VANDEN PLAS. 1982-90 (prod 81,870). 5-door 4-seater hatchback. F/F, 1275cc (S4 OHV). Max speed n/a, 0-60mph n/a. Purists might shudder, but with the aid of a few pieces of veneer, some leather, special coachlining and the name of coachbuilder Vanden Plas, BL managed to raise the Metro's image. It also had more power to make up for the extra weight, its 72bhp (instead of 63bhp) making it the quickest of the Austin-based Metros. But the four-speed AP-designed automatic transmission, severely blunted the performance edge. One for older folk...

MAXI. 1969-81 (prod 450,000). 5-door 5-seater hatchback. F/F, 1748cc (S4 OC). Max speed 97mph, 0-60mph 13.2sec. Almost all the right ingredients, but no one ever got the mix right. Practical, roomy five-door body was let down by dull interiors and careless build quality. Latterly only the larger (1750) version of the E4 single overhead camshaft engine was being used, although the five-speed gearbox – if you could find any of the gears – was there from launch. Wheel-at-each-corner long wheelbase design, with Hydrolastic suspension, gave surprisingly good handling and ride. This was the final relic of the late and unlamented BMC era.

ALLEGRO 1500/1750. 1973-83 (prod: see above). 4-door 4-seater saloon, 2-door estate. F/F, 1485/1748cc (S4 OC). Max speed 100mph, 0-60mph 11.4sec. They may have been given titles like Sport and Sport TC (for twin carburettors), but nothing could really disguise the fact that these were very ordinary cars. In the last days, with the facelifted MkIII launched in 1980, only the larger of the E-series engines (1750), first seen in the Maxi, was being used, with the five-speed gearbox. Appearance was never helped by the then-current vogue for vinyl roof trim. Doubtful build quality, indifferent reliability and rust became Allegro hallmarks.

ALLEGRO 1100/1300. 1973-83 (prod 478,000 all models). 2/4-door 4-seater saloon, 2-door estate. F/F, 1098/1275cc (S4 OHV). Max speed 87mph, 0-60mph 16.5sec. For all their faults, the earlier 1100/1300 models, which the Allegro replaced, at least had the saving grace of well-balanced, elegant looks. The blobby Allegro, with its piggy rectangular headlamps, had little attraction. At the rear, the 1300-only estate was an even unhappier conflict of lines. The lack of a front subframe led to lots of engine and road noise feeding through to the cabin, as well as windscreens coming out when the car was jacked up. Sturdy though the A-series engines were, they did not exactly add to the Allegro's refinement. All you can say in the Allegro's favour is that it was very economical to run. Dropped in 1983, ousted by the Maestro.

MARINA. 1971-82 (prod 1.0 million). 4-door 4-seater saloon, 5-door estate, 3-door coupé. F/R, 1275/1798cc (S4 OHV), 1695cc (S4 OC). Max speed 98mph, 0-60mph 12.5sec. No one could accuse the Marina of breaking any new ground when it came to engineering or design. Until the 'MkII' version in 1978, the 1275cc A-series and 1789cc B-series engines provided the power, with four-speed gearboxes – but the B-series TC (twin carburettor) version could outdrag the far heavier MGB. In 1978, B-series was replaced by 1.7 O-series engine. Suspension, with lever-arm front dampers and torsion bars, dated back to original Morris Minor design. Two-door coupé body was short on rear seat leg and headroom. Early pre-production Marinas were afflicted with terminal understeer, which BMC promised would be cured before the car went on sale. It wasn't, as many white-knuckled owners discovered.

ITAL. 1982-84 (prod 126,000). 4/5-door 4-seater saloon/estate. F/R, 1275cc (S4 OHV), 1695cc (S4 OC). Max speed 101mph, 0-60mph 11.7sec. The final fling for the Morris name, which was about to join Riley and Wolseley on Austin Rover's dusty shelf. Giugiaro's ItalDesign studio was given the task of keeping the Marina alive – hence the new name for this revamp for a further two years, until the Rover 200 was launched. The coupé was abandoned, leaving just saloon and estate. Underneath nothing really changed, but the A-series engine became the A-plus (with 60bhp) and the B-series was replaced by the 78bhp 1.7 O-series, both engines still with four-speed gearboxes. Saloon dropped in February 1984, with the estate staying on to the summer before being axed.

PRINCESS II. 1978-81 (prod 221,000 all models). 4-door 5-seater saloon. F/F, 1695/1993cc (S4 OC), 2227cc (S6 OC). Max speed 110mph, 0-60mph 12.6sec. The 'MkII' saw the end of the pushrod B-series engine, replaced by the 1.7 and 2.0 single overhead camshaft O-series engines, while the six-cylinder E-series continued unchanged. The original wedge design may have looked a little unusual, but having a transverse engine in a long wheelbase allowed leg-stretching room in the cabin. The BMC marketing department had decreed back in 1975 that a hatchback was too downmarket, and the Princess II stayed with the original head-clouting boot lid. Hydragas suspension gave predictable handling with reasonable ride.

AMBASSADOR. 1982-84 (prod 43,500). 5-door 5-seater hatchback. F/F, 1695/1993cc (S4 OC). Max speed 100mph, 0-60mph 14.3sec. At least one coachbuilder offered the Princess II with a hatchback conversion, and in its last two years, and with a new name, the model finally received the tailgate it always needed. The four-cylinder O-series engines stayed, with the E6 being finally abandoned. The 1.7 versions had 83bhp, while the 2.0 HL started with 92bhp but climbed to 100bhp when it was given the twin carburettor version used in the HLS. The top Vanden Plas model stayed with the lower output engine. Build quality problems were now almost a thing of the past, heralding the start of the new Rover image.

MAESTRO. 1983 to date (prod 596,000 to date). 5-door 5-seater hatchback. F/F, 1275cc (S4 OHV), 1598/1994cc (S4 OC). Max speed 100mph, 0-60mph 12.8sec. The name was the second choice in an in-plant suggestion scheme for ARG's new cars. Metro had already gone, so the new mid-range hatchback was Maestro. Third name was Match – whatever happened to that? The Maestro idea was sensible enough, with a practical five-door design. Like the Montego, it used steel springs rather than any rubber-based system. The aged A-plus engine was used, but this time with the gearbox end-on rather than in the sump. The 1.6 R-series engine was quickly replaced by the S-series, with belt-driven cam and VW Golf gearbox. The Vanden Plas version featured the digital, talking instrument panel, another idea which thankfully faded into memory.

MONTEGO. 1984-93 (prod 546,000 to date). 4-door 5-seater saloon. F/F, 1275cc (S4 OHV), 1598/1994cc (S4 OC), 1994cc turbo diesel (S4 OC). Max speed 116mph, 0-60mph 9.1sec. Last of what were then the Big Three challengers for volume in the important fleet market. Competition was fierce, with Ford and Vauxhall already in the ring with the Sierra and Cavalier. With conservative-minded fleet managers in mind, the Montego was designed along very conventional lines. Steel spring suspension was used front and rear. The 1.3 version struggled with the ageing A-plus engine and four-speed gearbox, while larger ones used S- and E-series engines, plus lusty but noisy turbo diesel. Essentially a good car, with plenty of room and, with bigger engines, adequate performance. Early build quality problems took time to overcome but were eventually conquered.

MONTEGO ESTATE. 1984 to date (prod: see above). 5-door 5-seater estate. F/F, 1598/1994cc (S4 OC), 1994cc turbo diesel (S4 OC). Max speed 113mph, 0-60mph 8.9sec. With the demise of the Ital estate, this was Austin-Rover's only big load carrier. Design was carried out by IAD of Worthing, Sussex. Smaller 1.6 S-series version phased out in 1991, while 2.0 models moved upmarket. Injection engines with 117bhp gave decent performance, while top Vanden Plas version even had self-levelling suspension. Squared-up rear end gave huge volume, while seating could be expanded with a pair of rear-facing seats for children. Petrol-engined version gradually dropped, leaving diesel and turbo diesel versions to carry on.

BENTLEY (GB)

The original company, founded by Walter Owen Bentley, lasted just 11 years, but in that short period a legend was created, mainly around a succession of five victories at Le Mans. Financial problems were never far away and in 1931 the company was acquired by Rolls-Royce. During the 1980s, Bentley started to regain its identity, with models like the Turbo R and Mulsanne.

CORNICHE/CONTINENTAL. 1971 to date (prod n/a). 2-door, 5-seater convertible. F/R, 6750cc (V8 OHV). Max speed 130mph, 0-60mph 7.9sec. British coachbuilding at its best, with original Corniche versions being hand-crafted by Mulliner Park Ward. Renamed Continental in 1984 mainly to avoid confusion with the Rolls-Royce Corniche, although mechanically identical. More subtle Bentley radiator grille seems to complement the lines. Power, always adequate, was made even more so in 1987 with fuel injection, with anti-lock brakes becoming standard. Power everything, with extras list even including having your initials discreetly painted on the doors.

T2-SERIES. 1977-80 (prod 558 standard, 10 long wheelbase). 4-door 5-seater saloon. F/R, 6750cc

(V8 OHV). Max speed 118mph, 0-60mph 10.9sec. Essentially nothing more than a badge-engineered version of the Roll-Royce Silver Shadow II, still using the Pressed Steel monocoque body unit with just the bonnet and grille pressings altered to accept the more restrained Bentley radiator shell and 'Flying B' badge, designed originally by Frank Gordon Crosby of *The Autocar*.

MULSANNE/MULSANNE S. 1980-92 (prod 2039). 4-door 5-seater saloon. F/R, 6750cc (V8 OHV). Max speed 123mph, 0-60mph 6.8sec. In some ways the last of the rebadged Rolls-Royces, this time on the Silver Spirit. But the Bentley ghost started to stir once more, with the Mulsanne Turbo in 1982 showing that the V8 engine really could pick up its skirts and, provided you owned an oil well, fly. The non-turbo Mulsanne was replaced by the S version in 1987, with more power – but still undisclosed – and a 170mph speedometer.

EIGHT. 1984-92 (prod: 1734). 4-door 5-seater saloon. F/R, 6750cc (V8 OHV). Max speed 129mph, 0-60mph 9.6sec. Costing some £10,000 less than the Mulsanne, this was a nice piece of marketing by Rolls-Royce as one of the first moves to push the Bentley name to the fore. The chrome mesh wire grille was reminiscent of the glory days at Le Mans, while the black rubber bumpers and terribly discreet front spoiler added to the image. Since Bentleys seemed so much less opulent than Rolls-Royces, sales soared through the 1980s.

TURBO R. 1985-92 (prod: 4815). 4-door 5-seater saloon. F/R, 6750cc (V8 OHV). Max speed 135mph, 0-60mph 6.6sec. W.O. Bentley regarded superchargers with contempt, so what would he have made of the Turbo R? Rolls-Royce at last lifted the veil on power outputs, this engine producing 320bhp and a massive 457lb ft torque. Since this fearsome powerhouse weighed almost 2.4 tonnes, speed had to be limited to 135mph because there were no suitable tyres to handle higher speeds. Drawing room comfort at not quite Concorde speeds.

BITTER (D)

Using components from the big Opels, Erich Bitter set about creating his own good-looking, hand-built, very expensive coupés, with Stuttgart-based coachbuilder Bauer making the first cars. The last cars sold in this country were even available with Ferguson four wheel drive and anti-lock braking systems.

SC COUPE. 1979-84 (prod n/a). 2-door 2+2-seater coupé. F/R, 2968/3457cc (S6 OHV). Max speed 142mph, 0-60mph 7.6sec. There was an Opel Senator floorpan underneath, but the supremely elegant coupé body on top certainly gave no hint of the fact. Attention to detail and finish was outstanding, while the basically sound handling and ride needed only fine tuning. The 180bhp 3.0 was joined by a 210bhp 3.5 version, which put top speed up to over 140mph and gave a 7.6sec 0-60mph time.

SC SALOON. 1984-87 (prod n/a). 4-door 5-seater saloon. F/R or F/4×4, 3457cc (S6 OHV). Max speed 139mph, 0-60mph 8.9sec. Essentially a long-wheelbase version of the coupé, the saloon had the same elegant, well-balanced lines and superb equipment. The 3.5 engine was standard, with the FF – Ferguson Formula – 4wd system among the extras. The SCs were built by Maggoria in Turin, with Steyr in Austria carrying out final trim and assembly.

BMW (D)

Bayerische Moteren Werke AG was formed in 1918, although the BMW initials did not come to prominence until 1936, with the 327 and better known 328. In the years after World War II, BMW concentrated on motorcycles, almost foundering financially during the 1950s. In the early 1960s fortunes changed with the new 1600 and 2002. The current model structure started in 1973 with the 5 series, followed in 1975 by the 3 series, the image car of the 1980s.

3 SERIES (four-cylinder). 1975-82 (prod 1,364,039). 2-door 5-seater saloon. F/R, 1573/1766/1990cc (S4 OC). Max speed 113mph, 0-60mph 9.6sec. It was the 1600/2002 models of the early 1960s which put BMW back on the road to success, and the 3 series was the natural successor. Clean, conservative two-door styling, with the suspension and engine range carried over from the earlier models, although rack and pinion steering became standard. The two smaller engines were carburettor only, but the 2.0 was available with carburettors (109bhp) or petrol injection (125bhp).

3 SERIES (six cylinder). 1977-83 (prod 410,552). 2-door 5-seater saloon. F/R, 1990/2315cc (S6 OC). Max speed 126mph, 0-60mph 8.3sec. The new generation of M-series engines, the six-cylinder M60, went into the 3 series in 1977 to produce the 320-6 and the 323i, with 122bhp and 143bhp respectively. Gearboxes were four-speed only at first, but the 323i was given a five-speed in 1980. As many drivers discovered, the 323i's power in conjunction with tail-happy rear suspension and the available tyres could make wet-road driving something of a white-knuckle ride.

3 SERIES MKII. 1983-91 (prod 1,167,130). 2/4-door 5-seater saloon. F/R, 1596/1766/1796cc (S4 OC), 1991/2315/2495cc (S6 OC). Max speed 135mph, 0-60mph 8.3sec. No dramatic changes in appearance, although there was now the choice of two or four doors. Perhaps more significant was a revised rear suspension which finally tamed those wayward handling tendencies. New M40 four-cylinder engines in 1987-88 put 316i and 318i power up to 102bhp and 115bhp, while at the six-cylinder end of the range the 2.3 was replaced by the 171bhp 2.5, a Sport version having a close-ratio gearbox. As a sought-after company car, the 3 series had no equal in the 1980s boom years.

3 SERIES BAUER CONVERTIBLE. 1981-85 (prod n/a). 2-door 4-seater convertible. F/R, 1991/2495cc (S6 OC). Max speed n/a, 0-60mph n/a. The Stuttgart-based coachbuilder Karl Bauer had produced factory-approved convertible versions of the MkI 3 series, but these had never been sold in the UK. While BMW was working on an in-house soft-top version of the MkII, Bauer went ahead with its own. Keeping the door frames and using a wide roll-over bar between the B-pillars helped retain torsional stiffness, but the steeply-sloping rear hood section reduced back seat headroom drastically.

3 SERIES CONVERTIBLE. 1986-93 (prod: see above). 2-door 4-seater convertible. F/R, 1991/2495cc (S6 OC). Max speed 135mph, 0-60mph 8.7sec. In a brilliant technical exercise, Munich produced one of the best-looking four-seater convertibles around. Carefully-calculated bracing in the screen pillar gave roll-over protection, leaving a flat, uncluttered waistline. The hood stowed completely out of sight under a steel closing panel, with status-enhancing power operation an option. Launched as the 325i, but the 320i came in 1987 and the 318i in 1991. Replaced in 1993 by the new-look version.

3 SERIES TOURING. 1988 to date (prod: see above). 3/5-door 4-seater estate. F/R, 1796cc (S4 OC), 1991/2495cc (S6 OC). Max speed 133mph, 0-60mph 8.8sec. A combination of clever design and marketing put the Touring in a class of its own. By keeping a low sill across the rear, body strength was maintained without need for much more stiffening, while the narrow-at-the-bottom tailgate made it not quite an estate – which is exactly what BMW wanted. For the UK market, Home Counties success was assured. Launched initially in six-cylinder 325i form, the new Touring – the 1977 original was a hatchback – was joined by the four-cylinder 318i in 1989 and the smaller 316i in 1991.

325iX. 1985-91 (prod: see above). 2/4-door 4-seater saloon. F/4×4, 2494cc (S6 OC). Max speed 126mph, 0-60mph 7.4sec. BMW was pinning its performance faith very much in the M3, so the 325iX, despite its figures, was considered very much more as a keep-you-going version of the 325i, with the 4wd system aimed more for people who lived up a snowy alp. Same 171bhp engine as the 2wd cars, with five-speed manual 'box. The all-wheel drive system was developed by BMW for today's models, but it proved to be a blind alley. Only made in left-hand drive, and with only a handful imported, they've already achieved endangered species status.

M3. 1988-91 (prod 17,184). 2-door 4-seater saloon. F/R, 2302cc (S4 OC). Max speed 143mph, 0-60mph 6.5sec. Ultimate volume production 'homologation special' bred for the track, although few creature comforts were missing. The 2.3 single-cam four-cylinder engine originally developed 200bhp, increasing to 215bhp in 1989 when a catalytic converter became standard. With a close-ratio gearbox, limited slip diff and squat tyres riding on taut suspension, this was the ultimate 3 series until the Evolution models arrived in 1990. Aerodynamic differences included a deep front air dam, a shallower rear window angle and a tail spoiler. Left-hand drive was just about the only drawback for UK buyers.

5 SERIES (four-cylinder). 1972-81 (prod 297,950). 4-door 5-seater saloon. F/R, 1766/1990cc (S4 OC). Max speed 110mph, 0-60mph 10.5sec. As research and development costs soared, BMW slowed its progress in the late 1960s, with the 5 series its first new mid-sized model in 10 years. Launched in time for the Munich Olympics, it initially had a four-cylinder 2.0 engine, first with carburettors, later with injection. Appeal was widened with the 518. These were spacious, comfortable saloons, with safe handling which showed none of the 3 series' tail-happy tendencies.

5 SERIES (six-cylinder). 1973-81 (prod: 261,113).4-door 5-seater saloon. F/R, 1990/2494/2788/2985cc (S6 OC). Max speed 133mph, 0-60mph 8.7sec. Appearing a year after the four-cylinder models, the sixes used the same bodyshell, but with slightly modified suspension and all-round disc brakes to handle extra performance. UK market cars were 525 and 528, with 145bhp and 176bhp; the 530i was for the North American market only. Despite up-market image, buyers found themselves facing a daunting list of extras from which to 'tailor' their cars to their liking – at a cost. When a six-cylinder 520 arrived in 1977, it needed a keen eye to spot that the 'i' was missing from the four-cylinder car's designation. The new M60 overhead camshaft engine used a single twin-choke Solex carburettor and developed 122bhp, marginally down on the 125bhp of the identical-capacity injection 'four' it replaced.

5 SERIES (four-cylinder). 1981-87 (prod: 722,328). 4-door 5-seater saloon. F/R, 1766cc (S4 OC). Max speed 112mph, 0-60mph 12.3sec. The 1766cc engine had appeared briefly at the end of the original 5 series' innings. In the revised car, it gave 105bhp in both its original carburettor and, from 1984, injection forms. And out went the tipped-forward grille and tall greenhouse, with the new car getting a smoother, lower appearance. The suspension used struts at the front, semi-trailing arms at the rear, with slightly old-fashioned worm and roller steering. Equipment was rather basic, but owners had the option to enhance their cars to suit their needs – at a price!

5 SERIES (six-cylinder). 1981-87 (prod: see above). 4-door 5-seater saloon. F/R, 1990/2495/2788/3420cc (S6 OC). Max speed 146mph, 0-60mph 7.7sec. With the six-cylinder version, BMW really opened up choices in the facelifted 5 series. The single-cam, 12-valve engines had outputs ranging from 125bhp in 1990cc form to 218bhp in the 3420cc 535i. Until 1987, the biggest engine was 2788cc/185bhp in the comparatively rare 528i. Five-speed gearboxes were standard, with three-speed automatics an option until the four-speed came with the 535i. Social status was unbeatable – but there was not that much room either in the rear seats or boot. Equipment increased with price, 528i and 535i having anti-lock brakes as standard.

525e. 1983-87 (prod: see above). 4-door 5-seater saloon. F/R, 2693cc (S6 OC). Max speed 115mph, 0-60mph 10.8sec. Engineers use the Greek letter *eta* – hence the e – to denote efficiency. The low-friction 2.7 six produced a long-legged 125bhp at just 4250rpm, driving through a high-geared four-speed automatic 'box. Drag was kept down with skinny 175HR/14 tyres – and the result was a car which could top 115mph and return 35mpg. This was not in most people's image of a BMW, although the few who drove this model were fascinated by its performance and economy.

M535i. 1985-87 (prod: 2241). 4-door 5-seater saloon. F/R, 3420cc (S6 OC). Max speed 152mph, 0-60mph 6.4sec. The 'go-faster' looks sat rather unhappily on the rather stately 5 series lines, but it all worked. M Technic spoilers, flared wheelarches, side skirts and, a matter of months after launch, M Technic suspension, plus 218bhp and a close-ratio gearbox, gave the M535i good performance, with handling to match. Several years were to pass before the new and very much quicker M5 came on the scene.

5 SERIES. 1988 to date (prod: 722,328). 4-door 5-seater saloon. F/R, 1990/2494/2986/3430cc (S6 OC). Max speed 146mph, 0-60mph 7.7sec. For many the new look was too reminiscent of the old model, but the elegant shape caught on quickly, even if there was not that much interior space and the boot shape was awkward. All six-cylinder engines during the 1980s, with the brilliant new 24-valve units and the cheaper four-cylinder 518 not arriving until 1990. The composed handling and outstanding ride matched the understated good looks. Thanks to tall gearing, refinement tended to come before outright performance.

6 SERIES. 1976-89 (prod: 80,361). 2-door 4-seater coupé. F/R, 2788/2985/3210/3430/3453cc (S6 OC). Max speed 140mph, 0-60mph 6.8sec. Hindsight would have revealed that the 6 series was based on the same chassis which would be used on the 7 series, launched a year later. During the 1980s the range was pruned back to the 628i, which ceased in 1987, and the 635CSiA. Equipment levels increased in line with the price, power for the 635 easing up from 218bhp to 220bhp in 1987. Comfortable grand tourers, but towards the end they were looking very dated.

7 SERIES. 1977-86 (prod: 285,029). 4-door 5-seater saloon. F/R, 2788/2985/3210/3430/3453cc (S6 OC). Max speed 130mph, 0-60mph 7.8sec. BMW had its eyes set firmly on the market which was being dominated by Mercedes-Benz and Jaguar. In the UK the cluttered range included 2.8/184bhp, 3.2/197bhp and 3.5/218bhp engines, the last with injection only from 1979, most being bought with the four-speed auto, with a five-speed option on the 732i. Big, comfortable cars with masses of equipment and well-balanced handling. Despite BMW's reputation, the 7 series never quite achieved the hoped-for status.

M635CSi. 1985-89 (prod: 5855). 2-door 4-seater coupé. F/R, 3453cc (S6 OC). Max speed 158mph, 0-60mph 6.2sec. Created as the ultimate 6 series, based on the 635CSi. Power was pushed up from 218bhp to 286bhp, and a close-ratio five-speed gearbox was fitted. M Technic body kit and alloy wheels, plus special seats and steering wheel, made it look the part. In the last two years luxury was improved with full leather trim, electric front seats and new spoilers. Something of a high-velocity dinosaur – but at least it did everything with style.

7 SERIES. 1986 to date (prod: 245,896). 4-door 5-seater saloon. F/R, 2986/3430cc (S6 OC), 4988cc (V12 DOC). Max speed 150mph, 0-60mph 7.3sec. Like the 5 series, the new 7 series had a lot of the old model about it but the range was slimmed down, initially with just two engines, 3.0/188bhp and 3.5/211bhp. In 1987 the technically brilliant and visually elegant 5.0/300bhp V12 was added, and distinguished from the outside by broader front grille 'kidneys'. At the same time a long-wheelbase version arrived, with 4in extra in the rear. Despite the size, handling was surprisingly agile, but the ride was considered rather too firm for a car of this class. Equipment? The list goes on and on…

M1. 1979-80 (prod 450). 2-door 2-seater sports coupé. M/R, 3453cc (S6 DOC). Max speed 162mph, 0-60mph 5.5sec. At Lamborghini's Sant'Agata plant you could see where M1 had been all but obliterated by the word Countach on the production line. The Italian company did develop the chassis, but production was eventually carried out by Bauer in Stuttgart, using a Giugiaro-styled glass-fibre body. Power came from a 277bhp twin-cam version of the in-line six, driving through a ZF five-speed 'box. Although never gaining Type Approval in the UK, around a dozen were imported. This hugely expensive exercise produced a wonderful car but little in the way of technical or publicity spin-off.

Z1. 1986-91 (prod 8000). 2-door 2-seater sports car. F/R, 2494cc (S6 OC). Max speed 140mph, 0-60mph 7.9sec. This car's life started as a 'mule' for the Z axle rear suspension being developed for the current 3 series. Then BMW's technical department gave it a high-tech body, with a steel and carbon-fibre monocoque clad in a glass-fibre skin, with slide-down doors. Until it was seen in public, there was never any intention of putting it into production – and then 8000 were built. Rare in the UK as it cost a huge £37,728. In the end the Z1's handling and performance never did quite live up to its looks.

BRISTOL (GB)

With many high-skilled craftsmen at its Filton factory and World War II over, the Bristol Aeroplane Co formed the Car Division in 1946, building unusual but elegant coupés. In 1955 Bristol Cars Ltd was formed, later becoming a subsidiary of Bristol Siddeley Engines. During 1960 the company was bought by Tony Crook, who continued to develop the series of big, very hand-built models, latterly all powered by massive Chrysler V8 engines.

412. 1975-82 (prod: n/a). 2-door 4-seater convertible/saloon. F/R, 5900cc (V8 OHV). Max speed 135mph, 0-60mph 7.8sec. Apart from detail changes, the box-type ladder-frame chassis remained much as it had been originally designed in the late-1940s. In 1978, the massive 6.6 Chrysler V8 was replaced by the 5.9 version, although power outputs, along with production figures, remained undisclosed. Zagato's bodywork was to form the basis of future models.

603. 1976-82 (prod: n/a). 2-door 4-seater coupé. F/R, 5900cc (V8 OHV). Max speed 128mph, 0-60mph 7.5sec. Old, familiar chassis, with the old, familiar 5.9 Chrysler V8 and three-speed Torqueflite transmission. Elegant, good-looking body reflected the amount of genuine hand craftsmanship which went into the building of these cars. Wishbone front suspension and torsion bar sprung live rear axle located by Watts linkage combined predictable handling with excellent ride.

BEAUFIGHTER. 1980-92 (prod: n/a). 2-door 4-seater saloon. F/R, 5900cc (V8 OHV). Max speed 150mph, 0-60mph 5.9sec. The Zagato styling of the 412 was modified, with a removable glass-fibre roof panel for fine-weather motoring. But the biggest change was to the Chrysler engine, which was turbocharged to an undisclosed degree. It was enough to push top speed to 150mph and put the car into the sub-6.0sec to 60mph club.

BRITANNIA. 1982 to date (prod: n/a). 2-door 4-seater saloon. F/R, 5900cc (V8 OHV). Max speed 140mph, 0-60mph 7.2sec. Second of the cars to draw upon the stock of names first used by the aircraft side of the business. Styling was based on the 603's fastback lines, with two rectangular headlamps in place of the former's four-lamp layout. The chassis, as ever, remained largely unchanged, as did the Chrysler V8 engine and transmission.

BRIGAND. 1983 to date (prod: n/a). 2-door 4-seater saloon. F/R, 5900cc (V8 OHV). Max speed 150mph, 0-60mph 5.9sec. The logical progression after the Beaufighter was to turbocharge the Britannia, renaming it Brigand. The chassis seemed able to handle the extra power, although the car was running with 7in rim alloy wheels. Because Bristols change so rarely and as most run with cherished numbers, spotting the new ones remains a problem.

BUICK (USA)

In the General Motors hierarchy, Buick fits in towards the top of the range, its slightly conservative, up-market image placing the cars somewhere below Cadillac, but ahead of Oldsmobile and Pontiac. Buick became part of the GM empire before World War I.

SKYLARK. 1979-83 (prod: n/a). 2/4-door 5-seater saloon/coupé. F/F, 2471cc (S4 OHV), 2828cc (V6 OHV). Max speed 109mph, 0-60mph 12.5sec.

Despite being over 15ft long, the Skylark was classified as a compact. Transverse engine layout was new, although power outputs were puny by European standards – the 2.5 four-cylinder produced 90bhp, the 2.8 V6 115bhp. Four-speed manual 'box was available, although the vast majority went out with the three-speed automatic. Strut front suspension was used, with a well-located dead axle at the rear.

Above: 1984 Buick Regal Grand National. Below: 1984 Buick Century Custom Wagon.

CENTURY/REGAL. 1981-85 (prod: n/a). 4/5-door 5-seater saloon/estate, 2-door 4-seater coupé. F/R, 3791cc (V6 OHV), 4344/4942cc (V8 OHV). Max speed 100mph, 0-60mph 10.5sec. Mainstream models, the Century name used for the saloon and station wagon, Regal for the coupé, all on the same 108in wheelbase perimeter frame chassis. Standard engine was the 3.8 V6, giving 110bhp. But with turbocharging, something GM had played with back in 1962 with the ill-fated Corvair, this was pushed to 170bhp for the Regal Sport. Traditionalists could still have a V8, with the big 4.9 giving a gas-swilling 140bhp.

RIVIERA. 1978-84 (prod: n/a). 2-door 5-seater coupé. F/R, 3791cc/4128cc (V6 OHV), 5033cc (V8 OHV), 5737cc diesel (V8 OHV). 112mph, 0-60mph 10.9sec. A classic from the early 1980s, with not over-generous seating for five at a pinch in a car 17ft 4in long. Distinctive GM 'hallmark' greenhouse styling, with steeply raked screen but near-vertical rear window plus, of course, a seemingly endless bonnet. V6 was available with turbocharger to give 180bhp, but few 5.0 V8s made it to the UK, and none of the 5.7 V8 diesels. The diesels were hangovers from the mid-1970s fuel crisis and, with just 105bhp, rapidly losing favour in the US.

CADILLAC (USA)

The name is synonymous with luxury and status - and General Motors has never done anything to dispel that image. In common with other GM marques, Cadillac did down-size many of its models during the 1970s and 1980s, while continuing to build vast saloons like the De Ville. Sales never came to much in the UK, but these and other GM models did well in Belgium and Switzerland.

SEVILLE. 1979-86 (prod: n/a). 4-door 5/6-seater saloon/limousine. F/F, 4128cc (V6 OHV), 6054cc (V8 OHV), 5737cc diesel (V8 OHV). Max speed 116mph, 0-60mph 10.4sec. Revolution was in the air for the new Seville. First, it had front-drive with automatic-only transmission. Second, the 'lead' engine was the lumbering 105bhp 5.7 V8 diesel. But the familiar perimeter frame chassis was retained, now with all-round independent suspension. The sharp-edged fastback styling was also new, a break with GM's taste for near-upright rear windows. As Americans realised that the end of their gasoline world was not nigh, the diesel quietly faded into oblivion.

DE VILLE. 1976-84 (prod: n/a). 2/4-door 6-seater saloon/coupé. F/R, 4128cc (V6 OHV), 6037cc (V8 OHV), 5737cc diesel (V8 OHV). Max speed 118mph, 0-60mph 10.3sec. Downsizing was the new Detroit watchword – and in the case of the de Ville the new car lost 8in of length – but it was still 18ft 5in long, tipping the weighbridge at close to 4200lb. Still with live rear axle and massive perimeter chassis. The 6.0 V8, with 140bhp, was standard, with the 5.7 diesel V8 and 4.1 V6 less popular options, all with automatic transmission. Fuel-saving measure involved electronically-controlled alternate cylinder cut-out, also used on other GM V8s. It was a great idea but did not work in practice.

FLEETWOOD BROUGHAM. 1976-84 (prod: n/a). 4-door 6/8-seater saloon/limousine. F/R, 6037cc (V8 OHV). Max speed 104mph, 0-60mph 11.0sec. The Fleetwood Brougham Limousine was, to many people, the Cadillac to be seen in and outlasted the saloon it was based on. With its chassis stretched to give a 144in wheelbase, and its formal limousine body complete with division and fold-away occasional seats, the car covered 20ft 4in of parking space. In order to cope with the extra weight, the coil-sprung live rear axle needed pneumatic self-levelling. The saloon with a 121.5in wheelbase wasn't that small either but obviously lacked the prestige of the Limo. To UK eyes, though, 15mpg might seem a little excessive.

ELDORADO. 1978-85 (prod: n/a). 2-door 5-seater coupé. F/F, 4128cc (V6 OHV), 6045cc (V8 OHV), 5737cc diesel (V8 OHV). Max speed 116mph, 0-60mph 9.8sec. The front-drive system originated in the Olds Toronado, with 6.0/140bhp V8 joined by fuel-saving 5.7/105bhp V8 diesel and rather more refined 4.1/125bhp V6. Half a ton lighter and over a foot shorter than its predecessor, but still over 17ft long. Many body panels were shared with Buick, but two-door version only. Despite power cut-back, it was still quick – but economical? At an average 13mpg, hardly...

SEVILLE. 1989-92 (prod: n/a). 4-door 5-seater saloon. F/F, 4900cc (V8 OHV). Max speed 125mph, 0-60mph 8.0sec. By some past Cadillac standards, this neat under-16ft saloon was soberly understated. Transverse 200bhp V8 matched to totally seamless automatic gave powerful acceleration and sensible top speed. Good handling let down only by need for better damping. The near-£32,000 price included everything, such as self-closing boot and outstanding air conditioning. To Europeans, the facia was delightfully old-fashioned and the upholstery tasteless.

CARBODIES (GB)

Although the name may not be too familiar, its main product is known almost worldwide as a symbol of London. Until the mid-1980s, when the first commercially viable rival appeared, Coventry-based Carbodies' FX4 'Black Cab' had the market to itself. But there was a car interest too...

CORTINA CONVERTIBLE. 1981-83 (prod n/a). 2-door 4-seater convertible. F/R, 1297cc (S4 OHV). 1593/1993cc (S4 OC). Max speed n/a, 0-60mph n/a. In a deal with David McMullan's Crayford Conversions firm in Kent, Carbodies set up a small line to produce a soft-top version of the three-door MkV Cortina. One immediate problem was that only the 1300 version of the three-door Cortina had UK Type Approval, so the stock computer at Cologne refused to release parts for larger-engined RHD cars. Approval was given to the convertibles, which still suffered from scuttle shake despite all the extra stiffening.

CATERHAM (GB)

Colin Chapman's original Lotus Seven, launched in 1957, was a classic piece of niche marketing. The Seven was about as basic as they come - and huge fun to drive. In 1973, as Lotus headed upmarket, Graham Nearn acquired the design rights, building the cars at Caterham in Surrey.

SUPER SEVEN. 1973 to date (prod: 3700 to 1990). 2-door 2-seater convertible. F/R, 1599cc (S4 OHV), 1599cc (S4 DOC), 1715cc (S4 OC). Max speed 112mph, 0-60mph 5.1sec. Starting from Colin Chapman's Seven base, the only way for Caterham to go was up. The combination of a simple but brilliant chassis and a variety of Ford engines, clad with minimal bodywork, is about as close as most people will ever get to single-seater motoring. De Dion rear suspension, optional from 1987, improved handling still further, but the entire car has steadily matured – and become quicker – thanks to painstaking development. Caterham's success inspired many copies, but legal action generally squashed them.

CHEVROLET (USA)

The backbone of the General Motors empire, with its high volume cars targeted at Detroit rival Ford. But it was one rather untypical car, the Corvette Stingray, which made Chevrolet's name on this side of the Atlantic. Less familiar were the big saloons and station wagons, which, with their born-in-the-USA handling and ride, looked and felt unhappy on the wrong side of the road.

CORVETTE. 1981-86 (prod: n/a). 2-door 2-seater sports coupé. F/R, 5733cc (V8 OHV). Max speed 142mph, 0-60mph 6.6sec. An unmistakable American icon. Emissions regulations slashed power of 5.7 V8 to 190bhp. Four-speed manual transmission or three-speed automatic, with Positraction limited slip diff. Separate chassis with all-round independent suspension, disc brakes and speed-variable power steering, clothed in swooping glass-fibre two-seater bodywork. Within limits – which tend to arrive suddenly in the wet – the handling is reasonable, backed by the distant thunder of the V8 engine. Although not officially sold in the UK, the ZR-1 with a Lotus-developed four-valve 5.7 V8 was launched in 1989 and was capable of nearly 180mph – the ultimate Corvette.

CAMARO Z28. 1981-86 (prod: n/a). 2-door 4-seater coupé. F/R, 5733cc (V8 OHV). Max speed 112mph, 0-60mph 9.2sec. The looks said power and performance, but the result was a bit different. With just 175bhp and a car weighing 3500lb, the V8 had to be worked hard to get much performance – and most owners opted for automatic too. Nor did the suspension quite match the looks: independent at the front, but at the rear there was just a live axle on semi-elliptic springs. Unlike the Corvette, the body was an all-steel monocoque.

MONTE CARLO. 1981-85 (prod: n/a). 2-door 4-seater saloon. F/R, 3751cc (V6 OHV), 4398cc (V8 OHV). Max speed 94mph, 0-60mph 11.3sec. Imposing two-door saloon, based on the chassis of the 108in wheelbase Malibu, which was never sold in the UK. Straightforward suspension, with front struts and coil-sprung live rear axle, still with drum brakes at the back. Neither version of the 3.8 V6 – 110bhp or 170bhp turbocharged – was sold here. Standard was 115bhp 4.4 V8, with three-speed automatic. Not really a car built for England's rolling roads...

CAPRICE. 1980-85 (prod: n/a). 4/5-door 5-seater saloon/estate. F/R, 3751cc (V6 OHV), 4398/5001cc (V8 OHV), 5737cc diesel (V8 OHV). Max speed 110mph, 0-60mph 11.9sec. Straight from Main Street, America. Big – 17ft 8in long – saloon and ever bigger station wagon, although only former sold here with 5.0/150bhp V8 and three-speed overdrive automatic transmission. Front discs, rear drums and live rear axle kept costs down, and were ideal for US motoring.

BLAZER. 1978-85 (prod: n/a). 3-door 5-seater off-road estate car. F/4×4, 4093cc (S6 OHV), 5012cc (V8 OHV). Max speed 90mph, 0-60mph 13.1sec. Rugged and relatively simple estate, built more for unmade roads and bad weather than getting too far off the beaten track. Live axles on semi-elliptic springs carried on a tough separate chassis, most with automatic transmission. In-line 4.1 'six' gave 115bhp, while 5.0 V8 managed 167bhp with a four-barrel carburettor. Ride surprisingly good, but handling was dictated by sheer bulk.

CHRYSLER (EUR)

In a shambles of takeovers and ill-founded marketing ideas, the ultra-British Rootes Group and Gallic Simca were heaped together under the single Chrysler Europe banner. Models were sold as Chrysler in the UK, Simca in the remainder of Europe. In 1978 Chrysler USA quit, handing over the operation to Peugeot. Quickly the Chrysler name was dropped, replaced by Talbot, as the new owners were faced with the task of re-establishing image.

2-LITRE. 1970-80 (prod 23,720). 4-door 5-seater saloon. F/R, 1981cc (S4 OC). Max speed 109mph, 0-60mph 12.1sec. When it came to character, this car came bottom of the list, lacking almost any appeal. Most of the body and chassis design came from the UK, with France developing the powertrain. Heavy styling and US-influenced interior simply did not fit in on European roads. Its one saving grace was that it could seat five in comfort, with quite a large boot. Even if you've never been in one, the overall shape just about sums up the handling characteristics.

CITROEN (F)

André Citroën's wonderfully idiosyncratic style of engineering and design blossomed in 1934 with the low-slung *Traction Avant* saloons and went on through creations as diverse as the 2CV and Maserati-engined SM. But financial problems led to tyre-makers Michelin taking a major slice of the company. The merger with Peugeot started in 1974, Citroën becoming a wholly-owned subsidiary of PSA in May 1976.

2CV6. 1949-90 (prod 3,872,600). 2-door 4-seater saloon. F/F, 602cc (HO2 OHV). Max speed 68mph, 0-60mph 24.6sec. Tears were shed as the last French-built 2CV6 rolled out of the doors at the Levallois plant in north-west Paris in 1988, but production continued in Portugal until 1990. Ultra-basic transport, with the tiny air-cooled flat-twin engine providing marginal performance, the 2CV was as Gallic as Gauloise and *pastis*. The ability to thrive on neglect and corner on its minimal door handles simply added to the appeal. Yet despite its apparent simplicity, it was neither an easy DIY proposition nor that environmentally friendly.

DYANE 6. 1968-85 (prod 1,443,013 all models). 4-door 4-seater saloon. F/F, 602cc (HO2 OHV). Max speed 67mph, 0-60mph 25.2sec. Although it was pure 2CV below, with the same breathless 602cc flat-twin engine and dashboard gearchange, the Dyane, with its roomier, more practical four-door body, was a 'sensible' car, lacking much in the way of charisma. No matter what the original colour might have been, all seem to have faded into a blue-grey matt finish.

GSA. 1970-85 (prod 2,475,150). 5-door 5-seater hatchback. F/F, 1299cc (HO4 OC). Max speed 99mph, 0-60mph 13.6sec. Citroën at this time was never a company to allow convention to influence its designs. So there was an all-new flat-four, air-cooled engine, located ahead of the front wheels, driving through a four-speed gearbox. The self-levelling oleo-pneumatic suspension was similar to that used on the CX, with disc brakes all round – unique at the time on a car of this size. Original facia design was a Citroën classic, with rotating-drum speedo and controls located where you would least expect them.

GSA ESTATE. 1972-85 (prod: 576,760). 5-door 5-seater estate. F/F, 1299cc (HO4 OC). Max speed 97mph, 0-60mph 13.8sec. Running on the same long 100in wheelbase, the estate version could swallow surprisingly large loads, with the self-levelling suspension maintaining ride height and attitude at all times. What was really lacking was power, because the GSA engine never grew beyond 1.3/65bhp. Aerodynamics gave good top speed, but the car took its time getting there.

VISA. 1978-89 (prod: 1,254,400). 5-door 4-seater hatchback/convertible. F/F, 652cc (HO2 OHV), 952/1124/1360/1580cc (S4 OC), 1769cc diesel (S4 OC). Max speed 114mph, 0-60mph 9.2sec. No mistaking the Citroën styling, but under the bonnet there was a gradual move towards Peugeot-designed engines as the merger between the two makers grew stronger. The *decapotable* (convertible) needed to keep the door frames and use a tie bar between the B-pillars to retain a semblence of stiffness. All-independent suspension used MacPherson struts at the front, semi-trailing arms at the rear, with steel springs. Power ranged from the 652cc flat-twin's 35bhp to the 1580cc GT's 115bhp. Petrol-engined models gradually dropped, leaving the 1.7 diesel to soldier on almost to the end of the decade.

LNA. 1983-85 (prod: 223,775). 2-door 4-seater hatchback. F/F, 1124cc (S4 OC). Max speed 87mph, 0-60mph 14.2sec. Despite the extra side mouldings and add-on plastic trim, few were fooled into thinking that the LNA was anything but a Peugeot 104 in disguise. For its domestic market, Citroën produced the base LN, with the 652cc flat-twin air-cooled engine. For the UK, the Peugeot 1.1 T-series engine, laid back at an angle of 72 degrees, was kept. Why those initials? With a Gallic accent, they say Helena. Are you any the wiser?

CX20/22/24/25D. 1982-89 (prod: 1,042,300). 4-door 5-seater saloon. F/F, 1995cc (S4 OC), 2165/2347cc (S4 OHV), 2500cc diesel (S4 OHV). Max speed 137mph, 0-60mph 8.0sec. Launched originally in 1972, there were bodywork revisions and new designations from 1982. Citroën's first transverse-engined model, complete with the all-hydraulic suspension, braking and steering systems developed for the DS. Quickest CX was the GTi Turbo, with 168bhp going through the protesting front tyres. Early high-pressure hydraulic reliability problems were eventually resolved, but not before many owners had experienced that sinking feeling.

CX SAFARI. 1982-91 (prod: see above). 5-door 5/8-seater estate. F/F, 1995cc (S4 OC), 2165/2347cc (S4 OHV), 2500cc diesel (S4 OHV). Max speed 121mph, 0-60mph 10.2sec. If you wanted to include the kitchen sink, the Safari was for you, while the Familiale provided seemingly endless rows of seats. Reprofiled roof line and uncompromisingly vertical stern ensured every inch of available space could be used, while the suspension dealt with impossibly heavy loads without flinching. Diesels continued until 1991, when the XM estate – with equally van-sized load area – arrived.

AX. 1987 to date (prod: 2,075,149). 3/5-door 4-seater hatchback. F/F, 954/1224/1360cc (S4 OC), 1360cc diesel (S4 OC). Max speed 109mph, 0-60mph 9.2sec. Underneath are straightforward PSA engines and suspension – but outside it is pure Gallic *chic*, straight from a *couturier* in Rue St Honoré. Launched as a three-door, with five-door versions added 12 months on. Compact 90in wheelbase does not give a huge amount of space inside. The 1.0/45bhp, 1.1/55bhp and 1.3/65bhp engines were joined in 1988 by 1.3/85bhp GT version. The original interior was a rabbit warren of cubbyholes and hideyholes, but this was revised in 1989 along with better pedal and seat layout, improved sound-deadening and a general beefing-up of the rather flimsy construction.

BX. 1983-93 (prod: 2,333,240). 5-door 5-seater hatchback. F/F or F/4×4, 1360/1580/1905cc (S4 OC), 1769/1905cc diesels (S4 OC). Max speed 134mph, 0-60mph 8.1sec. Brilliant planning by PSA launched the sufficiently Citroënesque BX around the same time as the Peugeot 309, so that every taste was catered for. The by now bug-free high-pressure hydraulic system served suspension, brakes and, where fitted, power steering, while the BX used the corporate PSA range of overhead cam engines, including the outstanding diesels. The 16V GTi versions catered for the performance end of the market, with sure-footed handling and good ride – and there was a 4wd model too. Plastic panels, including bonnet and tailgate, cut weight and risk of corrosion.

BX ESTATE. 1985-93 (prod: see above). 5-door 5-seater estate. F/F or F/4×4, 1580/1905cc (S4 OC), 1769/1905cc diesels (S4 OC). Max speed 117mph, 0-60mph 9.6sec. It would have been too easy to spoil the attractive lines of the BX with an uncompromising squared-off estate car stern. Instead, a clever extension was grafted on, extending carrying capacity but preserving the looks. Self-levelling suspension looked after maximum payloads without any tail-end sag. The bottom 1.4 and top 1.9 16V versions were missed out, but again the diesels excelled, with strong low-down torque and world-beating refinement.

XM. 1989 to date (prod: 256,790). 5-door 5-seater hatchback. F/F, 1998cc (S4 OC), 2975cc (V6 OC), 2088cc turbo diesel (S4 OC). Max speed 146mph, 0-60mph 7.5sec. Citroën kept the faith with advanced technology, but the XM was able to benefit from so many lessons learned from the ultra-complex CX. Self-levelling oleo-pneumatic suspension backed by computer control resulted in outstanding ride and handling. Two versions of 1998cc eight-valve engine gave 115bhp and 130bhp, while the PRV 3.0 V6 produced 170bhp in its 12-valve form and 200bhp with new four-valve heads. The 12-valve four-cylinder turbo diesels were among PSA's best. Sleek hatchback bodies (styled by Bertone), with inner rear window to protect passengers from elements when the tailgate was opened, joined by practical estate in 1991.

CLAN (GB)

Paul Haussauer and John Frayling left Lotus in 1970 to establish the Clan plant at Washington in what was then Co. Durham. The Crusader's monocoque glass-fibre body gave room for two, with a Sunbeam Stiletto engine providing the power. In 1974, with the double blow of VAT on kit cars and the panic caused by the OPEC oil crisis, Clan folded. A decade later Clan was revived in Northern Ireland with investment help from the authorities, but it only lasted for a couple of years.

CLAN II. 1984-86 (prod: 40 approx). 2-door 2-seater sports coupé. R/R, 875cc (S4 OC), 1286cc (HO4 OC). Max speed 100mph, 0-60mph 12.0sec. With its wider track, flared wheel arches and pop-up headlamps, the revised Clan II lost some of the original's perky looks. The Imp engine, still in production as an industrial unit, was used once more, although a few cars were built with rear-mounted 1.3 Alfasud engines and gearboxes. The new Clan had the makings of success, with sound build quality and nice handling, but fragile financing led the company to cease trading late in 1986.

CRAYFORD (GB)

David McMullan founded his business in Westerham, Kent, during the late 1960s, producing convertible Minis. Other ventures included a soft-top version of the Ford Fiesta, an estate car based on the Triumph TR7, and the Cortina convertible, made in conjunction with Carbodies (see pages 30-31).

CORTINA. 1981-83 (prod: n/a). 2-door 4-seater convertible. F/R, 1297cc (S4 OHV), 1593/1993cc (S4 OC). Max speed n/a, 0-60mph n/a. The Cortina project was based on the three-door MkIV, only sold briefly with the 1.3 engine in the UK. Bodyshell stiffening included inserting extra bracing into the sills via the rear wheel arches, plus more bracing under the rear seat and scuttle. After the prototype, a deal was agreed with Carbodies in Coventry for a limited production run, with the addition of 1.6 and 2.0 engines.

MERCEDES-BENZ 230CE/280CE. 1978-81 (prod: 12). 2-door 4-seater convertibles. F/R, 2307cc (S4 OC), 2746cc (S6 OC). Max speed 114mph, 0-60mph 10.4sec. The first car to be converted, for a Middle East customer, was not a full soft-top. Instead, only the section behind the rear seat passengers was made to fold flat. Later a handful of cars were produced as full convertibles, although the long cockpit opening made torsional stiffness difficult to achieve.

FIESTA. 1983 (prod: 21). 2-door 4-seater convertible. F/F, 957/1117cc (S4 OHV), 1298/1608cc (S4 OC). Max speed n/a, 0-60mph n/a. In the post-war years the motorcycle and sidecar was the alternative to the cheapest car, so the Fiesta Fly was seen as the modern alternative to the combination. The hatchback was removed by welding the lower part of the tailgate to the bodyshell, so adding extra bracing. More stiffening was added under the scuttle and across the engine bulkhead. The conversions were only done on secondhand Fiestas – and provided a cheap(ish) and cheerful introduction to fresh air motoring, provided you could tolerate the rattles and scuttle shake. Few of those built made it into the 1990s.

DACIA (ROM)

Unlike some other western European manufacturers, Renault was willing to let Romania produce its own versions of the 4, 5 and 18 while they were still being built in France, as well as the time-expired R12, none of which were sold in the UK. The state-owned organisation also produced the ARO 4wd vehicles, although the Duster was sold in the UK under the Dacia banner.

DUSTER 1981-90 (prod: n/a). 2-door 4-seater off-roader. F/4×4, 1397cc (S4 OHV). Max speed 73mph, 0-60mph 22.7sec. Price was one of the few things in favour of the Duster, which was sold in the UK either as the soft-top Roadster or the grandly-titled GLX estate. Underneath the utilitarian bodywork was a ladder type chassis, with independent suspension fore and aft. The Renault engine drove the front wheels, with the rear ones being clutched in for (limited) off-road driving. The increasing number of Japanese rivals did it all so much better...

DAIHATSU (J)

The foundations of the company date back to 1907, but the name was not adopted until 1951, and the first four-wheeled vehicle was not made until 1958. Daihatsu, how part of the Toyota group of companies, has always concentrated on small cars and compact 4wd off-roaders. In 1966, the Compagno had the distinction of being the very first Japanese car to be imported, briefly, for sale in the UK.

DOMINO. 1983-89 (prod: n/a). 3/5-door 4-seater hatchback. F/F, 617cc (S2 OC), 846cc (S3 OC). Max speed 85mph, 0-60mph 14.7sec. A tiny hatchback, initially with a diminutive 617cc twin-cylinder water-cooled engine producing a frenzied 32bhp. In 1986, the transverse engine gained a third cylinder and size went up to 846cc, with 44bhp, and there was now a five-speed gearbox. The five-door model was 6in longer than a Mini but the interior was far smaller – but fitting five doors into a body length of 10ft 6in was an achievement in itself. Lively handling – and an even livelier ride.

CHARADE. 1981-87 (prod: n/a). 3/5-door 4-seater hatchback. F/F, 993cc (S3 OC), 993cc diesel (S3 OC). Max speed 103mph, 0-60mph 10.3sec. Clean looks, and with the distinction of having three-cylinder 993cc overhead cam engines of amazing variety. Cooking petrol version gave 50bhp, the diesel – the smallest in the UK – 37.6bhp. With a turbo, petrol power went to 68bhp and the diesel to an amazing 46bhp, with outstanding economy and off-beat noises. While handling was fair, ride was over-firm and very fidgety.

CHARADE. 1987-93 (prod: 579,700). 5-door 4-seater hatchback. F/F, 993cc (S3 OC), 993cc diesel (S3 OC), 1295cc (S4 OC). Max speed 106mph, 0-60mph 10.5sec. An amazing amount of space was packed into the five-door hatchback body. Far more refined four-cylinder 1.3 engines supplemented the rackety three-cylinder originals, but the diesel remained unbeatable for economy.

Towards the end the interiors were starting to look rather angular and dated, while Japanese rivals were learning a thing or two about ride.

CHARADE GTti. 1987-93 (prod: 227,790). 3-door 4-seater hatchback. F/F, 993cc (S3 DOC). Max speed 113mph, 0-60mph 7.7sec. If there was ever a latter day Mini Cooper S, this was it. With fuel injection and a turbo, the little three-cylinder engine screamed out 99bhp, making this little three-door rollerskate huge fun to drive. Amazingly, it applied all that power to the road without too much wheelspin, while precise steering gave pin-sharp handling, although the over-firm ride could send it scuttling sideways on poor surfaces. An impossible act to follow...

CHARMANT. 1983-87 (prod: n/a). 4-door 4-seater saloon. F/F, 1290/1588cc (S4 OC). Max speed 96mph, 0-60mph 13.2sec. When it came to anonymous looks, the Charmant had to be among the top contenders. Bland three-box saloon used wishbone front suspension, with a Panhard rod-located dead rear axle. With 1.3/64bhp and 1.6/74bhp engines and five-speed gearboxes, performance was nothing special. Unusually, the larger-engined 1600GLX could be ordered with semi-automatic three-speed Diamatic transmission, which gave acceleration of the suck-it-and-see variety.

FOURTRAK. 1985 to date. (prod: 379,000). 2/3-door 2/4-seater off-roader. F/4×4, 1998/2765cc (S4 OC), 2765cc diesel (S4 OC). Max speed 83mph, 0-60mph 17.2sec. Slotting neatly between the 'supermini' off-roaders and the heavy metal, the Fourtrak had the options of 2.0/87bhp petrol, 2.8/72bhp diesel or 2.8/82bhp turbo diesel engines. Some early models made do with four-speed gearboxes, but 4wd plus low-ratio transfer boxes gave good off-road abilities. On-road handling rather matched the rugged looks.

SPORTRAK. 1989 to date (prod: 250,500). 3-door 4-seater off-roader. F/4×4, 1589cc (S4 OC). Max speed 92mph, 0-60mph 13.2sec. It did not take the Japanese long to move in on the 'leisure' market. Lively 1.6/85bhp engine and slick five-speed gearbox, joined by a 94bhp 16-valve version in 1990. Reasonable on-road handling and performance, while 4wd, with freewheeling front hubs, gave mild off-roading abilities.

DAIMLER (GB)

One of the older names in the British industry, although it has had many owners. It was part of the BSA Group in the 1950s, when some extraordinary gold-plated models were built for the chairman, Lord Docker, at the behest of his wife to publicise (or vulgarise) the name. Sold to

Jaguar in 1960, although for some time it retained its own identity, with a range of V8 engines. With Jaguar, Daimler was swallowed into the BMC empire in 1966, to go public in 1984.

SOVEREIGN SERIES III. 1979-86 (prod: 29,354). 4-door 5-seater saloon. F/R, 4235cc (S6 DOC). Max speed 126mph, 0-60mph 8.7sec. Pininfarina beautifully restyled the Series II 'greenhouse' to give the Series III a flatter roof and larger windows, while new triangular tail lamps provided further recognition. The 31-year-old XK six-cylinder engine soldiered on, with fuel injection pushing power up to 205bhp. In 1983 both the Vanden Plas and Sovereign titles were dropped, along with manual gearbox, with the lavishly-equipped Daimler model – distinguished by a different radiator grille – becoming the plain 4.2.

3.6/4.0. 1986 to date (prod: 28,775). 4-door 5-seater saloon. F/R, 3590cc/3980cc (S6 DOC). Max speed 131mph, 0-60mph 7.7sec. Once more the fluted top to the radiator grille and carefully tailored equipment managed to set the Daimler version apart from the Jaguar XJ6. Both handling and ride complemented the outstandingly graceful, elegant looks. Daimler models did not use the 2.9 version of the new single-cam AJ6 engine, starting with the 3.6/221bhp version and increasing to 4.0/235bhp in autumn 1989.

DOUBLE-SIX SERIES III. 1981 to date (prod: 14,270). 4-door 5-seater saloon. F/R, 5343cc (V12 OC). Max speed 150mph, 0-60mph 8.7sec. The name goes back to 1927, with Daimler's first V12 – or double-six. Essentially the same bodyshell and engines as the Jaguar, with the Pininfarina 'greenhouse' changes. The Vanden Plas version lasted just 18 months, replaced by the HE model with similar equipment. Power of the 5.3 V12 engine dropped from 295bhp to 260bhp in 1990 with the fitting of a catalyst. Only offered with GM 400 automatic transmission.

LIMOUSINE. 1979-92 (prod: 4305). 4-door 7-seater limousine/cabriolet. F/R, 4235cc (S6 DOC). Max speed n/a, 0-60mph n/a. A coachbuilding era ended with the demise of the Limousine in 1992. A stretched 420G floorpan and 4.2 XK engine, with just 164bhp provided the platform on which was mounted the imposing body, built by Motor Panels. Jaguar craftsmen completed the trim, with all cars being built very much to individual specifications. Outstanding ride, but handling at higher speeds can be judged from the appearance.

DELOREAN (GB)

The saga of John Z. DeLorean will long be remembered in Northern Ireland, where so many hopes were pinned on the success of the new car. Government money was poured into the project, against advice from practically every quarter. Lotus and Giugiaro were brought in to design the chassis and body, but the whole project foundered in a trail of debts, scandal and lost jobs. DeLorean himself, however, seemed to emerge unscathed from endless legal actions.

DMC-2. 1981-82 (prod: 8583). 2-door 2+2-seater coupé. R/R, 2849cc (V6 OC). Max speed 121mph, 0-60mph 10.2sec. John Z. went for the best, with Lotus designing the classic backbone chassis and Giugiaro responsible for the styling. But from the start things began to go wrong, with dreadful build quality, doubts over the safety of the gull-wing doors and the stainless steel veneer over the plastic bodyshell showing every fingerprint. The rear-mounted Renault V6 engine made handling tricky, while the car's weight stunted performance.

DE TOMASO (I)

Alejandro de Tomaso's involvement in Italy's motor industry has been wide and varied, encompassing Maserati, Innocenti and Moto Guzzi. His early models, the Vallelunga and Mangusta, were more interesting than successful. Unusual were the big saloons and coupés, which had more traditional lines than the evergreen Ford V8-engined Pantera.

PANTERA GTS. 1971-93 (prod: 10,000). 2-door 2-seater coupé. M/R, 5763cc (V8 OHV). Max speed 170mph, 0-60mph 5.2 sec. The sole 1980s survivor of the thundering herd of V8-engined continental supercars which flourished in the 1970s. The Dallara-designed chassis had its 5.8 Ford V8 engine mid-mounted, driving through a five-speed ZF transaxle. Tail-heavy weight bias made handling interesting, but the performance was undeniably in the soul-stirring category.

DEAUVILLE. 1971-89 (prod: 355 approx). 4-door 5-seater saloon. F/R, 5763cc (V8 OHV). Max speed 150mph, 0-60mph 8.6sec. A Jaguar XJ6 must have been passing the drawing office windows at Ghia's studio when they were seeking inspiration for the new long-wheelbase, four-door version of the Longchamps. The front was changed – for the worse – with a new four-headlamp layout. A 5.8 Ford V8 provided the power, with a three-speed automatic from the same stable. The Dallara-designed chassis meant independent suspension all round, plus big disc brakes. UK sales were tiny and faded virtually to oblivion before 1980 was more than a few months old – but manufacture continued at a trickle until 1989.

LONGCHAMPS. 1972-89 (prod: 400 approx). 2-door 4-seater saloon. F/R, 5763cc (V8 OHV). Max speed 150mph, 0-60mph 6.7sec. Once again the 5.8 Ford V8 supplied the power for this two-door short-chassis version of the big Deauville saloon, with Ghia responsible for the looks. Automatic was standard, although the GTS version, just a few of which made it to the UK, could have a five-speed ZF manual 'box. At £38,527, sales were few and far between.

DUTTON (GB)

The first Dutton - the name comes from founder Tim Dutton-Wooley - was made in 1968 at the Worthing, West Sussex, plant. The vast majority were sold as kits, with simple tubular chassis, a variety of existing suspensions, and glass-fibre bodywork reminiscent of, but not copying, the Lotus Seven.

Above: Dutton Phaeton. Below: Dutton Melos.

PHAETON/MELOS. 1983-91 (prod: n/a). 2/4-seater convertible. F/R, various engines. Max speed n/a, 0-60mph n/a. The Phaeton was a development of the Dutton B, which used a separate chassis, Triumph Spitfire suspension and almost any engine you chose to drop under the bonnet. The doorless but well-finished glass-fibre body owed something to the Lotus Seven, but was no slavish copy. The Melos used the same chassis, but the 'retro' body styling pre-dated even the Colin Chapman era.

ERA (GB)

The ERA initials are famous for pre-war voiturette racing cars like 'Romulus' and 'Remus', but they found themselves on a very different machine in the late 1980s. Attempting to evoke the Mini Cooper spirit, this Dunstable-based engineering consultancy went into limited production with a turbocharged, titivated Mini, but the special company formed to produce it folded in 1991.

MINI TURBO. 1989-91 (prod: 400 plus). 2-door, 4-seater saloon. F/F, 1275cc (S4 OHV). Max speed 115mph, 0-60mph 7.8sec. Power was provided by a 1275cc MG Metro engine, squeezed to 94bhp at 6130rpm, driving through the 'old faithful' in-the-sump four-speed 'box. Dennis Adams created the body mods, with fat 6in rimmed 13in wheels and suspension tweaked to cope. Performance was in the point-and-squirt class. Inside the Mini's classic bus driver seat/wheel relationship was drastically modified to make it all more driver friendly. At £11,950, it was not surprising that most went to Japanese Minimaniacs.

FERRARI (I)

In 1969 Fiat took a quiet 50 per cent share in what has to be the most instantly recognisable name in motoring, and acquired full control on Enzo Ferrari's death in 1988. The black-on-yellow prancing horse badge has appeared on some of the most sought-after high performance cars in the world, the ultimate being the 1962 250GTO short wheelbase Berlinetta.

400i/412i. 1979-89 (prod: 1308/576). 2-door 4-seater saloon. F/R, 4823/4942cc (V12 DOC). Max speed 158mph, 0-60mph 6.7sec. The Ferrari for the family, with proper seating for four. The chassis was based on a long wheelbase version of the 365GTC/4, with a classic Pininfarina body. The 400 used the 310bhp 4.8 V12, replaced in 1986 by the

340bhp 5.0 engine, both available with three-speed automatic transmission. In line with the looks, equipment included air conditioning, leather upholstery and, with the 412, anti-lock brakes. Those slightly sedate, but undeniably elegant, looks should not deceive, for the handling was quite delightful.

308GTB/GTS. 1975-81 (prod: 2897/3219). 2-door 2-seater coupé/'targa'. M/R, 2921cc (V8 DOC). Max speed 154mph, 0-60mph 6.5sec. During the late 1960s, the 246 Dino had been seen as the alternative to the Porsche 911, but the 308 which replaced it made it no contest. Virtually the same chassis was retained, with the 3.0 dry-sump V8, mounted transversely behind the seats, giving 250bhp. A 2.0 V8 version, the 208, was a turbocharged tax beater for the Italian market only. Pininfarina came up with the best-looking Ferrari to date, with the side air ducts looking exactly right. Until 1977, bodies were in glass-fibre, but (rust-prone) steel was used after that largely in deference to Ferrari's perception of what US customers wanted.

308GTBi/GTSi. 1981-85 (prod: 1242/4785). 2-door 2-seater coupé/'targa'. M/R, 2921cc (V8 DOC). Max speed 148mph, 0-60mph 6.9sec. Faced with tougher exhaust emission regulations, Ferrari switched to Bosch K-Jetronic fuel injection. The result was a drop in power from the original's 250bhp to just 214bhp. Performance fell off markedly, so that the magic 150mph was no longer attainable. The solution to the problem came one year later, with the more efficient four-valve (*quattrovalvole*) cylinder heads. Power returned to 240bhp and with it the 308's original performance.

328GTB/GTS. 1985-88 (prod: 1344/6068). 2-door 2-seater coupé/'targa'. M/R, 3195cc (V8 DOC). Max speed 163mph, 0-60mph 6.4sec. With the classic GTB/GTS in its final form, the capacity of the V8 engine was lifted to 3.2 litres and the *quattrovalvole* cylinder heads were kept. Power went to 270bhp, backed with a healthy 223lb ft torque. The result was that Ferrari's claims of over 160mph for its best-selling car ever were finally realised.

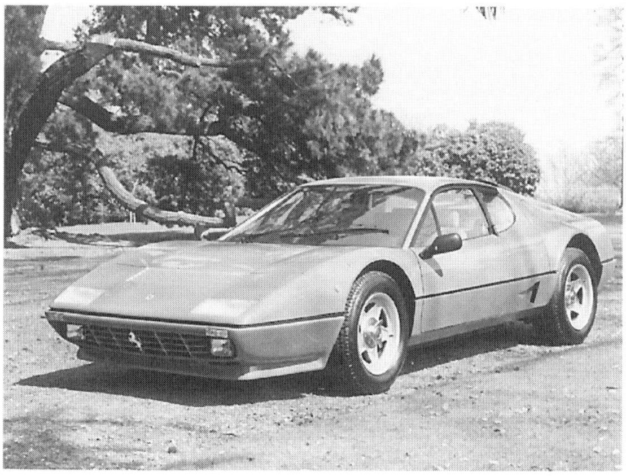

BB512/BB512i. 1973-85 (prod: 929/1007). 2-door 2-seater coupé. M/R, 4942cc (HO12 DOC). Max speed 188mph, 0-60mph 5.2sec. Those BB initials stood for Berlinetta Boxer, marking Ferrari's first use in a road car of the race-bred flat-12 engine. The purity of line achieved by the Pininfarina stylists gave the models that timeless beauty which continues to turn heads today. The 5.0 engine in early four Weber carburettor form produced the same power (360bhp) as the 1973-76 4.4 original, but torque was up 10 per cent. From 1981, Bosch K-Jetronic injection displaced carbs and took power up to 380bhp. Poise and handling were every bit as good as the looks. The only query seemed to be over the maximum speed, because few motoring magazines could get close to Ferrari's claimed 188mph. But with looks like that, does it really matter?

TESTAROSSA. 1984-92 (prod: n/a). 2-door 2-seater coupé. M/R, 4942cc (HO12 DOC). Max speed 181mph, 0-60mph 5.8sec. Successor to 512BB, unmistakable for its sheer size and distinctive – and much-copied – horizontal side slats directing air into the rear-mounted radiators. Most bodywork, save roof and door pressings, was in aluminium to save weight. Capacity of the all-alloy flat-12 engine was upped to 5.0, giving 390bhp. Pininfarina had used a wind tunnel to achieve the necessary downthrust, but even so the model's sheer size – width of 78in made it the broadest production car of its time – meant that plenty of wide open road was needed to exploit its amazing handling. Nevertheless, this was a Ferrari which anyone could feel comfortable in, with its light controls and user-friendly cabin.

MONDIAL 8/QV/3.2. 1980-89 (prod: 703/1145/ 987). 2-door 4-seater coupé. M/R, 2926cc (V8 DOC), 3195cc (V8 DOC). Max speed 155mph, 0-60mph 7.4sec. As the name implies, this was Ferrari's first 'world' car, designed to meet assorted regulations in potential markets. It was made on the 1970s 308GT4 floorpan, stretched by 4in to make it a full four-seater – despite having the V8 mounted behind the cabin. The transverse 3.0 engine's power went from 214bhp to 240bhp with the *quattrovalvole* (four valves per cylinder) version in 1982, and to 270bhp with the 3.2 in 1985. Its ease of driving and slightly ungainly looks marked it down in many people's books, but for some owners it was an ideal blend of practicality and vivacity.

MONDIAL CABRIOLET. 1984-94 (prod: 629). 2-door 4-seater cabriolet. M/R, 2926/3195cc (V8 DOC), 3405cc (V8 DOC). Max speed 155mph, 0-60mph 7.4sec. The 'world' image of the Mondial was strengthened with the soft-top version launched in 1984. Pininfarina-designed body looked at its best with the hood folded, with no roll-over bar spoiling clean lines. Larger 3.2/270bhp twin-cam V8 replaced original 3.0/240bhp in 1986, at same time as body and trim revisions. Big change was switch to 3.4/300bhp and transverse gearbox in summer 1989. Despite potential performance, amazingly easy to drive.

MONDIAL t. 1989-94 (prod: n/a). 2-door 4-seater coupé/cabriolet. M/R, 3405cc (V8 DOC). Max speed 158mph, 0-60mph 6.3sec. The external changes gave little clue to what had happened inside the Mondial. Engine size was increased 3405cc, with the V8 now located longitudinally and hitched to a new transverse five-speed gearbox. Electronically-controlled damping smoothed out the suspension and enhanced the already good handling. The new interior gave more room, with a far better control layout. But the Mondial still seemed lacking in one vital ingredient – the magic Ferrari image.

288 GTO. 1984-87 (prod: 273). 2-door 2-seater coupé. M/R, 2855cc (V8 DOC). Max speed 190mph, 0-60mph 4.0sec. Ferrari's most famous set of initials was revived for what was planned as a 200-off 'homologation special' Group B competition model – but the car was never to race seriously. Lines were similar to a 308, but the wheelbase was 4in longer to accommodate the north-south, rather than transverse, engine layout. Ferrari had tried turbocharging before, in the 2.0 208 Italian market tax-beater, but this was different. With twin IHI turbos, the V8 gave a massive 400bhp, plus 366lb ft of torque. Almost all were sold as road-going versions, a few with refinements like air conditioning and electric windows.

F40. 1988-92 (prod: n/a). 2-door 2-seater coupé. M/R, 2936cc (V8 DOC). Max speed 201mph, 0-60mph 3.9sec. Built to mark Enzo Ferrari's 40 years in the business – and hyped to be, at the time, the ultimate supercar. Based on the GTO floorpan, the F40 made extensive and innovative use of exotic composites to save body/chassis weight – a quest which explains the lack of carpets and door trim. With twin turbos, the short stroke 3.0 V8 developed 478bhp. But if you wanted more, the factory could arrange for a further 200bhp in exchange for several million lire. The performance was shattering – and so were the losses for people who hoped to make a killing on resale values. Until the arrival of the Lamborghini Diablo and Jaguar XJ220, this was the world's fastest production car. It was also the noisiest, the stripped-out cabin acting like a sounding box – but this was part of the F40's unforgettable character.

348tb/ts. 1989 to date (prod: n/a). 2-door 2-seater coupé/'targa'. M/R, 3405cc (V8 DOC). Max speed 170mph, 0-60mph 5.6sec. Stricter crash protection regulations, plus the need for new styling, resulted in a bigger, bulkier replacement for the 328. The familiar V8 engine, now in 3.4 form, was turned through 90 degrees so that it could be set lower in the chassis, which itself had been stiffened further to help handling. Although the engine was longitudinal, the five-speed gearbox was transverse (hence the 't'), as in contemporary F1 cars. Pininfarina's rather anonymous-looking body had outstanding aerodynamics, with Testarossa-style side radiator vents. The V8's 296bhp gave tremendous performance – but rivals were starting to catch up too quickly for Maranello's comfort.

FIAT (I)

Fiat is Italy - and Italy is Fiat. Giovanni Agnelli founded the company which was to become Fabbrica Italiana Automobili Torino in 1899, and it has stayed in Agnelli hands ever since. Since 1968, Autobianchi, Lancia, Ferrari and Alfa Romeo have all become members of the family. Until recently Fiat dominated sales in Italy, but market share has been pared back by imports. In the UK, the image of rusting cars has finally been laid to rest.

126. 1977-87 (prod: 1,970,000). 2-door 4-seater saloon. R/R, 594/652cc (S2 OHV). Max speed

65mph, 0-60mph 42.1sec. Matchbox motoring at its most minimal. Vertical twin 652cc/24bhp engine in the back did its tiny air-cooled best to provide some performance, which was slender even when going downhill. At sub-65mph speeds handling did not matter, while the ride made it hard to believe that there was all-round independent suspension. Fiat's domination of the Italian domestic market ensured high demand for a car whose roots could be traced to the original pre-war Topolino 500.

126 BIS. 1987-92 (prod: 879,500). 2-door 4-seater hatchback. R/R, 704cc (HO2 OHV). Max speed 72mph, 0-60mph 33.0sec. A new flat-twin 704cc engine meant more power – up from 24bhp to 26bhp. The under-the-floor location meant that the new model, by now being built by FSM in Poland, could finally get a hatchback and folding rear seats. The extra power meant that 70mph could just be exceeded if you had the time to spare. The 126 clung on into the 1990s while far better and, more importantly, more economical models were leaving it wandering in a motorised wilderness.

128. 1969-84 (prod: 2,776,000). 2/4-door 4-seater saloon. F/F, 903cc (S4 OHV), 1115/1290cc (S4 OC). Max speed 90mph, 0-60mph 13.9sec. Practical three-box body continued virtually unchanged for 15 years, although there were three-door 'sporting' versions in the 1970s. But those ordinary looks concealed several innovations, such as the new overhead cam engines and the end-on gearbox for front-drive. Handling, too, was something new, with tenacious grip and, for this size of car, outstanding ride from the all-independent suspension. Rust, rather than mechanical weariness, saw most head prematurely for the scrapyard.

127. 1971-83 (prod: 3,730,000). 3-door 4-seater hatchback. F/F, 903 (S4 OHV), 1049/1301cc (S4 OC). Max speed 91mph, 0-60mph 11.9sec. Smaller by 9in in the wheelbase than the 128, the 127 became one of Fiat's most successful models. Crisp styling contained plenty of room for occupants and, with sensibly sized hatchback, their luggage. Front-drive layout initially used 903cc pushrod engine, later with Fiat Brazil's 1049cc overhead cam unit, and finally with the 75bhp 1300 Sport version. If the ride could not quite match the 128's, the handling more than equalled. But the spectre of rust was never far away.

X1/9 1500. 1978-89 (prod: 180,000). 2-door 2-seater sports coupé. M/R, 1498cc (S4 OC). Max speed 111mph, 0-60mph 10.3sec. When it came to style, this pretty little mid-engined sports-car, designed and built by Bertone, was a winner. Image was exactly right, with pop-up headlamps and lift-off roof panel. The chassis was clearly able to handle more than the rather puny 85bhp the transversely-mounted engine was able to provide, so that many luke-warm hatchbacks could outrun it – but it was always fun to drive. Right to the end, with the last models named Gran Finale, rust remained the eternal problem.

STRADA. 1978-88 (prod: 1,790,000). 3/5-door 4-seater hatchback. F/F, 1116/1301/1498 (S4 OHC), 1585cc (S4 DOC). Max speed 111mph, 0-60mph 9.4sec. No one could accuse Fiat of styling conservatism with its new model, called Ritmo everywhere except in the UK, where it was better know as Strada. It ran alongside the 128, using much of that model's running gear. Fiat's first real venture into the hot hatchback field was with the twin-cam 105TC and 125TC. Handling and ride were good, but the original styling, thankfully more restrained with the Mk2 version, of this famously robot-built car was too weird for many tastes.

STRADA CABRIOLET. 1983-85 (prod: see above). 2-door 4-seater convertible. F/F, 1498cc (S4 OC). Max speed 103mph, 0-60mph 10.3sec. With the sudden interest in convertibles, Fiat hurried in with its contender. Built by Bertone (who also called it the Palinuro), the two-door Strada version was built round the 1.5/82bhp engine. Stiffness was helped by a roll-over bar between the B-pillars, and a closed-in rear end in place of the hatchback opening. Low demand in Italy and on export markets brought the project to an end after just two years. This rag-top may have been able to beat a Golf cabriolet on price, but it couldn't touch it for quality or ability.

STRADA 130TC. 1984-88 (prod: see above). 3-door 4-seater hatchback. F/F, 1995cc (S4 DOC). Max speed 117mph, 0-60mph 7.9sec. Abarth's scorpion badge on the back said it all. A wonderful scruff-of-the-neck car, with a brace of gobbling, gurgling Weber carburettors feeding the fiercely exciting 2.0 twin-cam engine. Recaro front seats kept you in place as you explored the limits of grip while your vision blurred with the rock-hard, race-track ride, keeping the rev counter on the red line with the aid of the close-ratio gearbox. Short on refinement, long on sheer driving exuberance. So much a driver's car that only contortionists could squeeze past the Recaros into the back seats...

REGATA 1984-90 (prod: 1,970,000). 4-door 4-seater saloon. F/F, 1299/1585cc (S4 OC), 1585cc (S4 DOC), 1929cc diesel (S4 OC). Max speed 109mph, 0-60mph 9.9sec. After the styling novelty of the original Strada, the three-box Regata saloon looked almost plain by comparison. Same floorpan as the hatchback, even to the unusual transverse leaf spring independent rear suspension. Early models included fuel-saving engine cut-off systems, with re-start operated by clutch pedal; they did not last long. Turbo diesel was quick if slightly agricultural.

REGATA WEEKEND. 1985-90 (prod: see above). 5-door 4-seater estate. F/F, 1585cc (S4 OC), 1585cc (S4 DOC). Max speed 113mph, 0-60mph 10.6sec. Product planners slipped, because almost a year elapsed between the Mirafiori estate being pensioned off and the Weekend arriving. On the same wheelbase as the Regata saloon, it proved to be a useful load carrier, with just the 1.6 single-cam (85bhp) and twin-cam (100bhp) engines for the UK market during the '80s. Unusual was the split tailgate, carried on to the Tempra SW in the 1990s.

MIRAFIORI. 1978-84 (prod: 1,850,500). 4/5-door 4-seater saloon/estate. F/R, 1367/1585cc (S4 OC), 1995cc (S4 DOC). Max speed 110mph, 0-60mph 10.1sec. After using numbers as model designations for years, Fiat switched to names. Mirafiori may sound exotic, but it was simply the name of the factory where the car was built. Successor to the hugely successful 124, although it lacked much driving excitement in either handling or performance. The 2.0/112bhp twin-cam Supermirafirori estate clung on until 1984, although rust has claimed most by now.

124 SPIDER. 1972-82 (prod: 140,000). 2-door 2+2-sports car. F/R, 1592/1995cc (S4 DOC). Max speed 115mph, 0-60mph 9.8sec. Although the coupe version of the 124 vanished a couple of years before the saloon, the open spider, both designed and built by Pininfarina, lived on (although only as LHD personal imports in the UK), with the twin-cam 2.0 engine providing the performance its looks always deserved. The handling was everything that the front-engined, rear-drive layout dictated, but these sporting Fiats were always overshadowed by their Alfa Romeo rivals.

132/ARGENTA. 1972-84 (prod: 975,970). 4-door 5-seater saloon. F/R, 1585/1592/1856/1995cc (S4 DOC), 1995cc (S4 OC). Max speed 110mph, 0-60 10.5sec. Among grey cars, this had to be the greyest. Yes, there was plenty of room within the square-rigged shape, and the larger engines gave a modicum of performance, but dull handling and indifferent ride just about sums it up. The 132 version seemed to be relaunched almost annually, but the result was usually the same – universal apathy. Changing the name in 1982 to Argenta did not fool anyone…

PANDA. 1980 to date (prod: 2,740,350). 2-door 4-seater hatchback. F/F, 903cc (S4 OHV), 769/999cc (S4 OC). Max speed 87mph, 0-60mph 16.0sec. Someone unkindly said the Panda looked like the box it came in. Squared-up body with flat glass all round made maximum use of interior space, and the facia design was refreshingly different. The tiny 652cc/30bhp 126-engined version was never sold in UK. Original and simple semi-elliptic rear suspension gave a harsh ride, but Lancia Y10-style 'Omega' suspension, along with the new FIRE range of overhead-cam engines, improved ride, performance and image.

PANDA 4x4. 1984-92 (prod: see above). 2-door 4-seater hatchback. F/4×4, 965cc (S4 OHV), 999cc (S4 OC). Max speed 83mph, 0-60mph 16.7sec. Land Rover had nothing to fear. Built by Steyr Puch in Austria, the 4×4 normally drove through the front wheels, with an ultra-simple 4wd system adding rear-drive to tackle ice, snow and mud. Higher ground clearance and knobbly tyres helped in bad conditions, but this Panda never had off-roader pretensions. The extra weight and height made cornering feel a little top heavy – but with so little performance it never really mattered.

UNO SELECTA. 1987-93 (prod: see above). 3/5-door 4-seater hatchback. F/F, 1108cc (S4 OC). Max speed 96mph, 0-60mph 15.0sec. Fiat and Ford joined forces to develop an entirely new version of the original Van Doorne inspired stepless, continuously-variable automatic transmission, using a steel segment belt in place of the original flexible rubber bands. The MkI versions suffered from poor cold-start drive away, snatchy take-up and noise – but pointed the way to future developments which really did work, and others were to copy.

UNO. 1983 to date (prod: approx 6.5 million to 1994). 3/5-door 4-seater hatchback. F/F, 903cc (S4 OHV), 999/1108/1116/1299/1301cc (S4 OC), 1697cc diesel (S4 OC). Max speed 102mph, 0-60mph 12.0sec. Style-setter when it first appeared, with tall Giugiaro-penned outline and lots of glass. Surprisingly large inside too, with the original facia design wonderfully off-beat. Overhead-cam FIRE engines from 1985, 1.7/58bhp diesel from 1987. McPherson strut front suspension and torsion beam axle at the rear gave crisp, agile handling, with a comfortable ride. Body revisions and new facia in 1990, but the magic was starting to fade by then. One of the biggest-selling cars of the 1980s.

UNO TURBO. 1982 to date (prod: see above). 3-door 4-seater hatchback. F/F, 1299/1301/1372cc (S4 OC). Max speed 123mph, 0-60mph 7.9sec. There was little doubt that the Uno chassis was capable of taking the extra power, but the Turbo never quite managed to get into Division One of the hot hatches. With injection and turbo, the 1.3 engine gave 102bhp. In 1990, capacity increased to 1.4, with 118bhp. Be-spoilered tailgate, Turbo decals and alloy wheels did little to conceal what was rather too much of a boy racer image.

TIPO. 1988 to date (prod: 970,740). 5-door 4-seater hatchback. F/F, 1108/1373/1580cc (S4 OC), 1697/1929cc diesels (S4 OC). Max speed 106mph, 0-60mph 11.7sec. If the original Strada's styling was plain weird, the Tipo's was simply unusual – but it worked. And with all exterior body panels galvanised, the rusting curse was finally lifted. Long 100in wheelbase means plenty of room for passengers and luggage, with five doors only until 1993. The 1.1/56bhp version never sold in the UK, while 1.8 and 2.0 *sedicievalvole* (16-valve) models did not arrive until early 1990s. Outstanding if slightly rough-at-the-edges turbo diesel was fastest Tipo in 1980s. Well-mannered handling and good ride were plus points, but initial build quality achieved at Casino plant, near Naples, was not.

CROMA. 1986 to date (prod: 643,400). 5-door 5-seater hatchback. F/F, 1995cc (S4 DOC). Max speed 131mph, 0-60mph 8.2sec. Fiat's second Type Four model – the first was the Lancia Thema. Spacious hatchback using variations on the 2.0 twin-cam engine theme, with power of 90bhp or 120bhp with carburettor or injection, or up to a furious wheel-spinning 155bhp in turbo form. Very roomy, with sensible load-carrying abilities. Equipment levels became better and better throughout its life, but build quality was always hit-and-miss. Nice safe handling in general, but the turbo could suffer from horrendous torque steer. True to form, Fiat still seemed unable to make a genuinely competent big car.

FORD (GB)

The first Model Ts were built in the UK at Trafford Park, Manchester, in October 1911 - and since then Ford has not looked back. The Dagenham plant, built on reclaimed marshland in Essex alongside the Thames, opened in 1931. Ford marketed the first £100 car in 1935. While British Leyland foundered from the 1960s and Vauxhall was reorganising, Ford dominated the important company car business in the UK with models like the Cortina, Escort, Sierra and Granada.

CORTINA MkV. 1979-82 (prod: 1,131,850, inc MkIV). 2/4-door 5-seater saloon/estate. F/R, 1297cc (S4 OHV), 1593/1993cc (S4 OC), 2293cc (V6 OHV). Max speed 103mph, 0-60mph 10.5sec. In truth little more than a slightly face-lifted version of the MkIV, which three years before had itself replaced the Coke-bottle profiled MkIII. A more straightforward mechanical layout would be hard to find, faithful to the front-engined, rear-drive basics, complete with live rear axle. But with a wide assortment of trim levels, from L through to Ghia, it was ideal for the job it was designed to do – to sell and sell.

CAPRI III. 1977-86 (prod: 324,045 all models). 3-door 4-seater coupé hatchback. F/R, 1297cc (S4 OHV), 1593/1993cc (S4 OC), 2792/2994cc (V6 OHV). Max speed 127mph, 0-60mph 7.9sec. Even with the new four-headlamp front, looks were becoming dated. And as hot hatches began to make their mark, pruning had to start. The 1300s went in 1982, while the new 2.8 V6 replaced the potent 3.0 in 1981. The 1.6/2.0 Laser versions and the 2.8i Special soldiered on to 1987, when the axe finally fell on the car which Ford, 18 years before, had told us that we had always promised ourselves.

TICKFORD CAPRI. 1984 (prod: n/a). 3-door 4-seater coupé hatchback. F/R, 2792cc (V6 OHV). Max speed 133mph, 0-60mph 7.1sec. Little chance of missing this curiosity, with its all-white bespoilered bodywork and blankly-staring closed-in grille. The turbocharged 2.8 V6 gave 205bhp, against the standard car's 160bhp. Some clever changes to the rather basic original rear suspension also gave the Capri the handling it had always cried out for. Lots of leather and walnut inside – and a strange triangular-spoke steering wheel design. An icon for Essex Man?

CAPRI 280. 1987 (prod: 500). 3-door 4-seater coupé hatchback. F/R, 2792cc (V6 OHV). Max speed 127mph, 0-60mph 7.9sec. To mark the end of Capri production, Ford produced the 280 as the final limited edition. Mechanically absolutely standard, with the 160bhp 2.8 V6 engine and five-speed gearbox. But visually it was resplendent in Brooklands Green metallic paint, with 280 badging and special alloy wheels. Inside, there was full grey leather trim, piped in burgundy. One of the best Capris, and probably the most sought-after today.

FIESTA. 1976-83 (prod: 1,750,000). 3-door 4-seater hatchback. F/F, 957/1117/1298cc (S4 OHV). Max speed 94mph, 0-60mph 13.7sec. A milestone for Ford, with its first supermini and first transverse-engined front-drive model. New Valencia – after the name of the new Spanish factory – 1.0 and 1.1 OHV engines plus Kent 1.3 for UK mainstream models, all with four-speed gearbox. Neat three-door only body, with McPherson struts at front. With the Ford badge on the front, it had to succeed.

XR2. 1981-83 (prod: see above). 3-door 4-seater hatchback. F/F, 1598cc (S4 OHV). Max speed 104mph, 0-60mph 9.4sec. Barely lukewarm hatchback and a curious example of apparent indecision on Ford's part. It had the looks – alloy wheels, wheel arch extenders, black grille, sports seats and a rev counter. But with the Kent 1.6 OHV engine giving only 84bhp and just a four-speed gearbox, performance never sparkled. After less than two years, the XR2 project was temporarily shelved.

FIESTA. 1983-89 (prod: 1,980,100). 3-door 4-seater hatchback. F/F, 957/1117cc (S4 OHV), 1298/1392cc (S4 OC), 1608cc diesel (S4 OC). Max

speed 102mph, 0-60mph 10.6sec. A mid-term facelift gave the Fiesta a new, more rounded bonnet line, with a different grille, neater wrap-round indicators and a revised facia. The new front added a couple inches to overall length. While the smaller engines stayed unchanged, newcomers were the 69bhp 1.3 and, from 1986, the 75bhp 1.4 CVH (Compound Valve Hemispherical) units, with five-speed gearboxes. In 1987, the stepless CVT transmission, developed jointly with Fiat, was offered on some 1.1 models, but there were few takers.

XR2. 1984-89 (prod: see above). 3-door 4-seater hatchback. F/F, 1597cc (S4 OHC). Max speed 109mph, 0-60mph 9.5sec. With the new-look body and a 1.6 version of the CVH engine, the XR2 came to life. Still on carburettors but now with 95bhp and a five-speed gearbox, there was more than enough performance to outrun lesser Fiestas. The combination of safe, forgiving handling, sporty ride and the right looks made it an instant success, although over-sensitive steering was a criticism. The ability to withstand hard use and, in later life, the efforts of DIY owners, made it a firm favourite.

FIESTA. 1989 to date (prod: 1,697,000). 3/5-door 4-seater hatchback. F/F, 999/1118/1297cc (S4 OHV), 1392/1596cc (S4 OC), 1753cc diesel (S4 OC). Max speed 109mph, 0-60mph 10.0sec. Ford added an essential missing ingredient to the Fiesta recipe – size. The new bodyshell, 6in longer, offered three and five doors for the first time. The suspension stayed much as before, but new were the 1.0 and 1.1 HCS (High Compression Swirl) engines, designed to meet pre-catalyst EC emissions regulations. If the extra interior space was appreciated, the low-geared steering and indifferent handling were not to everyone's tastes.

FIESTA XR2i. 1989-92 (prod: see above). 3-door 4-seater hatchback. F/F, 1596cc (S4 OC). Max speed 114mph, 0-60mph 8.7sec. Made in three-door form only, the fuel-injected version of the 1.6 CVH engine, with 110bhp, gave the XR2i the performance previous carburettor versions had always lacked. With tautened suspension and wider wheels – alloys did not become standard until mid-summer in 1990 – handling was better than standard models' abilities. But in the competitive small hot hatch market, the XR2i was never among the front runners in terms of user-chooser popularity.

ESCORT MKII. 1975-80 (prod: 631,828 all types in UK, over 2 million worldwide). 2/4-door 4-seater saloon/estate. F/R, 1098/1297/1599cc (S4 OHV). Max speed 93mph, 0-60mph 12.9sec. While the new front-drive Escort was taking shape behind locked doors at Dunton, the front-engined, rear-drive version reached its final stages. The looks may have been a bit anonymous, while the engineering hardly caused even a slightly raised eyebrow. The Ghia name appeared, to replace the E, while the Sport took the place of the GT. The chassis was improved with all versions having discs at the front.

ESCORT RS2000 MKII. 1976-80 (prod: n/a). 2-door 4-seater saloon. F/R, 1993cc (S4 OC). Max speed 109mph, 0-60mph 8.6sec. Clever use of cosmetics, with a standard two-door Escort body prettied with a four-headlamp front, neat boot-top spoiler and alloy wheels. Less costly version later, with steel wheels. Power supplied by 110bhp 2.0 litre Pinto engine, but still with four-speed transmission. Suspension was tightened just enough to make handling very neat, so in its time it was considered very much a driver's car – and a favourite for club rallying. The RS, incidentally, stood for *Rallye*, not *Rennen* (racing) Sport.

ESCORT. 1980-86 (prod: 1,857,000). 3/5-door 4-seater hatchback/estate. F/F, 1117/1297cc (S4 OHV), 1296/1392/1597cc (S4 OC), 1608cc diesel (S4 OC). Max speed 101mph, 0-60mph 11.1sec. With the Fiesta filling the gap at the bottom of Ford's market, the switch from rear-drive to front-drive for the Escort should have come as no surprise. McPherson strut suspension was used front and rear, with a 94.6in wheelbase. As usual, Ford bracketed the market with a whole range of models, from base 1.1/1.3 to top Ghia versions. Both handling and ride were revelations after the dull, rear-drive, run-of-the-mill Escorts, and the shape was smart too. It became a firm favourite in the UK best-seller lists.

ORION. 1983-86 (prod: see above). 4-door 4-seater saloon. F/F, 1296/1597cc (S4 OC), 1608cc diesel (S4 OC). Max speed 115mph, 0-60mph 9.7sec. Product planning at its best, just as people were looking for a saloon alternative to the hatchback Escort. Based on same 94.6in wheelbase, but boot overhang added 9in to overall length. Image was 'adjusted', with no 1.1 version, although there was a 1.6/54bhp diesel. But it never managed to achieve anything like the volumes reached by the Escort, and the name was shelved in 1993.

ESCORT XR3/XR3i. 1981-86 (prod: see above). 3-door 4-seater hatchback. F/F, 1597cc (S4 OC). Max speed 116mph, 0-60mph 8.6sec. Ford had established a tradition of high-performance versions of its more mundane previous-model Escorts, but this was the first taste of the 1980s 'XR' philosophy. The 1.6 CVH engine, first in carburettor/96bhp form, then post-1983 with injection/105bhp, gave it the legs over lesser versions. It looked the part too, with black grille and window surrounds, alloy wheels and a tailgate spoiler. Slightly tautened suspension and low-profile tyres really put a shine on the already good handling. All that spoiled it was the tacky 'boy racer' following it attracted as the years went by.

ESCORT RS1600i. 1983 (prod: 8659). 3-door 4-seater hatchback. F/F, 1597cc (S4 OC). Max speed 117mph, 0-60mph 8.7sec. One of Ford's shorter-lived Escort variants, launched at the beginning of 1983 and gone by September, but only because demand was so strong. Ford originally planned to build 5000 for Groups A/N competition eligibility, but in the end 8659 were made. Power of the 1.6 CVH injection engine was upped to 115bhp, matched to a close-ratio five-speed transmission. This was a model you could hardly miss, with its 'strobe' bonnet striping, RS alloy wheels, Recaro front seats and chubby RS leather-trimmed steering wheel. Few and far between in the UK (around 700 came over from Cologne), but it did prove how basically good the Escort chassis was.

ESCORT RS TURBO. 1984-90 (prod: 8604). 3-door 4-seater hatchback. F/F, 1597cc (S4 OC). Max speed 122mph, 0-60mph 8.1sec. The RS1600i had been a foretaste of things to come. The RS Turbo used the same basic engine, but turbocharged (by Garrett AiResearch) to give 132bhp, which remained unchanged throughout its life. Until 1986 facelift, available only in white. It certainly packed a punch, although the handling was rather from the scruff-of-the-neck school. Anti-lock brakes added at the facelift, with spec improving right to the end.

ESCORT CABRIOLET. 1984-90 (prod: 27,900). 3-door 4-seater cabriolet. F/F, 1296/1597cc (S4 OC). Max speed 107mph, 0-60mph 10.3sec. Coachbuilders Karmann created the good-looking soft-top Escort, using a roll-over bar between the B-pillars to help retain stiffness – although the body was never very rigid. Power hood operation was available on most models. Carburettor 1.3 and 1.6 versions lacked power, but 105bhp 1.6 injection had the performance to match looks. XR3i and Ghia designations came in 1986, but Ghia dropped a year later. A capable, appealing car, but saddled with a 'hairdresser' image.

ESCORT. 1986-90 (prod: 1,855,000). 3/5-door 4-seater hatchback/estate. F/F, 1117/1297cc (S4 OHV), 1392/1597cc (S4 OC), 1608/1753cc diesel (S4 OC). Max speed 111mph, 0-60mph 9.7sec. Mid-term revisions included a new, softer look, especially at the front, with the bonnet sloping down between the headlamps and replacing the previous model's black radiator grille. Changes inside included a new facia design and seats. The CVH engine range was expanded with a 1.4/75bhp added to the 1.6/79bhp unit, while the 1.1 was dropped in 1987. Capacity of the primitive diesel was also increased from 1.6 to 1.8, with 60bhp.

ORION. 1986-90 (prod: see above). 4-door 4-seater saloon. F/F, 1297cc (S4 OHV), 1392/1597cc (S4 OC), 1752cc diesel (S4 OC). Max speed 115mph, 0-60mph 9.3sec. Although the styling changes were the same as for the Escort, the Orion's image was starting to fade against increasingly better rivals. In autumn 1988 the distinguished 1600E title, created for the limited-run MkII Cortina, was cynically revived, with leather and wood veneer trim, and the injection 1.6/105bhp engine. Like the Escort, the stepless automatic transmission was available in a limited number of top-range models.

SIERRA. 1982-87 (prod: 467,900). 3/5-door 5-seater hatchback, 5-door 5-seater estate. F/R, 1294/1593/1796/1993cc (S4 OC), 2304cc diesel (S4 OHV). Max speed 114mph, 0-60mph 9.9sec. No one outside Ford was quite prepared for the shock of the Sierra, with its 'jelly mould' lines so totally different from the ultra-conservative Cortina it was replacing. Underneath, it used McPherson strut front suspension and a new independent layout at the rear. Low demand in the UK saw the end of the three-door after just two years, but five-door sales built strongly after a sluggish start, when Ford must have questioned the wisdom of such radical styling. Engines were mainly carried over from the Cortina, with the 2.3 diesel coming from Peugeot. Efficient through the air, but lack of cross-wind stability was something which Sierra drivers quickly learned about.

SIERRA 2.3. 1982-84 (prod: see above). 5-door 5-seater hatchback/estate. F/R, 2294cc (V6 OHV). Max speed 109mph, 0-60mph 11.9sec. Ford had been shoehorning the 2.3 V6 into the Cortina since the mid-1970s and continued with the Sierra. The 115bhp engine gave reasonable performance, especially for the full-laden estate car, with the Ghia version getting self-levelling suspension as standard. But poor demand made this a short-lived model which faded away in 1984.

SIERRA XR4i. 1983-85 (prod: 27,400). 3-door 5-seater hatchback. F/R, 2792cc (V6 OHV). Max speed 128mph, 0-60mph 7.7sec. This was certainly not a case of Ford hiding its light under any bushels. The distinctive biplane spoiler perched on the tailgate made it absolutely clear that the XR4i was about performance. To cope with the 2.8 V6's 150bhp, the suspension was stiffened, while the huge spoiler conquered the cross-wind instability. Even so, with just rear-drive, wet-road handling could become interesting.

SIERRA XR4×4. 1985-90 (prod: 23,540). 5-door 5-seater hatchback. F/4×4, 2792/2933cc (V6 OHV). Max speed 127mph, 0-60mph 8.2sec. The 4wd system developed for the Sierra and Granada had little in common with the one in the RS200. It used a transfer off the side of the gearbox to take the drive forward, with the normal propshaft being retained to the rear, and a centre diff to split torque. The problem of the engine being in the way of the front driveshafts was solved simply by running them in a tunnel laterally through the sump. Traction problems were finally solved, even if refinement was never very high. A significant mainstream contribution to the temporary 1980s popularity of 4wd as a performance aid.

SIERRA RS COSWORTH. 1985-86 (prod: 6021). 3-door 5-seater hatchback. F/R, 1993cc (S4 DOC). Max speed 145mph, 0-60mph 8.2sec. If the XR4i had shown how well the Sierra chassis could be persuaded to handle, the arrival of the 2.0 twin overhead camshaft Cosworth turbo engine, with 204bhp, showed just how quickly it could be made to go. With its mesh grille, bonnet-top air vents and huge (but this time just one-piece) rear spoiler, all squatting over low-profile tyres and alloy wheels, the RS Cosworth looked every inch a road racer in the tattoed-forearm manner. The short production run ensured that they remain sought-after today.

SIERRA COSWORTH RS500. 1987 (prod: 500). 3-door 5-seater hatchback. F/R, 1993cc (S4 DOC). Max speed 149mph, 0-60mph 6.0sec. The original three-door Sierra was dropped because sales fell through the floor. But that one had just 60bhp. Boost the standard-issue 'Cossie' 204bhp to a muscle-flexing 224bhp, add even bigger spoilers and wider intakes under the front bumper (to cool the massive discs), and you have the RS500. Designed very much with competition in mind, so power steering and anti-lock brakes, standard on the RS, were options. The power output was just for starters: chipped and tweaked, 300bhp was there for the asking. Very, very collectible – but make sure it has the right engine under the bonnet!

SIERRA. 1987-92 (prod: 974,400). 5-door 5-seater hatchback/estate. F/R, 1593/1769/1993cc (S4 OC), 1998cc (S4 DOC), 2304cc diesel (S4 OHV). Max speed 116mph, 0-60mph 9.8sec. If the new-look bonnet, dropping down to bumper level between bigger headlamps and wrap-round indicator units, was the most obvious change, the most significant was at the back. Rather than fit a spoiler, which would have solved the stability problem, Ford used small aerodynamic 'fences' on the tailgate to redirect airflow – and they worked. In June 1989, the single-cam 2.0/105bhp engine was replaced by the new 2.0/125bhp twin-cam and MT75 five-speed gearbox.

SAPPHIRE. 1987-92 (prod: see above). 4-door 5-seater saloon. F/R, 1593/1769/1993cc (S4 OC), 1998cc (S4 DOC), 2304cc diesel (S4 OHV). Max speed 112mph, 0-60mph 8.6sec. By the time Sapphire arrived, the shock of the Sierra was very much a thing of the past. The booted version had the same 103in wheelbase, but was 2in longer. Chassis and engine range too were identical, and as with Sierra, the new twin-cam 2.0 replaced the single-cam unit in summer 1989. The following February, it had its only face-lift, with a new grille and indicator glasses, black rear light covers and bumper pinstripe inserts. A dated design – but fleet managers loved it.

SAPPHIRE RS COSWORTH. 1988-90 (prod: 11,000). 4-door 5-seater saloon. F/R, 1993cc (S4 DOC). Max speed 143mph, 0-60mph 5.8sec. Great though the original Sierra RS Cosworth had been, its three-door shell did not make it the most practical of cars. So the new four-door Sapphire saloon was the most obvious alternative home for the 2.0 twin-cam turbo engine. The meanness of the looks was refined into something less aggressive, while equipment was improved. Handling matched the performance, which was unbeatable at the price. Perhaps inevitably, the 'Cossie' also gained a reputation as one of the UK's most stolen cars.

SAPPHIRE RS COSWORTH 4×4. 1990-92 (prod: 9250). 4-door 5-seater saloon. F/4×4, 1993cc (S4 DOC). Max speed 143mph, 0-60mph 5.5sec. Good as it was, the rear-drive RS Cosworth was being left behind by 4wd rivals in rallies. With the new all-wheel drive system, Ford upped the power of the Cosworth twin-cam from 204bhp to 220bhp, giving it a new 16-valve head. The extra power and vastly improved traction meant the Sapphire 4×4 had few rivals on the road. Ford added an alarm system and improved the specification still further, even running to full leather trim at extra cost. But attention from the light-fingered community grew, escalating insurance premiums reducing demand to a trickle by the end.

GRANADA MKII. 1977-85 (prod: 918,969). 4/5-door 5-seater saloon/estate. F/R, 1993cc (S4 OC), 2293/2498/2792cc (V6 OHV). Max speed 117mph, 0-60mph 8.9sec. With clean, neat lines, this was the best-looking of all the Granadas. The floorpan and suspension, independent all round, were carried over from the MkI. Performance was hardly stirring with the 2.0/105bhp single-cam engine, but improved considerably with the V6 versions of 2.3/114bhp and 2.8/150bhp. On the Ghia and Ghia X models, equipment levels became almost embarrassingly lavish.

GRANADA/SCORPIO. 1985 to date (prod: 250,000). 5-door 5-seater hatchback. F/R, 1796/1993cc (S4 OC), 1998cc (S4 DOC), 2394/2792/2933cc (V6 OHV), 2498cc diesel (S4 OHV). Max speed 124mph, 0-60mph 10.4sec. Once more Ford went out on its own limb, with the Sierra-like, hatchback-only Granada a shock to the styling system. But underneath all those sweeping curves, things had not changed that much, with all-round independent suspension and rear-drive – although this was the world's first volume production model to have anti-lock brakes as standard across the range. New to the Granada was the 1.8/90bhp engine, which hardly impressed on the performance front and was dropped in 1987. The 2.4 V6 was also dropped with the arrival of the 2.0/125bhp twin-cam, while the 2.8 V6 was replaced by the more efficient 2.9 in 1987. Saloon and estate car versions were to be added during the 1990s.

GRANADA/SCORPIO 4×4. 1985-92 (prod: see above). 5-door 5-seater hatchback. F/4×4, 2792/2933cc (V6 OHV). Max speed 126mph, 0-60mph 9.4sec. The 4wd system was essentially the same as that used in the Sierra, with the addition of a limited slip diff. Unlike the rear-drive 2.8/2.9 Granadas, on which automatic was virtually standard and the five-speed manual a rarely-chosen no-cost option, the 4wd models always came with a manual 'box – hence the better performance figures. Only made in Ghia and Scorpio specification, they were finally dropped in 1992 as the market lost its taste for 4wd.

RS200. 1985-86 (prod: 200). 2-door 2-seater coupé. M/4×4, 1803cc (S4 DOC). Max speed 140mph, 0-60mph 6.0sec. One of the more practical Group B rally cars, with fully-trimmed road-going versions made to encourage sales. FF Developments did much of the 4wd system design, with the turbocharged Cosworth BDT 1.8 engine providing the power, which started at 250bhp and ran to 650bhp for track use. Unusually, the gearbox was totally separate from the mid-mounted engine, and sited immediately behind the front differential. For strength and to save weight, much of the monocoque was fabricated in Kevlar and carbon fibre. With only 200 made, collectibility will eventually be assured.

FORD (USA)

Henry Ford's one-model policy, with just the Model T being produced for 18 years to 1927, left the company vulnerable when the Detroit plant was completely closed to re-tool for the Model A. Despite creating the names Mercury and Lincoln, Ford has always run a close second to the multi-marque General Motors.

MUSTANG. 1978-84 (prod: n/a). 2-door 4-seater coupé. F/R, 2301cc (S4 OC), 3273cc (S6 OHV), 4183cc (V8 OHV). Max speed 99mph, 0-60mph 12.1sec. A far cry from the original glory days, with the Mustang down-sized almost to Shetland pony dimensions. Despite turbocharging, the 2.3 'four' could only manage 116bhp and less than 100mph – Ford never dared bring the 88bhp version to the UK! The 4.2 V8, too, was a shadow of its former 300bhp plus, its clean exhaust cutting power to only 115bhp. Suspension, still with live rear axle and leaf springs, had not changed much.

LTD. 1979-83 (prod: n/a). 2-door 5-seater coupé; 4-door 5-seater saloon; 5-door 5-seater estate. F/R, 4183/4942cc (V8 OHV). Max speed 119mph, 0-60mph 10.3sec. LTD stood for 'Limited Edition', but Ford sold lots of them. One step up from the bread-and-butter Fairmont, all with either 4.2/120bhp or 4.8/130bhp V8 engines and four-speed overdrive automatic transmissions. Still with perimeter-frame chassis, using independent front suspension and a coil-sprung live axle at the rear. Upright looks defied aerodynamics, but with 55mph speed limit in the USA that did not matter. Handling was in line with 17ft 5in length and 3600lb kerb weight.

MONARCH. 1982-86 (prod: n/a). 4-door 5-seater saloon. F/R, 4942cc (V8 OHV). Max speed 102mph, 0-60mph 13.5sec. Regal title for what was essentially yet another variation on the Ford parts warehouse. Big, imposing four-door saloon, on LTD's 114in wheelbase platform, with one of the fading 'gas guzzler' 4.9 V8s managing just 122bhp, driving rear wheels through three-speed automatic. Powered just about everything, but the sheer size (well over 17ft from chromium-plated stem to stern) and handling (designed more for wide-open US roads than our twisting country lanes) meant that few were sold in the UK and even fewer survive.

FSO (PL)

The initials were adopted during the decade as the name Polski-Fiat was dropped. Fabryka Samochodow Osobowych was set up as a state company in 1946, building two-stroke Warsawa and Syenra cars. In 1968 a deal with Fiat resulted in the 125p, created from an amalgamation of the 125 body and pre-1960s mechanicals. Rock bottom pricing could not help FSO's final decline in the UK during the early 1990s.

125p. 1968-91 (prod: 724,000). 4/5-door 5-seater saloon/estate. F/R, 1299/1481cc (S4 OHV). Max speed 89mph, 0-60mph 17.5sec. While Fiat shuffled the time-expired 124 off to the Soviet Union to become the Lada, the bigger 125 went to Poland. But underneath lurked the suspension and engines of an even older Fiat. The 1300 and 1500 engines, as well as the wishbone front suspension and live rear axle, were from the eponymous saloons and estates which dated back to 1960. Not even bargain basement pricing could disguise the grinding engines and dated suspension.

POLONEZ. 1975-92 (prod: 440,500). 5-door 5-seater hatchbacks. F/R, 1481/1589cc (S4 OHV). Max speed 96mph, 0-60mph 12.8sec. With no alternatives to the aged Fiat engines and suspensions, FSO set about designing its own hatchback on the 125p floorpan. The narrow track looked out of place under the bulky body, but it was a brave effort given the ingredients. But someone forgot to tell the design team that a hatchback is meant to have a folding rear seat – the omission was corrected on later models! Plunging depreciation from a low base spelled the end, before an unexpected revival in 1993 under new management.

GINETTA (GB)

Unlike Lotus, the Walklett family, which founded Ginetta in 1958, preferred to get on with building its specialist sports cars rather than expand the empire. Simple but well-sorted chassis, clad in good looking glass-fibre bodies, with mainly Ford engines, gave many drivers their first taste of circuit racing. Moved from Witham, Essex, to new owners in Scunthorpe in 1989.

G32. 1989-92 (prod: n/a). 2-door 2-seater sports coupé. M/R, 1597cc (S4 OHV). Max speed 120mph. 0-60mph 8.2sec. The chassis was made up from box-section steel, with double wishbone and coil spring front suspension, and struts (Fiesta-type) at the rear, all of which gave terrific handling. Years of experience had taught Ginetta all about making good-looking, well-finished glass-fibre bodywork. Standard G32s ran with a 1.6/110bhp XR2i engine/gearbox, mid-mounted and turned round to drive the rear wheels. An open version was launched in 1990, shortly before financial problems began to bite.

HONDA (J)

It was the tidal-wave of cheap, reliable Honda two-wheelers during the late 1950s and 1960s which effectively swamped the British motorcycle industry. The earliest cars reflected the motorcycle influence, until the arrival in 1972 of the Civic as the first 'real' car. Honda aimed for the discerning end of the market, rather than high volume with its broad range of cars, which were all transverse-engined and front-drive in the 1980s. Links with BL (Honda had a 20 per cent stake in Rover until BMW stepped in during 1994) started in 1979, with the Triumph Acclaim version of the Ballade starting an increasingly strong association.

CIVIC. 1980-83 (prod: 3,336,983). 3-door 4-seater hatchback. F/F, 1335/1488cc (S4 OC) Max speed 100mph, 0-60mph 12.6sec. Neat hatchbacks for the UK market, with transverse single overhead cam 1.3 and 1.5 engines with five-speed gearbox or optional three-speed semi-automatic Hondamatic. Suspension used struts front and rear. The Ballade three-box saloon version was assembled in the UK, but wearing Triumph Acclaim badges – and offering rather better ride characteristics than the Civic. As with so many early Japanese imports, rust was a problem.

CIVIC. 1983-87 (prod: 1,573,907). 3/5-door 4-seater hatchback. F/F, 1335/1342/1488cc (S4 OC). Max speed 113mph, 0-60mph 8.9sec. Still sold only as hatchbacks in the UK, although the Ballade saloon was offered elsewhere. The lines were still over-fussy, but Honda's 'hallmark' build quality set the cars above other Japanese rivals. Low-emissions 12-valve engines came in 1984, with 1.3/71bhp or, in the new Sport models, 1.5/85bhp – the latter rose to 100bhp in the following year with the GT. Honda, however, still had things to learn about ride comfort.

CIVIC. 1987-91 (prod: 2,016,669). 3-door 4-seater hatchback. F/F, 1342/1396cc (S4 OC), 1590/1595cc (S4 DOC). Max speed 122mph, 0-60mph 8.1sec. The new design brought one of the best-looking small hatchbacks, with a neat, almost estate-style body. All the engines were now 16-valve units, the 1.3/75bhp and 1.4/90bhp versions having a single camshaft. The two 1.6 engines both had twin overhead cams, the 150bhp version with Honda's innovative variable valve-timing V-TEC system. Great performers, but at a price. Handling was good, but the ride still over-firm.

CIVIC SHUTTLE. 1984-88 (prod: inc in Civic figures). 5-door 4-seater estate. F/F or F/4×4, 1488cc (S4 OC). Max speed 100mph, 0-60mph

11.2sec. Lots of new thinking, with the shape designed more for people than looks. Upright stance made it 6in taller than the hatchback. The only engine available was the 1.5/85bhp single-cam 12-valve unit. The pricey but technically-clever 4wd initially had a part-time system, with a six-speed gearbox, the lowest ratio being a mud-plugging 4wd-only crawler. In 1987, it became a full-time system with a centre diff.

CIVIC SHUTTLE. 1988-91 (prod: inc in Civic figures). 5-door 4-seater estate. F/F or F/4×4, 1396/1590cc (S4 OC). Max speed 111mph, 0-60mph 9.9sec. If the body style remained essentially unchanged, Honda was playing the permutations game with its engines. The front-drive version now had the 1.4/90bhp 12-valve engine, while the 4wd used a detuned version of the 1.6i 16-valver, producing 118bhp with a rather less peaky torque curve. Power steering had become standard, while the 1.4 was available with a four-speed automatic as an option to the standard five-speed manual 'box.

JAZZ. 1984-85 (prod: 26,419). 3-door 4-seater hatchback. F/F, 1231cc (S4 OC). Max speed 90mph, 0-60mph 11.6sec. Mini Honda, just over 11ft long, renamed the Jazz for the UK because Austin-Rover used the original City name here. Short 87in wheelbase, with McPherson struts at the front, semi-trailing arms at the rear. To European eyes, the 1.2/56bhp engine, with three valves per cylinder and tunnel-shaped stratified-charge combustion chambers (all in the pursuit of cleaner exhaust emissions), was amazing in a car like this. UK import restrictions and the fact that higher profits were made selling more expensive cars meant a short life for the Jazz.

CIVIC 1.5 CRX. 1984-86 (prod: 269,719). 3-door 2+2-seater coupé. F/F, 1488cc (S4 OC). Max speed 112mph, 0-60mph 8.5sec. Honda seemed able to conjure cars and engines from the proverbial hat to fill market niches. The same 93in wheelbase as the hatchbacks, but with a fastback coupé body, making accommodation strictly two-seater in everything but name. The injected, 12-valve 1.5 engine gave a storming 100bhp, driving through a close-ratio five-speed gearbox. Handling was impressively precise, although the ride was more akin to a go-kart's.

CIVIC 1.6i CRX/V-TEC. 1986-91 (prod: 420,741). 3-door 2+2-seater coupé. F/F, 1590/1595cc (S4 DOC). Max speed 129mph, 0-60mph 7.5sec. Although it packed an almost fearsome punch with the new twin-cam 16-valve engine developing 125bhp, the price of the car and high insurance ratings tended to push the CRX beyond the pockets of many younger drivers. The novel V-TEC engine raised power to 150bhp, with flexible performance to match. Outstanding handling, but the ride remained as firm as before.

ACCORD 1976-83 (prod: 1,170,712). 3/4-door 4-seater hatchback/saloon. F/F, 1599/1602cc (S4 OC). Max speed 95mph, 0-60mph 12.4sec. Logical development of the Civic theme, initially made only as a three-door hatchback but with a four-door saloon on the same floorpan added in 1979. Single-cam engine design, with five-speed manual or two-speed semi-automatic Hondamatic transmission, drove through front wheels. Equipment not outstanding, but quality and finish were building Honda's reputation.

ACCORD DX/EX 1983-85 (prod: 1,510,932). 3-door 4-seater hatchback, 4-door 4-seater saloon. F/F, 1598/1602/1829cc (S4 OC). Max speed 95mph, 0-60mph 12.4sec. Short-lived interim models which showed just how fast the Accord was maturing. The 1602cc eight-valve engine in the EX was replaced by the larger 12-valve 1.8/100bhp unit in spring 1984, with the new, larger hatchback and saloon bodies. Equipment was starting to pile in, the EX getting air conditioning and cruise control.

ACCORD 2.0. 1985-89 (prod: 1,799,382). 4-door 5-seater saloon. F/F, 1955cc (S4 OC), 1958cc (S4 DOC). Max speed 114mph, 0-60mph 9.9sec. Moving steadily upmarket and now all with 2.0 engines. The single-cam 12-valve version gave 106bhp with carbs or 122bhp with injection, while the twin-cam 16-valve 2.0i-16 produced 137bhp. All had speed-variable power steering, central locking and electric windows, while anti-lock brakes were standard on EX models. But the interior was not very spacious and the handling did not sparkle.

AERODECK. 1985-89 (prod: inc with Accord). 3-door 4-seater hatchback/estate. F/F, 1955cc (S4 OC). Max speed 112mph, 0-60mph 9.8sec. Appealing looks, but what role was it fulfilling? It was no estate car because the load space was too small, while the ordinary handling and ride, despite performance potential, did not make it a sports car. The single-cam 1955cc 12-valve engines were as used in the regular saloons, with the 122bhp injection EXi the best equipped, having anti-lock brakes. As with the saloon, Honda had moved from strut to wishbone suspension.

ACCORD. 1989-92 (prod: 1,717,208). 4-door 5-seater saloon. F/F, 1997/2156cc (S4 OC). Max speed 132mph, 0-60mph 8.4sec. Last of the Japanese-built Accords, before production started at the new Swindon plant. Bigger and better, packed with equipment. The 2.2/150bhp version had the four-wheel steering system pioneered in the Prelude. Build quality and feel were unbeatable, but Honda still had not managed to reach European standards of handling or ride.

INTEGRA. 1986-89 (prod: 1,027,180). 5-door 4-seater hatchback. F/F, 1488cc (S4 OC), 1590cc (S4 DOC). Max speed 116mph, 0-60mph 9.6sec. After the full hatchback Accord was dropped, Honda filled the gap with the five-door Integra. Rather ordinary styling, using the basic Accord all-independent suspension layout. DX, with 1.5/85bhp 12-valve engine, was improved with power steering after a couple of years. Top version was the EX16, with 1.6/125bhp 16-valve engine. The usual Honda story of the time: strong on build quality, not so good on dynamics.

BALLADE. 1986-89 (prod: 73,842). 4-door 4-seater saloon. F/F, 1488cc (S4 OC). Max speed 106mph, 0-60mph 9.9sec. Almost as a dummy run for Concerto production, the Ballade was built alongside its sister Rover 213/216 models at Cowley, on the 'MkII' shell with the bonnet opening to bumper level. Slightly different grille and interior from the Rover, but the same suspension. Power steering, not available on any Rover equivalent, was standard on the top EXi version. The 1.5 engine – offering 85bhp on carbs or 100bhp in 12-valve injection form – was only used on the Ballade.

CONCERTO. 1989 to date (prod: 198,500). 4/5-door 4-seater saloon/hatchback. F/F, 1396/1493/1590cc (S4 OC), 1590cc (S4 DOC). Max speed 122mph, 0-60mph 8.9sec. Rover and Honda really got their act together, with the new designed-for-Europe Concerto being built on the same line as the latest 200/400 Rovers. But while the smaller Rovers used the new K-series engine, the Concerto had Honda's own 16-valve units. The 1.4, 1.5 and less powerful 1.6 had single overhead camshafts, the 1.6-16 twin cams and 130bhp maximum. Honda image was retained by slightly different ride and handling, and generally better equipment price-for-price against Rovers. Power steering, for instance, was standard across the range. All Concertos had their final pre-delivery check out at Honda's Swindon plant.

PRELUDE. 1978-83 (prod: 264,842). 2-door 2+2-seater coupé. F/F, 1602cc (S4 OC). Max speed 98mph, 0-60mph 11.3sec. A variation on the Accord theme, using the same floorpan and suspension, plus the larger 1.6 engine. Body far enough away from the Accord's to have a slightly sporting appearance, even down to the bonnet-top vents. Performance was reasonable, but the Prelude was distinctly short in rear seat leg and headroom. Long on price, thereby crossing itself off many people's shopping lists.

PRELUDE. 1983-86 (prod: 623,630). 2-door 2+2-seater coupé. F/F, 1882cc (S4 OC). Max speed 103 mph, 0-60mph 10.9sec. Once more the Accord's 96.5in wheelbase floorpan was used. With the 1.8 12-valve engine giving a modest 103bhp, performance was not tyre threatening. But the clean, uncluttered lines of the 2+2 body, with faired-in pop-up headlamps and an airy greenhouse, slotted it straight into a waiting – but middle-aged – market niche. Easy to drive, good to look at and, loaded with equipment in Executive trim, it was a sure success.

PRELUDE. 1986-92 (prod: 637,132). 2-door 2+2-seater coupé. F/F, 1958cc (S4 OC), 1958cc (S4 DOC). Max speed 120mph, 0-60mph 8.9sec. The exterior had not changed that much, but there was a major revolution underneath. The all-mechanical four-wheel steering system on the top version was simple and effective, endowing almost uncanny handling. The single-cam 1.9 engine gave just 114bhp, but the 16-valve twin-cam's output progressed from 137bhp to 150bhp. Despite the potential performance, the image remained far from youthful.

LEGEND SALOON. 1986-91 (prod: 538,611). 4-door 5-seater saloon. F/F, 2493/2675cc (V6 OC). Max speed 128mph, 0-60mph 9.4sec. Honda's first limo-sized car, designed alongside Rover's 825 Sterling. Transversely-mounted V6 engine started as 2.5/172bhp, but torque characteristics were too peaky for a big saloon. In spring 1988, it was replaced by a silky 2.7/177bhp version, matched to an equally smooth automatic. Ride and handling, as ever, from the leatherbound Japanese handbook which defined mediocrity in such matters. Over-fussy interior was Honda's idea of 'class', with never-ending equipment. By common consent, nowhere near as good as the Rover alternative.

LEGEND COUPE. 1987-91 (prod: see above). 2-door 4-seater coupé. F/F, 2675cc (V6 DOC). Max speed 137mph, 0-60mph 8.2sec. Coupé version of Legend (with no Rover equivalent) used 24-valve 2.7 V6 five months before the saloon. Very quick, but let down badly by podgy ride and over-light steering. A couple of inches shorter than the saloon, with no-cost option of five-speed manual or dual-range four-speed automatic. Masses of equipment, but the hefty price put it in the same bracket as Jaguar's XJ-S, so not many takers in the UK.

HYUNDAI (ROK)

For its first decade, the car-building offshoot of this huge South Korean industrial group assembled Cortinas. But in 1976, its first Pony model, using Mitsubishi engines and running gear, appeared. The first 'in-house' Hyundai, the Stellar, was launched in 1983. Highly competitive pricing and increasing sophistication have become Hyundai hallmarks in the UK market.

PONY. 1982-90 (prod: 3,230,378). 3/5-door 4-seater hatchback, 4-door 4-seater saloon. F/F, 1238/1439/1468cc (S4 OC). Max speed 95mph, 0-60mph 12.3sec. Hyundai chose to walk before even thinking of running, so turned to Mitsubishi for engines, gearboxes and running gear for its Pony hatchbacks and saloons. The ex-Lancer bits were well-proven, so these reasonably spacious hatchbacks and saloons handled and rode fairly well. With 71bhp at the best, performance was modest enough, but reliability and pricing won the day.

STELLAR. 1984-91 (prod: 405,459). 4-door 5-seater saloons. F/R, 1597cc (S4 OC). Max speed 98mph, 0-60mph 14.7sec. Call it a Korean Cortina and you would not be far wrong, because Hyundai assembled these evergreen Fords for years. Classic front-engined, rear-drive layout, with McPherson strut suspension at the front, live axle on coils at the back. Mitsubishi engine and gearbox meant reliability, with the simple mechanical layout making servicing easy. Handling and ride matched the looks, which were anonymous almost to the point of invisibility – even if some pundits likened it to a scaled-down Maserati Quattroporte.

SCOUPE. 1989 to date (prod: n/a). 3-door 4-seater coupé. F/F, 1468cc (S4 OC). Max speed 107mph, 0-60mph 12.1sec. If what was underneath was little different from the normal X2 Pony, the Scoupe body, from Hyundai's own in-house design team, at least looked smartly different. Same ex-Mitsubishi engine and transmission as the hatchbacks, with straightforward eight-valve heads. In 1990s, injection pushed power from original 82bhp to a peak of 114bhp with multi-point fuel injection. The let-down came with the rather uninspired handling and indifferent ride.

SONATA. 1989 to date (prod: 576,833). 4-door 5-seater saloon. F/F, 1795/1997/2351cc (S4 OC). Max speed 112mph, 0-60mph 11.2sec. Mitsubishi power once again, now the transverse units from the front-drive Galant. But this time Hyundai had set its sights a lot higher – and so nearly got it right. Clean, if unremarkable, styling gave a spacious saloon body, but the smaller engines – 1.8/95bhp and 2.0/100bhp – did not give much performance. The big 2.4 'four', with 115bhp, just about made it. Equipment levels out-gunned any European rivals at the price – but the let-down was sloppy handling and a wallowy 'trans-Atlantic' ride.

ISUZU (J)

An unlikely merger in 1937 between the company which made Wolseleys under licence in Japan and the Tokyo Gas and Electric Company resulted in Isuzu being created. GM took a minority share in the company in 1971, but the name remained unfamiliar in the UK until 1985, when the high-performance Piazza was launched, to be followed, slightly incongruously, by the tough four-wheel drive Troopers.

PIAZZA. 1986-90 (prod: 114,000). 2-door 2-seater sports coupé. F/R, 1994cc (S4 OC). Max speed 126mph, 0-60mph 8.6sec. During the late 1970s, Giugiaro's Ace of Clubs styling exercise, based on Isuzu mechanicals, was seen at several international shows. In 1981, with the exterior largely unchanged, Isuzu put it into production. At first, the potent turbo engine simply outran the undeveloped chassis, but after Lotus was called in to sort both ride and handling the Piazza became vastly better. Interior design was rather contrived and untidy. Original UK importers went bust, and by the time International Motors took on the Isuzu concession the Piazza was no more.

TROOPER. 1987-91 (prod: 577,000). 3/5-door 5-seater off-roader. F/4, 2254/2559cc (S4 OC), 2238/2771cc diesels (S4 OC). Max speed 93mph, 0-60mph 14.0sec. With prices undercutting the pricey Shogun, the Trooper found a ready market. Short- and long-wheelbase versions were offered with petrol or turbo diesel engines, plus dual-range five-speed transmissions. On the road they were well-mannered enough, although they lagged behind the Range Rover as off-roaders when the going got really tough. Interiors were almost car-like, but with rather scattered controls and awkward umbrella-type handbrake.

JAGUAR (GB)

In 1980, the title Jaguar Cars Ltd was restored to the Browns Lane works in Coventry after six wilderness years under the nationalised British Leyland. And four years later the company, founded by Sir William Lyons, was back in private hands. During the 1980s, major steps were taken to restore the damaged reputation for reliability and quality. In 1990, Jaguar passed into Ford's ownership.

XJ-S 5.3. 1975 to date (prod: 19,140). 2-door 4-seater coupé. F/R, 5343cc (V12 OC). Max speed 152mph, 0-60mph 7.8sec. After the inspired E-type, the XJ-S followed from a very different design mould. Based on the XJ floorpan, with the 5.3 fuel-injected V12 initially developing 285bhp, rising to 295bhp with the HE version from 1981. All but a handful had automatic transmission. Looks were not to everyone's taste, and space in the rear seats was very restricted. Outstanding ride, but the fuel consumption could easily decline towards single figures if full use was made of the performance.

XJ6 SERIES III. 1979-86 (prod: 122,452). 4-door 5-seater saloon. F/R, 3442/4235cc (S6 DOC). Max speed 131mph, 0-60mph 8.6sec. Sir William Lyons' original design was brought up to date by Pininfarina in 1979, with bigger windows, a flatter roof and a different nose. The 3.4 version of the XK engine gave 162bhp, the 4.2 205bhp. In 1985, with just a year to run, the two models lost their engine size designation and gained some trim improvements (even more walnut and stainless steel) aimed at maintaining buoyant sales right to the last moment.

XJ12 SERIES III/SOVEREIGN 5.3. 1979-93 (prod: 92,750). 4-door 5-seater saloon. F/R, 5343cc (V12 OC). Max speed 135mph, 0-60mph 8.9sec. The Pininfarina changes simply made the original lines more elegant. The Sovereign title replaced the XJ initials in 1983, but the car became known as the V12 again in 1989. HE power went to 295bhp, but dropped to 264bhp with catalyst option. After the arrival of the 'XJ40' in 1986, the V12 went silently and comfortably on and on simply because the new design specifically precluded use of the V12 engine. No manual gearbox, so three-speed GM automatic with slim selector was standard.

XJ-S 3.6. 1983-91 (prod: 92,750). 2-door 4-seater coupé. F/R, 3590cc (S6 DOC). Max speed 136mph, 0-60mph 7.1sec. Almost any increase in petrol prices seemed to affect V12-engined XJ-S sales adversely, but the outlook improved with the new six-cylinder version. The 3.6, twin overhead cam, 24-valve AJ6 engine, with 228bhp and manual gearbox, gave better acceleration than the V12 with far smaller fuel bills. The four-speed automatic, with the new J-gate selector, became an option in 1987. In 1991, with a catalyst now standard, engine capacity was raised to 4.0/223bhp.

XJ-S 3.6 CABRIOLET 1983-87 (prod: see above). 2-door 2-seater cabriolet. F/R, 3590cc (S6 DOC). Max speed 134mph, 0-60mph 7.3sec. Jaguar had been without an open model since the last of the E-types, a gap of eight years. But the XJ-S had never been designed with a soft-top version in mind, so the shell needed considerable bracing to reinstate the rigidity needed. The design was unusual, with Targa-type lift-out roof panels and a folding rear screen, with flexible window. Dropped in 1987, but reappeared in 1991 with the new 4.0 AJ6 engine.

XJ-S 5.3 CABRIOLET. 1985-87 (prod: 16,790). 2-door 2-seater cabriolet. F/R, 5343cc (V12 OC). Max speed 150mph, 0-60mph 8.0sec. A couple of years after the 3.6 Cabriolet appeared, Jaguar followed with the V12 version. The same twin-panel Targa top was used, with a dual-layer folding rear section. Power was reduced marginally in 1987, down from 295bhp to 291bhp in the pursuit of improved exhaust emissions. Like the 3.6 version, production ceased later that same year.

XJ-S 5.3 CONVERTIBLE. 1988-91 (prod: 7420). 2-door 2-seater convertible. F/R, 5343cc (V12 OC). Max speed 150mph, 0-60mph 7.9sec. This XJ-S, a proper convertible, had rather more than just a new hood mechanism, for the front of the structure was stiffened further with a new subframe which eliminated what little scuttle shake there had been. The cabriolet's two-part roof was replaced by a more conventional single-piece folding hood, with electric operation. With the new model, anti-lock brakes were part of the standard package. The most desirable XJ-S of all.

XJ6 2.9/3.2/3.6/4.0. 1986 to date (prod: 143,740). 4-door 5-seater saloon. F/R, 2919/3239/3590/3980cc (S6 DOC). Max speed 141mph, 0-60mph 8.3sec. Major step for Jaguar, with the worthy but aged XK engines finally replaced by fuel-efficient twin-cam, 24-valve AJ6s, in a brand new – but not that roomy – 'XJ40' saloon body. Initially with 2.9/165bhp and 3.6/221bhp engines, but 3.6 replaced by 4.0/235bhp in 1989 and 2.9 replaced by 3.2/200bhp in 1990. Four-speed automatic, with unusual J-gate selector lever (nicknamed the 'Randle handle' after Jaguar's chief engineer) was option to standard five-speed manual. Lighter weight and better aerodynamics gave stronger performance than old XJ6, while handling and ride were even more accomplished.

XJR 3.6/4.0. 1988-92 (prod: n/a). 4-door 5-seater saloon. F/R, 3590/3980cc (S6 DOC). Max speed 143mph, 0-60mph 8.2sec. Jaguar Sport version of the standard car, with sports suspension, black grille, deeper front spoiler and sill mouldings. No change in power for 3.6 engine, but 4.0 output was pushed from 235bhp to 251bhp, dropping to 248bhp when a catalyst became standard in 1990. Every possible extra: 3.6 was auto only, but 4.0 had choice of transmissions and limited slip diff as standard. New facia replaced the old messy design in 1989 made a good car even better.

XJR-S 5.3/6.0. 1988 to date (prod: 9390). 2-door 4-seater coupé. 5345/5993cc (V12 OC). Max speed 158mph, 0-60mph 5.6sec. The 5.3's engine power remained at 291bhp, but there was now a Jaguar Sport modified body with a discreet rear spoiler, front spoiler and sill mouldings in body colour, and Speedline alloy wheels. In 1989, engine capacity was opened up to 6.0 and 318bhp, still with the three-speed GM 400 automatic transmission. In 1991, power was eased even higher, to 333bhp – and that was with twin catalysts.

JEEP (USA)

The quarter-ton general purpose vehicle designed for the US Defense Dept at the start of World War II quickly became known by its initials - GP. So the Jeep name was born. American Motors acquired Jeep Corp in 1980, but after an unhappy liaison with Renault, AMC sold out in 1987 to Chrysler, itself a 'born-again' corporation following a period which bordered on extinction. Updated and with new looks, official Jeep imports restarted in the UK early in 1993.

CJ-7. 1978-86 (prod: n/a). 3-door 4-seater off-road estate. F/4×4, 4235cc (S6 OHV), 4981cc (V8 OHV). Max speed 93mph, 0-60mph 14.1sec. Basic construction had not changed a great deal from the 1940s original, using a tough chassis with live axles on semi-elliptic springs front and rear, although front brakes were discs. Normally rear wheel drive, with front axle added in when needed. Transmission refinements included full 4wd with centre diff – but at extra cost. The basic engine was 110bhp/4.2 in-line six, with 119bhp/5.0 V8 also available.

WAGONEER. 1978-86 (prod: n/a). 5-door 6-seater off-road estate. F/4×4, 4235cc (S6 OHV), 5896cc (V8 OHV). Max speed 100mph, 0-60mph 12.6sec. Rugged estates, built rather more for backwoods tracks than cross-country off-road exploring. Live axles on semi-elliptic springs could absorb huge punishment, and squared-up, spacious estate body was carried on a Forth Bridge chassis. Only 15ft 3in long, but close to 6ft high. Most had 110bhp/4.2 in-line six, with just a few sold in the UK with the big 5.9 V8. The full-time 4wd layout was only available with the V8.

JENSEN (GB)

Coachbuilding was the way Jensen started, with the first car produced in 1936. In post-war years, it build bodies for the Austin A40 Sports and the first of the Big Healeys. The ultimate Jensen was the FF, with four-wheel drive and Dunlop Maxaret anti-lock braking - a technological marvel from such a small company. In the 1970s an attempt was made to broaden appeal with the Jensen-Healey, but this bland-looking two-seat roadster never sold well. After closing in 1976, Jensen did produce a few cars in the 1980s, finally putting up the shutters as a manufacturer in 1993.

INTERCEPTOR. 1988-93 (prod: n/a). 2-door. 4-seater sports coupé/convertible. F/R, 5900cc (V8 OHV). Max speed 135mph, 0-60mph 7.5sec. Had the original Interceptor been a great car, recreating it in the 1980s might have been a good idea. But for the same price in 1988 (£52,000) you could buy a Ferrari 328 and get £6000 change. Vast Chrysler V8 engine, with automatic transmission, provided the power. Hand-built craftsmanship accounted for much of the cost, but in return you got a car which never did handle that well and drank fuel at a budget-breaking rate. A story of misplaced optimism from a company that was essentially a parts/service operation in the 1980s.

LADA (USSR/CIS)

In a deal with Fiat during the late 1960s, most of the 124 production facility was shifted from Turin to Togliatti, west of Moscow. With a rugged Soviet-designed engine, the Lada - the Shiguli in its home country - was born. High demand and little competition meant few changes. The front-drive Samara is a far more modern design, although quality and dynamics are reflected in rock-bottom prices.

1200/1300/1500/1600. 1970 to date (prod: n/a). 4/5-door 4-seater saloon, estate. F/R, 1198/1294/1452/1570cc (S4 OC). Max speed 97mph, 0-60mph 14.0sec. While there have been trim, engine and even name changes – Riva from 1984 – the car underneath always remained essentially the original Fiat 124, down to the switchgear and even the grey-cased tool kit. Tough, gruff engine also did not change much, apart from the stroke lengthening to increase capacity. These primitive cars serve as a salutary reminder of just how far the motor industry in the west has progressed in terms of ride, handling, engine efficiency and refinement.

NIVA 1500/1600. 1979 to date (prod: n/a). 3-door 4-seater off-roader. F/4×4, 1452/1570cc (S4 OC). Max speed 80mph, 0-60mph 18.9sec. The rush of small Japanese off-roaders put the Niva in the shade as far as quality was concerned. But over the rough, this tough little Russian left them standing. It used the same engines as the Lada saloon, but with an in-house 4wd system. Endless axle articulation gave leech-like traction in impossible conditions, but on-road handling needed much more attention. Originally LHD only, but larger engine, five-speed gearbox and RHD came in 1983.

SAMARA. 1984 to date (prod: n/a). 3/5-door 4-seater hatchback. F/F, 1099/1288/1499cc (S4 OC). Max speed 97mph, 0-60mph 14.0sec. A superb engineering achievement, considering the years of technical isolation the Soviet Union motor industry had faced. Everything was new – engine, gearbox, body. But beneath the sea of dreadful plastic and shoddy finish, the Samara lacked much in the way of dynamic qualities, with dull performance, indifferent handling and a bouncy ride. Low, low prices did not leave much room for depreciation.

LAMBORGHINI (I)

Ferruccio Lamborghini made his money from gas cookers and tractors, but his real love was high-performance cars - and he wanted his to be even better than Enzo Ferrari's. Financial problems led to the company passing through various hands (notably Chrysler's), although production continued. BMW's M1 was to have been built at the Sant'Agata factory, but never materialised.

COUNTACH LP400S 1978-82 (prod: 150). 2-door 2-seater sports coupé. M/R, 3929cc (V12 DOC). Max speed 170mph, 0-60mph 5.6sec. 'Countach' is, politely, a Piedmontese expression of astonished amazement – which just about sums up this incredible device. The mid-mounted V12 quad-cam engine, worth 375bhp, was mounted in a tubular chassis with the gearbox ahead of it, rather than behind. Marcello Gandini's extrovert styling used 'shark's gill' air intakes aft of the lift-up doors. The handling was totally in line with the huge performance and incredible looks.

COUNTACH LP500/LP500S QV. 1982-91 (prod: 459). 2-door 2-seater sports coupé. M/R, 5167cc (V12 DOC). Max speed 178mph, 0-60mph 4.9sec. While there was no significant power boost with the increase in engine size from 4.0 to 5.1, driveability was improved with better torque. From 1985, four-valve heads pushed power up to 455bhp and in the right places 200mph was claimed, although the best timed road speed was 178mph. The need for more cooling meant even larger radiator intakes, but the rear wing, a hugely expensive extra, did absolutely nothing except blunt performance and boost fragile egos.

JALPA P350. 1981-91 (prod: 179). 2-door 2-seater sports coupé. M/R, 3485cc (V8 DOC). Max speed 153mph, 0-60mph 7.0sec. Financial troubles were looming as this reworked Silhouette, itself based on the Urraco, was pushed into production. Giulio Alfieri, brought in from Maserati, worked on the transverse 3.5 V8 engine, working power up to 255bhp. Within the constraints of available space, the interior redesign put controls where the driver could at least reach them. On the outside, the tacked-on front spoiler did little for the Silhouette's already rather unhappy appearance.

LANCIA (I)

The 'quality' sector of the high-volume Fiat empire, which had owned it since 1969. For a time Lancia managed to retain its individuality, with models such as the Gamma, Montecarlo and Integrale. But rationalisation has seen many Lancia models become too closely related to those originally designed to wear the Fiat badge. UK sales struggled throughout the 1980s, Lancia finally ceasing to import early in 1994.

BETA SALOON. 1972-81 (prod: 194, 916). 4-door 5-seater saloon. F/F, 1297/1301/1438/ 1585/1592/1756/1995cc (S4 DOC). Max speed 118mph, 0-60mph 9.6sec. After a lifetime of loss-making but fascinating engineering, Lancia finally had to toe Fiat's corporate line with the Beta. Power came from gutsy twin-cam derivatives of Fiat engines, with outputs between 82bhp and 122bhp. Like most immediate predecessors, the Beta had front-wheel drive, with a transverse engine. Despite hatchback looks, the Beta was a saloon with well-balanced handling. But the albatross which still hangs round Lancia's neck, in the UK at least, was the way rust started almost before the cars were off the production line – but the car's finish was otherwise excellent. This model, more than any other, killed Lancia's fortunes outside its home market.

BETA COUPE/SPIDER. 1973-84 (prod: 111,801/ 9390). 2-door 2+2-seater coupé/convertible. 1297/1301/1367/1438/1585/1592/1756/1995cc (S4 DOC) Max speed 124mph, 0-60mph 9.0sec. Although the engines mainly paralleled those in the saloons, the image was very different. With wheelbase reduced from 100in to 92.5in, the good-looking in-house styling had a sporting appeal. The semi-convertible spider was the first open Lancia for decades, but had a shorter life than the coupé between 1975-83. As time ran out, engine options were reduced to leave just the 2.0 injection (122bhp) or ingenious supercharged Volumex (135bhp) versions.

BETA HPE. 1975-84 (prod: 71,258). 3-door 4-seater estate. F/F, 1585/1995cc (S4 DOC). Max speed 124mph, 0-60mph 9.3sec. After steps had been taken to beat the rust problem, the Beta name was quietly dropped from the tailgate in 1979. Distinctive, high-speed estate image was just what Lancia's slightly tarnished reputation needed, initially with 1.6/100bhp engine, later with the same 2.0 injection and supercharged Volumex choices as the coupé and spider. A good-looking and practical sports estate, but BMW's later 3 series Touring hit the same target far more successfully.

TREVI. 1981-84 (prod: 40,628). 4-door 4-seater saloon. F/F, 1585/1995cc (S4 DOC). Max speed 115mph, 0-60mph 9.4sec. At first glance a logical extension of the Beta theme, with a spacious if somewhat conservatively-styled saloon body on the same 100in floorpan, but now with a new single vertical-bar grille on what was essentially a Beta saloon front. Only the 1.6 and 2.0 engines were offered, with the chassis well able to handle more power. Inside, the Trevi's weird 'Gruyere cheese' facia, littered with recesses for instruments and switches, went into the archives as one that did not work. In fact, the same could really be said of the entire car...

MONTECARLO. 1981-84 (prod: 7595). 2-door 2-seater coupé. M/R, 1995cc. Max speed 119mph, 0-60mph 9.8sec. Although launched in 1975, the Montecarlo was put into production limbo in 1978 while handling and braking were refined (it was terribly easy to lock the front brakes). Reappeared in the UK in summer 1981. The transverse 1955cc engine was mid-mounted and drove the rear wheels. Code named X1/20, it was blessed with arresting Pininfarina styling with Fiat X1/9 overtones, but performance never quite managed to live up to the looks. Eager if slightly nervous handling. The main drawback was the driving position and lack of foot space around the pedals. Now rare – and starting to attract collectors.

GAMMA SALOON. 1976-84 (prod: 15,296). 4-door 4-seater saloon. F/F, 1999/2484cc (HO4 OC). Max speed 118mph, 0-60mph 10.1sec. With no engine over 2.0 in the Fiat parts catalogue, Lancia designed an all-new unit for this prestige saloon. The real surprise was that it was a flat-four, but, as with all contemporary Lancias, driving the front wheels. An uprated version of the British-designed four-speed AP automatic, originally destined for the Mini and 1100/1300 models, was an option. Despite the 2.5/140bhp engine, performance never impressed. The model was relaunched at regular intervals in the UK in an effort to boost feeble sales, but do you ever remember seeing one?

GAMMA COUPE. 1976-84 (prod: 6789). 2-door 4-seater saloon. F/F, 1999/2484cc (HO4 OC). Max speed 122mph, 0-60mph 9.6sec. Wonderfully graceful coupé shape, Pininfarina styling at its best. With floorpan shortened by 4.5in, the balance of wheelbase to overall length looked much better. Engines the same as in the saloon, although even with the 2.5 performance did not live up to looks. As with the saloon, corrosion and engine unreliability became problems which pushed down used values too quickly for comfort.

DELTA. 1980-90 (prod: 193,473). 5-door 4-seater hatchback. F/F, 1299/1498cc (S4 OC), 1585cc (S4 DOC). Max speed 115mph, 0-60mph 10.0sec.

Although it used Fiat-based engines, the Delta had little in common with the similar-sized Fiat Strada. With a 97in wheelbase, the model used McPherson strut-type suspension front and rear. Capacity of the 1300 mysteriously dropped from 1301cc to 1299cc – so moving it into what was then the lowest UK company car taxation class. Good handling and ride, but lacked the interior space of its rivals despite a practical five-door layout. Facia design, too, always seemed a little dated.

DELTA HF TURBO. 1984-90 (prod: see above). 5-door 4-seater hatchback. F/F, 1585cc (S4 DOC). Max speed 122mph, 0-60mph 8.5sec. After going out on a limb with its Volumex supercharger system, Fiat took the turbo route for the Delta. In carburettor form, the 1.6 twin-cam engine gave 130bhp, but fuel injection pushed this up to 140bhp in mid-1986. The white, be-striped Martini version, from 1988, was hardly subtle in appearance, but reasonably successful – by Lancia standards – in the UK. With tuned suspension, the HF Delta handled delightfully, although putting all that power through the front wheels in a hurry could turn heads. But ultimate refinement was spoiled by sudden turbo power delivery.

PRISMA. 1983-90 (prod: 150,577). 4-door 4-seater saloon. F/F or F/4×4, 1498/1586cc (S4 DOC). Max speed 114mph, 0-60mph 9.5sec. On paper it had to make sense, this booted, four-door version sitting on the same floorpan as the Delta. The 85bhp/1.5 engine was dropped in 1985, leaving just the 105bhp 1.6 – power went up to 108bhp in mid-1986 with injection. Same crisp handling as the Delta hatchbacks, but the British were wary of exactly where this practical and quick saloon actually fitted into their lives.

INTEGRALE. 1987-94 (prod: n/a). 5-door 4-seater hatchback. F/4×4, 1995cc (S4 DOC). Max speed 134mph. 0-60mph 5.7sec. For the first eight months it was known simply as the HF 4WD, with the 165bhp 2.0 turbo engine driving through a sophisticated 4wd system. Overnight, though, it became the Integrale, wearing flared wheel arches and winning international rallies. Yet this fireball had five doors and remained a practical family hatchback, even though it was made only with left-hand drive. In 1989 power was pushed from 185bhp to 200bhp with a 16-valve cylinder head, and later went to 210bhp. Handling, balance and performance were unbeatable. In the showrooms and on special stages, this was a success story to lighten Lancia's gloom.

Y10. 1985-92 (prod: 136,743). 3-door 4-seater hatchback. F/F, 999/1049/1108/1301cc (S4 OC). Max speed 112mph, 0-60mph 9.5sec. At the shopping basket end of the market, people want cars that are practical. The abruptly chopped-off tail certainly looked different – but with it went rear seat leg room and load space. A wide variety of engines, from 45bhp FIRE to less-than-fire-breathing 85bhp turbo. Interior had plenty of Lancia *chic*, but the let-down came with the open-road handling and jiggly ride. Others were doing it far, far better. Most in mainland Europe were Autobianchi-badged.

THEMA. 1985 to date (prod: 135,700). 4-door 5-seater saloon. F/F, 1995cc (S4 DOC), 2445cc turbo diesel (S4 OC). Max speed 133mph, 0-60mph 8.1sec. First of the Type Four cars, developed jointly by Fiat – the Croma and Alfa Romeo 164 were to come later – and Saab. In the event, it was a brief liaison. Fiat-based twin-cam engines again, the fierce turbo version with 165bhp providing equally fierce performance – but the chassis was generally able to handle it. Lots of room, but the over-conservative looks and doubts about longevity and reliability – misplaced with hindsight – did nothing for the Thema's reputation or depreciation.

THEMA V6. 1985-88. (prod: 4888). 4-door 5-seater saloon. F/F, 2849cc (V6 OC). Max speed 123mph, 0-60mph 9.2sec. With an eye on the luxury end of the market, Lancia shoehorned the PRV (Peugeot, Renault, Volvo) 2.8 V6 under the Thema's bonnet, the first time it had been used in a transverse position. The luxury image was continued by making this model automatic only – but with a three-speed unit the 150bhp had a struggle to achieve much performance.

THEMA 8.32. 1988-90 (prod: 2370). 4-door 5-seater saloon. F/F, 2927cc (V8 DOC). Max speed 140mph, 0-60mph 6.8sec. On paper a great idea, with the Ferrari 308 engine mounted transversely in the ultimate Q-car. With 215bhp performance was shattering for such a sedate-looking car. Despite all that power going through the front wheels, torque steer was non-existent, while the electronically-controlled damping looked after ride in town and country. The interior was in keeping, with lots of wood and leather. But at £43,200 and with left-hand drive only, few were sold in the UK.

LAND ROVER (GB)

There cannot be many countries left in the world where Land Rover has not set wheel. The 1946 Jeep-inspired original has matured considerably but still does the job for which it was designed. The Range Rover set new standards in on- and off-road manners, while the Discovery has simply added to Land Rover's 4wd arsenal.

RANGE ROVER. 1970 to date (prod: 307,781). 3/5-door 5-seater off-roader. F/4×4, 3528/3947cc (V8 OHV), 2392/2495cc turbo diesels (S4 OC). Max speed 108mph, 0-60mph 11.3sec. Difficult to believe that when it was launched, the price was under £2000. The basic concept has stayed unchanged: massive separate chassis, live axles hung on long-travel coil springs, a full-time 4wd system and the ubiquitous Rover V8 engine.

Originally three door only, with five-door versions from 1981. Four-cylinder turbo diesels were added in 1986. From the original rubber mats and dog-proof interior, equipment and trim levels have simply improved year by year, although at a price.

DISCOVERY. 1989 to date (prod: 106,032). 3/5-door 5/7-seater off-roader. F/4×4, 3528cc (V8 OHV), 2495cc diesel (S4 OC). Max speed 107mph, 0-60mph 11.6sec. With increasing competition from Japan, Discovery was brought in to fill the gap between the rugged Land Rovers and pricey Range Rovers. Same chassis, V8 or turbo diesels, plus a distinctive kick-roof body style. Conran Design put new thinking into the interior, although colour schemes were unusual. As unstoppable as the Range Rover off-road, it also shared similarly well-mannered on-road handling. With Japanese imports still restricted, success was ensured.

LAND ROVER SIII. 1971-85 (prod: approx 805,006 all versions). 2-door, various body styles on 88in/109in wheelbase chassis. F/4×4, 2286cc (S4 OHV), 2286cc diesel (S4 OHV), 2625cc (S6 OHV), 3528cc (V8 OHV). Max speed 84mph, 0-60mph 16.9sec. A rugged as ever, with massive chassis and uncompromising leaf-spring suspension. New was the low-compression carburettor V8 engine in long-wheelbase chassis only, although all-synchromesh gearbox was used on all models. New facia design made interior rather more civilised.

NINETY/ONE-TEN. 1985 to date (prod: see above). 2-door, various body styles, 90in/110in wheelbase chassis. F/4×4, 2495cc diesel (S4 OHV), 3528cc (V8 OHV). Max speed 86mph, 0-60mph 14.7sec. Refinement comes to Land Rover, with Range-Rover coil spring suspension, although still with live axles front and rear, and full-time 4wd for the first time. Diesel power and torque was increased with turbocharger, while 3.5 V8 gave massive lugging power – and heavy fuel bills. Off-road as capable as ever, but new chassis finally made the on-road handling less spine-jarring.

LONSDALE (AUS)

To protect its domestic motor industry, Australia imposed severe duty penalties on imported cars. So along with Nissan and Toyota, Mitsubishi set up manufacturing facilities in the country and sold cars under its own name. The Lonsdale name was created for the few cars which were exported to the UK to expand the Mitsubishi range.

LONSDALE. 1983-84 (prod: n/a). 4/5-door 5-seater saloon/estate. F/R, 1507/1995/2555cc (S4 OC). Max speed 111mph, 0-60mph 11.2sec. Behind the Lonsdale badge lurked nothing more exotic than the old-model Mitsubishi Sigma. Four-cylinder engines ranged from 1.6 with 81bhp to thumping 2.6 which managed a mere 102bhp, all driving the rear wheels. The 1.6 came with four-speed manual 'box only, but others had five-speed manual or three-speed automatic. MacPherson struts at the front and live axle at the rear completed the conventional picture. During the brief 13-month life, most sold were estates.

LOTUS (GB)

A name forever associated with founder Colin Chapman. His brilliant designs included the too-advanced original Elite, the agile, so-good-looking Elan, and the Esprit. Reliability was a long-term problem, sheer driving fun never. Bought out by General Motors in 1986 - and now sold on to a name from the past, Bugatti.

ELITE. 1974-83 (prod: 2531). 2-door 4-seater coupé. F/R, 1973/2174cc (S4 DOC). Max speed 124mph, 0-60mph 7.5sec. A major change of thinking for Chapman, with his sights moving further upmarket. But the backbone chassis, pioneered on the original Elan, and glass-fibre body were retained, as was all-round independent suspension with double wishbones at the front. The Lotus-designed 2.0 16-valve twin-cam engine was new, developing 160bhp. Capacity rose to 2.2 in 1980, with Getrag gearbox replacing the BL casing fitted with Lotus ratios. Automatic was an option, but very few ever sold.

ECLAT. 1975-85 (prod: 1522). 2-door 2+2-seater coupé. F/R, 1973/2174cc (S4 DOC). Max speed 129mph, 0-60mph 7.8sec. Take off that fastback 2+2 body and you would find exactly the same chassis as used on the Elite. But the reduced weight of the glass-fibre body meant overall weight dropped by around 100lb. With more efficient aerodynamics, this gave slightly better top speed. On the downside, there was rather less boot space beneath that shallower tail. Handling was as secure as ever, but Lotus had still to overcome its major headache of poor reliability.

EXCEL. 1985-92 (prod: 2074). 2-door 2+2-seater coupé. F/R, 2174cc (S4 DOC). Max speed 135mph, 0-60mph 6.8sec. To avoid the cost of obtaining new Type Approval, it was launched as the Excel Eclat. Same chassis and suspension as the Eclat, but with the bodywork's sharp edges smoothed out. But the Toyota five-speed gearbox and brakes were new, and the rear suspension was modified too. The 160bhp 2.2 version was joined by the SE (with 180bhp) in 1985, and the SA automatic a year later. Steadily improved with maturity.

ESPRIT S1/S2. 1976-81 (prod: 2092). 2-door 2-seater coupé. M/R, 1973/2174cc (S4 DOC). Max speed 124mph, 0-60mph 8.4sec. It was inevitable that Lotus would take the mid-engined route once more; the first time was with the Europa. The familiar backbone chassis was retained, this time with the composite plastics bodywork designed by Giugiaro's ItalDesign studio. Initially with the 2.0 engine, later the 2.2 version, both mated with a five-speed Citroën SM gearbox. The S1's overheating and vibration problems were finally sorted with the 1979 S2. With a revised engine installation, handling simply became better.

ESPRIT TURBO. 1980-87 (prod: 1658). 2-door 2-seater coupé. M/R, 2174cc (S4 DOC). Max speed 152mph, 0-60mph 5.5sec. Rather than invest huge sums in a new engine, Lotus turned to turbocharging. Although it stayed with the 2174cc four-cylinder layout, the engine was mostly new. The Garrett T3 turbo, plus charge cooling, put power up to 210bhp, rising to 215bhp from 1986. The stiffer chassis, with larger wheels and brakes, was made even better with the more powerful engine, with the front wishbone and coil spring layout revised. By now there was little anyone could teach Lotus about handling.

ESPRIT S3. 1981-87 (prod: 767). 2-door 2-seater coupé. M/R, 2174cc (S4 DOC). Max speed 134mph, 0-60mph 6.7sec. Although it stayed with the normally-aspirated 2.2 engine, the S3 appeared with most of the Turbo's chassis and suspension changes. At the rear there was new suspension, using lower wishbones, upper links and trailing arms. During this period Lotus was moving its image even further upmarket, the Esprit becoming pricier and better equipped.

ESPRIT SE. 1987-90 (prod: 385). 2-door 2-seater coupé. M/R, 2174cc (S4 DOC). Max speed 138mph, 0-60mph 6.5sec. With the original Giugiaro styling now 12 years old, drastic changes were needed – and Peter Stevens' subtle in-house redesign was accepted. Heavier by 500lb, but very much more aerodynamic, the beautifully finished composite bodywork was an immediate success. Transmission was changed to a Renault GTA transaxle.

ESPRIT TURBO. 1987 to date (prod: 2735). 2-door 2-seater coupé. M/R, 2174cc (S4 DOC). Max speed 163mph, 0-60mph 4.7sec. Beneath the smooth new Stevens body the chassis had been stiffened, mainly to cope with the extra power of the 228bhp turbo engine. As if 0-60mph in 5.3sec was not quick enough, Lotus launched the even quicker SE in spring 1989. This version's massive 264bhp – still from the four cylinder 2.2 – gave it affordable supercar status.

ELAN. 1989-92 (prod: 3855). 2-door 2-seater convertible. F/F, 1588cc (S4 DOC). Max speed 136mph, 0-60mph 6.5sec. If the original Elan was the prettiest Lotus ever made, the new one was perhaps the saddest. A more advanced backbone chassis and composite body structure was used, with Peter Stevens creating the shape and former GP driver John Miles designing novel interactive wishbone front suspension. Power came from Isuzu, with the four-cylinder 1.6 twin-cam engine developing 130bhp in normally-aspirated form (very few built) or 165bhp as the turbo SE. The front-drive caused raised eyebrows, but the chassis was so outstanding that handling was almost tediously good. But crashing sales and a poor response in the US, caused by the late-1980s recession, saw the whole Elan project shelved after just two years, although Bugatti's ownership brought a further run of 800 'Series 2' cars – built from existing supplies of components – in 1994.

MARCOS (GB)

A survivor among the small producers, thanks mainly to the distinctive looks of the cars. In 1972 financial problems led to the interruption of activities until 1981, when founder Jem Marsh made a comeback with updated versions of his enduring coupés. Rather like Morgan, Marcos relies on a traditional recipe except that its cars recall the 1960s.

3.0 LITRE. 1981-90 (prod: n/a). 2-door 2-seater sports coupé. F/R, 2792cc (V6 OHV). Max speed 130mph, 0-60mph 8.1sec. In effect, the 3-litre picked up the thread which had been dropped a decade before. The same square-section steel tube chassis was used, with wishbone front suspension. At the rear, the live axle was located by radius arms and a Panhard rod. Few changes were made to the glass-fibre bodywork, originally styled by Dennis Adams back in 1964. Massive grip tended to enhance the handling, but ride remained as 'sporting' as ever. Virtually all cars were sold in kit form.

MANTULA. 1984 to date (prod: n/a). 2-door 2-seater sports coupé/convertible. F/R, 3528/3947cc (V8 OHV). Max speed 150mph, 0-60mph 5.4sec. Since the existing body showed a tendency to lift at high speed with the extra performance of the 3.5 Rover V8 engine, a new nose (with deeper air dam) and side skirts was developed. In 1989, the 185bhp fuel-injection 3.9 V8 was installed, as well independent rear suspension with disc brakes.

MASERATI (I)

The trident badge has similar magic to Ferrari's prancing horse, yet Maserati's image started to fade in the latter part of the 1960s, with too many models chasing too few customers. Citroën money rescued Maserati in 1968, but the company was soon on its own again, really struggling in the wake of the 1973-74 oil crisis. De Tomaso's take-over in 1975 was later helped with Fiat finance, with the product range latterly being based around the Biturbo models. But 1980s sales in the UK were always sluggish.

BORA. 1971-80 (prod: 571). 2-door 2-seater sports coupé. M/R, 4719/4930cc (V8 DOC). Max speed 160mph, 0-60mph 6.5sec. Maserati's first mid-engined model, graced by ItalDesign's very distinctive all-steel body, with glassed-in 'flying buttresses' behind the the rear window. Wishbone and coil spring suspension all round, and Citroën high-pressure hydraulics for the brakes. Weber carburettor V8 engine, worth 320bhp in later 4.9 form, drove though ZF five-speed transaxle. Handling may have lacked Ferrari refinement, but was still impressive.

MERAK 2000/3000. 1972-83 (prod: 1832). 2-door 2+2-seater sports coupé. M/R, 1999/2965cc (V6 DOC). Max speed 135mph, 0-60mph 8.2sec. Maserati set its sights a little lower – and as a result brought into being its best-selling model. The Bora underpinnings and some body panels were used (but those flying buttresses were not glazed), with the 3.0/220bhp engine and transmission taken from the Citroën SM. The 2.0 version was an Italian market tax-beater. SM interior too in early days, later switched to something more conventional. Not hugely quick, but handling was impeccable.

KHAMSIN. 1974-82 (prod: 421). 2-door 2+2-seater sports coupé. F/R, 4930cc (V8 DOC). Max speed 151mph, 0-60mph 6.8sec. Reluctant to make the complete break with the classic front-engined, rear-drive format, Maserati used Bertone to style and build the Khamsin chassis and bodyshell. The big 4.9 V8 developed 320bhp, driving through a ZF manual gearbox or, on a few models, three-speed automatic. While the coil spring and wishbone suspension was conventional enough, the super-sensitive Citroën SM steering, hydraulic clutch and feather-touch brakes were not. But once you had come to terms with them, this big, heavy car could be handled with great ease – and its dart-like shape looked terrific.

KYALAMI. 1976-83 (prod: 150). 2-door 2+2-seater saloon. F/R, 4136/4930cc (V8 DOC). Max speed 147mph, 0-60mph 7.6sec. With the arrival of new owner Alejandro de Tomaso, the Maserati range gained an 'instant' new model. The de Tomaso Longchamps bodyshell, with some cosmetic changes by Ghia, was transformed into the Kyalami. Independent suspension front and rear, with the de Tomaso's Ford V8 replaced initially by Maserati's 4.1/255bhp V8 and, from 1978, the 4.9/280bhp version. The production figure tells the rest of the story.

QUATTROPORTE III/ROYALE. 1977-87 (prod: n/a). 4-door 5-seater saloon. F/R, 4136/4930cc (V8 DOC). Max speed 122mph, 0-60mph 9.1sec. While the Quattroporte name continued, ItalDesign replaced Bertone as the designer, using the Kyalami floorpan, engines and suspension. Best described as a sporting limousine – but it always looked rather cumbersome. Production trickled along in penny numbers, with the model being renamed the Royale in 1987, with an improved specification. Never officially imported into the UK, although a a handful found their way here as personal imports.

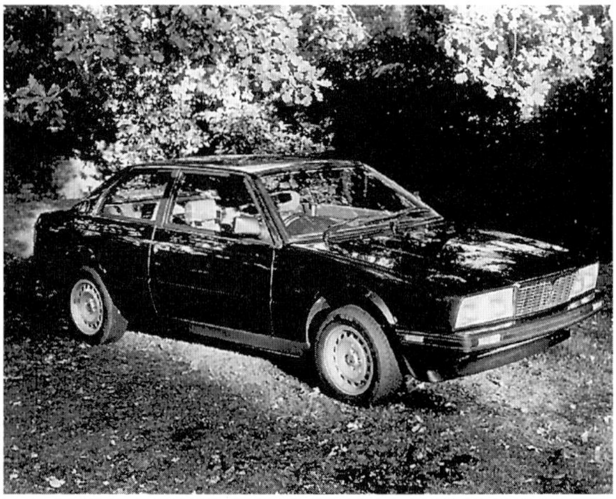

BITURBO. 1981-87 (prod: n/a). 2-door 4-seater saloon. F/R, 1996cc (V6 OC). Max speed 132mph, 0-60mph 7.8sec. In an attempt to widen appeal, Maserati designed the Biturbo along very conventional lines. The twin-turbo 2.0 V6 18-valve engine produced 180bhp, driving the rear wheels through a five-speed ZF gearbox, with McPherson strut suspension front and rear. After the head-turning looks of models like the Bora and Khamsin, the Biturbo looked quite dull – like an Italianate BMW 3 series. Image was not helped by severe turbo lag and indifferent handling. One peculiarity of the lush interior was a huge, glitzy clock in the centre of the facia.

BITURBO 420/425. 1983-91 (prod: n/a). 4-door 4-seater saloon. F/F, 1996/2491cc (V6 OC). Max speed 138mph, 0-60mph 6.6sec. A development of the Biturbo theme, with a very conventional looking four-door body using the same suspension layout as the two-door original. While the 420 stayed with the three-valve-per-cylinder 2.0 V6, the 425 used a larger 2.5/196bhp version. The 425 had the option of a three-speed ZF automatic in place of the five-speed manual 'box. Mediocre handling and the degree of turbo lag remained unchanged.

BITURBO SPYDER. 1984-91 (prod: n/a). 2-door 2-seater convertible. F/R, 1996/2491cc (V6 OC). Max speed 135mph, 0-60mph 6.7sec. The original Biturbo coupé had been designed with an open version in mind, but three years went by until it was added to the range. The 2.5 V6 version appeared a year after the launch of the 2.0. Good looking and outstandingly well equipped in a wood-and-leather manner, but it had far more of the sedate cabriolet feel about it than the Maserati name deserved.

MATRA (F)

A complex history for Matra, involving one of Jackie Stewart's three F1 World Championships and a trio of victories at Le Mans. In 1970, Simca took control of the production car division, but in the early 1980s Simca was sold to Peugeot, who in turn sold it on Renault. With Matra's aerospace connections, some very advanced techniques were used in the design of the Espace, which it continues to build for Renault.

BAGHEERA 1973-80 (prod: 47,802). 2-door 3-seater sports coupé. M/R, 1442cc (S4 OHV). Max speed 100mph, 0-60mph 12.3sec. If the construction was advanced, with a tubular spaceframe clad with glass-fibre bodywork and all-round independent suspension with torsion bars, the engine was not. From 1977, a mid-mounted 1442cc Simca four-cylinder was used, putting out a mere 90bhp, which resulted in performance certainly not in keeping with the looks. Odd seating layout, with two narrow passenger seats alongside the driver's. LHD only, but a few came to the UK.

MURENA 1980-83 (prod: 10,613). 2-door 3-seater sports coupé. M/R, 1592/2155cc (S4 OHV). Max speed 121mph, 0-60mph 9.3sec. The same basic construction as in the Bagheera was retained, but now with coil springs in place of torsion bars. Good-looking slippery coupé had a Cd factor of just 0.32, excellent for its day. Standard engine was the 1.6 Alpine unit, but the real power came from the 2.2 Chrysler unit, putting out 118bhp but a good deal more torque. The same three-abreast seating layout was used, with just five cars converted to RHD.

MAZDA (J)

After the 1973 OPEC oil crisis, Mazda was the only company to keep faith in the Wankel rotary engine. Indeed, so much money had been invested in the project that the company had little alternative. In the UK market, all its cars with the exception of the RX-7 now have conventional reciprocating engines.

121. 1988-91 (prod: 222,398). 3-door 4-seater hatchback. F/F, 1139/1324cc (S4 OC). Max speed 99mph, 0-60mph 11.3sec. Breakaway design, with tall, upright styling making best use of space within the 137in overall length. Suntop version had full-length electrically-operated sunroof. Independent suspension all round, using struts at the front. Base L version had 1.1/56bhp engine, the remainder a 1.3/65bhp unit, both transverse and driving the front wheels through a five-speed gearbox. Replaced in 1991 with retro-look Austin A35 version.

323. 1977-80 (prod: 904,573). 3/5-door 4-seater hatchback. F/R, 985/1272cc (S4 OC). Max speed 89mph, 0-60mph 14.2sec. Mazda seemed to be ignoring the move to front-drive. Utterly conventional layout, with McPherson struts at the front, live axle on coil springs at the rear. Frontal styling was an odd mix, with circular headlamps looking as if they had been specified as a last-minute afterthought. Practical enough, but just about as dull as they come on the handling side.

323. 1981-85 (prod: 2,567,162). 3/5-door 4-seater hatchback, 4-door 4-seater saloon. F/F, 1071/1296/1490cc (S4 OC). Max speed 101mph, 0-60mph 10.7sec. Mazda's first front-drive model and new from stem to stern. Overhead cam engines, initially with just four-speed gearboxes, going to five-speed on large engines with minor facelift in spring 1983. GT 1500 hatchback and saloon stayed with just 88bhp, but had alloy wheels and rev counter. Strut front suspension, twin transverse links at the rear. The Ford connection went as far as the 323 wearing the blue and white oval in Pacific markets.

323 ESTATE. 1982-86 (prod: inc above). 5-door 4-seater estate. F/R, 1490cc (S4 OC). Max speed 97mph, 0-60mph 12.3sec. With curious perversity, the 323 estate differed from the hatchback in styling with the front-engined, rear-drive layout. Only made with the 1.5/70bhp engine, but with five-speed gearbox or optional three-speed auto. Suspension layout was the same as the front-drive hatchback, so rear diff resulted in a rather high load floor level. Reputation for reliability and ease of driving meant it sold surprisingly well.

323. 1985-87 (prod: 1,578,755). 3/5-door 4-seater hatchback; 4-door 4-seater saloon; 5-door 4-seater estate. F/F, 1071/1296/1490/1597cc (S4 OC). Max

speed 112mph, 0-60mph 9.6sec. The body may have been new, but it needed a keen eye to spot the difference – and the old rear-drive estate continued to plough its lonely, dated furrow until finally replaced in 1986. New was the fuel-injected 1600FI, with 1597cc engine giving 105bhp, but it was only a 'tepid hatchback', lacking much flair.

323 1600 TURBO 4×4. 1985-89 (prod: see above). 3-door 4-seater hatchback. F/4×4, 1597cc (S4 DOC). Max speed 125mph, 0-60mph 7.9sec. Designed very much with rallying in mind. New twin-cam, 16-valve head was developed, with IHI turbocharger, intercooler and injection raising power of 1597cc engine to 148bhp. Simple but effective 4wd system with fixed 50/50 torque split. Four-wheel disc brakes and wider wheels coped with extra power and performance. Looked nothing special, but handling was huge fun.

323. 1987-89 (prod: see above). 3/5-door 4-seater hatchback; 4-door 4-seater saloon; 5-door 5-seater estate. F/F, 1296/1490cc (S4 OC). Max speed 112mph, 0-60mph 9.1sec. Money-spinning hatchback design continued, with smaller engines now absent from UK market, leaving 1.3/66bhp and 1.5/83bhp for mainstream models, including new front-drive estate. All but base models got power steering in 1988. The 1.6i stayed with 105bhp. Good range, but being left behind by European cars with better ride and handling.

323. 1989 to date (prod: n/a). 3/5-door 4-seater hatchback; 4-door 4-seater saloon; 5-door 4-seater fastback. F/F, 1324/1598cc (S4 OC), 1840cc (S4 DOC). Max speed 120mph, 0-60mph 8.2sec. Rearrangement of the body line-up, 323F 5-door fastback, with pop-up headlamps, joining usual hatchback and saloon. New 1.8 injection engine with twin-cam head gave 137bhp in fastback body. Upmarket hatchback was 1.6SE Executive, with huge equipment list. Underneath, suspension remained basically as before. Outstanding build quality, but ride comfort still deficient.

MONTROSE/626. 1978-82 (prod: 723.709). 4-door 5-seater saloon; 2-door 5-seater coupé. F/R, 1586/1769/1970cc (S4 OC). Max speed 104mph, 0-60mph 12.9sec. Worried that number designations would not sell, Mazda in the UK arbitrarily named the first 626 the Montrose. Good looks concealed essentially a very ordinary car, with single-cam engines, and choice of five-speed manual or three-speed automatic for 2.0 litre. Coil-spring live rear axle and struts at the front added up to unexceptional but basically sound handling.

626. 1983-87 (prod: 1,373,766). 4-door 5-seater saloon; 5-door 5-seater hatchback; 2-door 4-seater

coupé. F/F, 1586/1970/1998cc (S4 OC). Max speed 124mph, 0-60mph 8.6sec.** Mazda's wardrobe was being quickly brought up to date, with good-looking saloon, hatchback and coupé bodies and new front-drive layout. The 1970cc/90bhp engine was dropped after a year, replaced by new 1998cc unit, with 102bhp (carburettor) or 120bhp (injection). Good equipment and even better build quality was giving Mazda an improving image.

626. 1987-92 (prod: n/a). 4-door 5-seater saloon; 5-door 5-seater hatchback/estate; 2-door 4-seater coupé. F/F, 1789/1998cc (S4 OC), 1998cc (S4 DOC), F/4×4, 1998cc (S4 DOC). Max speed 130mph, 0-60mph 8.3sec. High technology four-wheel drive and four-wheel steering starting to overshadow the bread-and-butter models. Smooth looks with well-equipped interiors, plus usefully lively 1.8 and 2.0 engines. The 2.0i/148bhp GT, some with all-wheel steering, was very quick. The 4wd 2.0 estate, with 114bhp, was a sensible if pricey workhorse.

929 ESTATE. 1981-87 (prod: 103,426). 5-door 5-seater estate. F/R, 1970cc (S4 OC). Max speed 101mph, 0-60mph 13.2sec. This seemed to become a permanent resident in the price lists, although few were ever seen in the UK. Started life as the 2000 (a long-wheelbase version of the original rear-drive 626), becoming 929 in 1981, staying on for another six years. Utterly conventional, with dull handling and ride.

RX-7. 1978-86 (prod: 570,000). 2-door 2+2-seater coupé. F/R, 2292cc equivalent (2-rotor Wankel). Max speed 119mph, 0-60mph 9.5sec. Sole survivor in the UK of Mazda's affair with the Wankel engine. Clean-cut 2+2 coupé lines looked pretty, but performance was not too hot with original 105bhp engine – and an increase to 115bhp in 1981 did not help much. Engine apart, it was rather ordinary underneath, with strut front suspension and a well-located live axle at the rear. Nevertheless, the handling was amazingly agile.

RX-7. 1986-89 (prod: 197,180). 2-door 2+2-seater. F/R, 2254cc equivalent (2-rotor Wankel). Max speed 128mph, 0-60mph 8.4sec. With the new 13B engine producing a healthy 148bhp and a new chassis, the RX-7 came alive. The strut front suspension stayed, while at the rear a complicated but very effective independent system resulted in handling worthy of the new Porsche-cloned looks, although the ride was not that good. Hard-driving fuel consumption remained the Achilles heel of the Wankel engine, although power was seamlessly delivered.

RX-7 TURBO. 1988-92 (prod: n/a). 2-door 2+2 seater coupé, 2-seater convertible. F/R, 2254cc equivalent (2-rotor Wankel). Max speed 148mph, 0-60mph 6.7sec. Mazda had been turbocharging the Wankel engine for some time before it came to the UK. With 200bhp, the RX-7 was able to prove just how good its chassis could be. Scoops on the bonnet and new alloy wheels made it look the part too. The two-seater cabriolet came in summer 1989, with power hood but no anti-lock brakes. On the debit side, fuel consumption was even more alarming.

MX-5. 1989 to date (prod: n/a). 2-door 2-seater convertible. F/R, 1597cc (S4 DOC). Max speed 114mph, 0-60mph 9.1sec. Seen by many as what a new MG sports car should have been, with a pretty shape unashamedly inspired by the original Lotus Elan. Not quite as simple underneath as it might appear, with engine, gearbox and final drive carried on a separate subframe beneath the neat two-seater body. Double wishbone suspension gave neat handling, spoiled only by over-light power steering and, for some, lack of performance from the 114bhp engine. Inexpensive, fun – and a huge success.

MERCEDES-BENZ (D)

Daimler and Benz joined up in 1926 to form Mercedes-Benz, very soon establishing the company's products right at the top of the tree. The 1928 SSK's reputation was more feared than fearsome, while at the other end of the scale the first diesel model, the 260D, appeared in 1935. Only a year after the end of World War II, the Stuttgart factory was back in production. In the UK careful marketing quickly re-established the Mercedes-Benz name for sheer quality and reliability.

280S/280SE 1972-80 (prod: 122,848/150,775). 4-door 5-seater saloon. 2746cc (S6 DOC). Max speed 118mph, 0-60mph 10.2sec. Designated W116 (the W stands for nothing more exciting than *wagen* or car) the new S-class was to set new standards in comfort and safety. Timeless design, now with the trailing arm suspension from the SL range. At 3500lb in standard trim, it was no lightweight. Impeccable handling, composed ride and reasonable performance, even with the in-line six.

350SE/450SE/450SEL. 1972-80 (prod: 51,140/41,604/59,575). 4-door 5-seater saloon. F/R, 3499/4520cc (V8 OC). Max speed 124mph, 0-60mph 9.9sec. From any angle the S-class looked entirely right, even in its long-wheelbase (4in extra) 450SEL version, which had longer rear doors and more legroom in the back. V8 engines were matched to automatic transmission. Well-mannered handling and firm but smooth ride were hallmarks of the S-class. Well over a decade later, they still look as good as they did on day one.

450SEL 6.9. 1977-80 (prod: 7380). 4-door 5-seater saloon. F/R, 6834cc (V8 OC). Max speed 136mph, 0-60mph 6.9sec. The badge, if you had not had it removed before taking delivery, said it all. Mighty and unique 6.9 V8 (shared with 600) gave 286bhp, performance figures appear almost unseemly for a car of this size, even with compulsory automatic transmission. Air-over-oil suspension with self-levelling gave unflustered ride and impeccable handling. In its own way, a collector's car.

280SE/300SE/300SEL. 1980-91 (prod: 73,970 all versions). 4-door 5-seater saloon. F/R, 2746cc (S6 DOC), 2962cc (S6 OC). Max speed 131mph, 0-60mph 9.1sec. If the previous S-class had been good, its replacement was simply better. Just under 16½ft long, on a 116in wheelbase, but beautifully proportioned and visually exactly right. All the extra room in the long-wheelbase SEL version was in the rear, with wider doors and more legroom. With injection, the twin-camshaft 2.8 six gave 156bhp, while the single-cam 3.0 six produced 185bhp. Manual gearboxes were available, but the majority of owners opted for the far nicer automatic.

400SE/SEL, 420SE/SEL, 500SE/SEL. 1986-91 (prod: 46,350 all versions). 4-door 5-seater saloon. F/R, 3839/4196/4973cc (V8 OC). Max speed 146mph, 0-60mph 7.3sec. With the light-alloy V8 engine matched to the in-house four-speed automatic, these became the flagship models of the S-class range. Expensive, yes, but in return for your money you enjoyed imperceptible depreciation and exquisite engineering. Self-levelling suspension on all models, the layout remaining wishbones at the front and trailing arms at the rear, with coil springs. Largest 5.0 V8 went from 211bhp to 262bhp during its lifetime.

560SEL. 1986-91 (prod: 8435). 4-door 5-seater saloon. F/R, 5546cc (V8 OC). Max speed 156mph, 0-60mph 6.9sec. Powered everything in this ultimate expression of Stuttgart engineering. Long-wheelbase version only, with 5.6 V8 giving 300bhp and eyebrow-raising performance. The price – £62,120 in its final days – reflected the sort of car you were buying. Of course, items like anti-lock brakes, cruise control, air conditioning and memory front seats were standard. You had to wait until 1987 for an electrically-adjustable steering column and the following year for heated front seats. A spirit level was, and is, needed to detect depreciation.

380SEC/500SEC. 1981-86 (prod: 17,940). 2-door 4-seater coupé. F/R, 3839/4973cc (V8 OC). Max speed 143mph, 0-60mph 7.8sec. To some eyes an even better balanced, outstanding looking car than the S-class saloon on which it was based. Same 116in wheelbase, with steeply-sloped windscreen easing into fastback rear quarters. Pillarless layout gave airy, uncluttered look with windows up or down. V8 engines only, both matched to four-speed automatic. Well-mannered handling, with typically firm but smooth Mercedes ride. Highly sought-after, even today.

420SEC/500SEC/560SEC. 1981-91 (prod: 15,790). 2-door 4-seater coupé. F/R, 4196/4973/5547cc (V8 OC). Max speed 156mph, 0-60mph 6.8sec. Essentially the same floorpan and suspension layout, with an even more elegant two-door coupé body. The 4.2/218bhp V8 replaced the smaller 204bhp unit of the 380SEC, while 500 power rose from 240bhp to 245bhp. This was the first time that the 5.6/300bhp V8 had been used in the coupé body. Prices reflected the outstanding equipment list – the 560SEC went out of the price lists at a shade under £70,000.

600/600 PULLMAN. 1963-80 (prod: 2190/487). 4-door 6-seater limousine; 6-door 8-seater limousine. F/R, 6332cc (V8 OC). Max speed 116mph, 0-60mph 11.6sec. No penny-pinching here, with almost all body panels unique to the 600. Endless 126in or 153in wheelbase, bearing cliff-faced six/eight-seater limousine body on all-round independent pneumatic suspension. V8 engine (which had nothing in common with any other M-B V8) and automatic transmission resulted in sprightly performance – and 600 users did not have to worry about fuel consumption. The only real rivals were the Daimler Limousine and Rolls-Royce Phantom VI.

200/230. 1975-84 (prod: 419,170). 4/5-door 5-seater saloon/estate. F/R, 1987/1997cc (S4 OC). 2307/ 2299cc (S4 OC). Max speed 114mph, 0-60mph 11.6sec. Until the 190 arrived, the W123 range made up Mercedes' entry-level models. Nothing revolutionary about the looks, with horizontal rectangular headlamp cowls and conservative styling, plus practical T (for Transporter) estate version. All on 110in wheelbase, with semi-trailing arm suspension layout at the rear. New 2.0 and 2.3 engines from 1980, replacing carry-over originals. Real rivals in space, if not performance, to BMW's 5 series.

250/280E. 1975-84 (prod: 179,640). 4/5-door 5-seater saloon/estate. F/R, 2525cc (S6 OC), 2746cc (S6 DOC). Max speed 124mph, 0-60mph 10.4sec. Logical extension of the W123 theme, with six-cylinder engines. The 250's was a new single-cam engine with 140bhp, while the 280 used the existing 185bhp twin-cam unit. The latter's suffix E stands for *einspritzung* (fuel injection). Although manual transmission was standard, most were sold with cost-extra four-speed automatic. Undemanding to drive, but could become a bit of a handful at the wet-road limit.

200D/240D/300D. 1976-84 (prod: 563,420). 4/5-door 5-seater saloon/estate. F/R, 1988/2399/ 2402cc diesel (S4 OC), 3005cc diesel (S5 OC). Max speed 93mph, 0-60mph 15.2sec. Mercedes-Benz had been making diesel cars since the 1930s, and low fuel prices on the other side of the Channel ensured good sales. The 300 was the first with the five-cylinder diesel, essentially a 240-plus-one-pot. Turbocharged versions with 125bhp were available in the USA, but UK buyers had to make do with a lethargic 88bhp. For the adventurous, you could even specify automatic...

230CE/280CE/300CE. 1980-88 (prod: 187,367). 2-door 4-seater hardtop coupé. F/R, 2299cc (S4 OC), 2746/2962cc (S6 OC). Max speed 125mph, 0-60mph 9.4sec. With a shortened W123 floorpan (by 3.3in), and two-door hardtop coupé body, the result was not one of the greatest designs from Mercedes-Benz. After 1980, all had the same range of larger fuel injection six-cylinder engines as the saloon equivalents. The CEs never captured buyers' imaginations in this country, so they are fairly rare.

200E/230E. 1987 to date (prod: 523,600). 4/5-door 5-seater saloon /estate. F/R, 1997/2299cc (S4 OC). Max speed 127mph, 0-60mph 9.2sec. The W124 range came to fill the gap between the smaller 190 and the S-class. Appearance was similar to the 190, but on 5in longer wheelbase with most of the extra space being used in the rear. Distinctive diagonal boot shut line between rear lamps. Estate arrived a year after the saloon, and 2.0 engine saw injection (122bhp) replace carburettors (102bhp) from autumn 1988. Build quality was from the classic Mercedes-Benz school.

250D/300D. 1985 to date (prod: 497,870). 4/5-door 5-seater saloon/estate. F/R 2497cc diesel (S5 OC), 2996cc diesel (S6 OC). Max speed 118mph, 0-60mph 13.7sec. Turbochargers had finally been admitted at the Stuttgart factory – but not for UK cars. Smaller 250 managed just 90bhp but larger 3.0 reached 105bhp, which gave acceptable if not notable performance. Majority were sold in estate car form. An oddity, as on all W124 models, was the foot-operated parking brake – the US influence showing through. With long-lived diesel engines and outstanding build quality, these cars approach immortality.

300E. 1985 to date. (prod: 173,240). 4/5-door 5-seater saloon/estate. F/R, 2962cc (S6 OC). Max speed 136mph, 0-60mph 8.4sec. Although engine capacity was intruding into S-class territory, the size of the 300E did not impose. Made in both saloon and estate bodies, with up-market trim and rather more equipment. Anti-lock brakes became standard in 1987 across the whole range. In autumn 1989 the 188bhp 12-valve engine was joined by fire-breathing 231bhp 24-valve version, still with just a single camshaft.

300E 4-MATIC. 1988-92 (prod: 15,490). 4/5-door 5-seater saloon/estate. F/4×4, 2962cc (S6 OC). Max speed 136mph, 0-60mph 8.6sec. Determined to be different, Mercedes-Benz developed its very own four-wheel drive system, with 'Vier-matic' system sensing torque drop and automatically putting power where it was needed. Same engine as the rear-drive 300E, with the manual gearbox being dropped in 1990 to leave just a four-speed automatic. Unbeatable traction and grip – but the £6000 4wd price premium in the UK meant that it was far from being a best-seller.

300CE. 1987 to date (prod: 19,320). 2-door 4-seater hardtop coupé. F/R, 2962cc (S6 OC). Max speed 145mph, 0-60mph 7.8sec. So-elegant hardtop coupé based on W124 floorpan, shortened by 4in. First sold with 12-valve 3.0 engine, giving 188bhp, joined in late 1989 by 24-valve version with 231bhp. Both available with manual or automatic, most being sold with latter. Steeply sloping rear quarters did not give rear seat passengers much light or headroom. Poised handling, with pleasantly firm ride which matched those sporting looks.

190. 1983-93 (prod: 1,900,000). 4-door 5-seater saloon. F/R, 1797/1997cc (S4 OC), 2599cc (S6 OC), 1997cc diesel (S4 OC), 2497cc diesel (S5 OC). Max speed 119mph, 0-60mph 10.6sec. Sights at Stuttgart were lowered just a little to target the smaller BMWs – and the lucrative taxi market. In the UK, the 190 was seen rather differently, with less sporting appeal but more prestige than rival BMWs. Compact at a shade under 14½ft long, the 190s had surprisingly little rear seat leg room. Single-cam petrol engines ranged from 90bhp carburettor 2.0 'four' to 166bhp fuel-injected 2.6 'six'; later joined by 113bhp injection 1.8. Diesels, 2.0 and 2.5, followed Mercedes tradition. No change in outstanding build quality, mechanical strength and predictable handling.

190 16-V. 1985-93 (prod: see above). 4-door 5-seater saloon. F/R, 2299/2496cc (S4 DOC). Max speed 143mph, 0-60mph 6.7sec. Cosworth's cylinder head expertise was used for this four-valve-per-cylinder-design. Original 2.5 gave 180bhp, going to 2.6 with 197bhp in 1988. Manual gearboxes only – and performance to suit. Lowered, stiffened suspension, plus limited slip diff, with air-controlled self-levelling at the rear on the 2.5-16, gave classic rear-drive handling, even if the car was not that agile.

280SL/300SL. 1980-85 (prod: 160,011). 2-door 2-seater convertible. 2746cc (S6 DOC), 2962cc (S6 OC). Max speed 124mph, 0-60mph 9.6 sec. A far cry from the 300SL models of the mid-1950s. The SL initials originally stood for *sehr leicht* (very light), which these later cars were anything but. Originally with twin-cam 2.8/185bhp, replaced by single cam 3.0/188bhp in 1985. Majority sold with M-B's own four-speed automatic. Low bonnet line and distinctive three-pointed star incorporated in radiator grille were features. Smaller-engined versions looked better than they either performed or handled.

380SL/420SL/500SL/560SL. 1980-89 (prod: 106,215). 2-door 2-seater convertible. F/R, 3939/4196/4973/5547cc (V8 OC). Max speed 142mph, 0-60mph 6.9sec. Same chassis as the six-cylinder versions, but with V8 power. First was the miserably under-powered, de-toxed 380, with just 155bhp. Replaced in 1985 by 218bhp 420. Best-seller was the massive 5.6/227bhp version, with prodigious fuel thirst. Very much an 'image' car, with few sporting pretensions.

350SLC/450SLC. 1972-80 (prod: 45,664). 2-door 2+2-hardtop coupé. F/R, 3499/4520cc (V8 OC). Max speed 137mph, 0-60mph 7.4sec. Elegant version of the SL stretched by 14in, now with attractive fixed hardtop, with distinctive slatting behind rear quarter window. Amazingly, weight was up by just 110lb over the two-seater SL. Sufficient – just – room for two in the back made this a practical alternative to the bigger saloon and CE versions. V8 engines were matched to four-speed automatic transmission, with no manual option. Nice if slightly sedate handling.

450SLC/500SLC. 1977-81 (prod: 2769). 2-door 2+2-seater hardtop coupé. F/R, 4990/4973cc (V8 OC). Max speed 141mph, 0-60mph 7.4sec. With 14in longer wheelbase, weight cut by 250lb with alloy body panels, and light alloy V8 with three-speed automatic transmission, this 'homologation special' was aimed at rallying. And despite size, it almost succeeded. This model was dropped in favour of the standard SLC range, which paralleled the main SL family.

SL300. 1989-93 (prod: 29,990). 2-door 4-seater convertible/coupé. F/R, 2960cc (S6 OC), 2960cc (S6 DOC). Max speed 146mph, 0-60mph 8.4sec. One of the very best-looking cars from the Stuttgart factory, with outstandingly balanced lines. Standard 3.0 engine gave 190bhp, twin-cam 24-valve 231bhp, both with four-speed, dual-range automatic as standard (no manual option in UK). Power hood, naturally, with pop-up roll-over bar which rose automatically in potential accident situations. Anti-lock brakes standard, speed-lowering suspension extra. Replaced in 1993 by 280/320SL, with same power.

SL500. 1989 to date (prod: 19,373). 2-door 4-seater convertible/coupé. F/R, 4973cc (V8 DOC). Max speed 160mph, 0-60mph 5.9sec. Until joined by the V12 SL600 in 1992, this was the ultimate modern SL expression. Hugely quick and refined, with V8 engine and dual-range four-speed or even five-speed automatic transmission. As expected,

handling and ride were outstanding. Power everything, including hood. All SLs available with rear wind deflector to keep occupants' hair in place. Destined to become an instant classic.

G-WAGEN. 1979 to date (prod: 98,130). 3/5-door 4-seater off-road estate. F/4×4, 2299cc (S4 OC), 2746cc (S6 OC), 2998cc diesel (S5 OC). Max speed 102mph, 0-60mph 12.0sec. Little of the Land Rover's 'friendly farmer' image here. Rugged chassis using coil-sprung live axles and normal rear-wheel drive, with front-drive and low-ratio transfer 'box added when conditions demanded. Slab-sided, rather militaristic-looking bodywork and 'soldier-proof' interior. Despite unpromising looks, on-road handling was good. Appearance apart, hefty price and increasing competition from Japan did not help sales. More user-friendly versions came in 1991.

MG (GB)

When the MG plant at Abingdon-on-Thames closed in 1980, many felt that an era had ended. But to be fair, it had ended many years before, with both factory and product outdated thanks to British Leyland negligence. The MGB was simply too slow and too expensive as it staggered towards its demise in 1980, while the 'badge-engineered' performance saloons and hatchbacks failed to capture the original magic.

MGB II. 1974-80 (prod: 155,698). 2/3-door 2/2+2-seater convertible/coupé. F/R, 1798cc (S4 OHV). Max speed 105 mph, 0-60mph 12.1sec. Almost reluctantly, the once-loved MGB dragged itself into the 1980s, weighed down with lumpen black rubber bumpers to meet US safety regulations. With less power from the aged B-series engine and more weight to lug about, performance suffered, and handling also deteriorated in the 'rubber-bumper' phase. Overdrive was standard, while the final cars were sold with LE – Limited Edition – badging. Just months after production ceased, the Abingdon factory was demolished.

MG METRO. 1982-90 (prod: 37,500) 3-door 4-seater hatchback. F/F, 1275cc (S4 OHV). Max speed 100mph, 0-60mph 12.2sec. In a rather forlorn attempt to placate MG enthusiasts, the Metro was dressed up with the famous octagon badge, tweaked suspension, alloy wheels and red seat belts. Output of the venerable 1275cc A-plus engine was coaxed up to 72bhp (from the standard Metro's 62bhp), giving a 100mph top speed. The alloy wheels – replaced by steel ones in 1987 – made handling even better. Towards the end, MG logos ran riot inside and out.

MG METRO TURBO. 1983-89 (prod: 29,610). 3-door 4-seater hatchback. F/F, 1275cc (S4 OHV). Max speed 110mph, 0-60mph 10.3sec. Just what inspired Austin Rover to develop the Metro Turbo must remain a mystery. Power was kept down to a savagely-delivered 93bhp in an effort to preserve the gearbox – only a four-speed – and engine mounts, both of which expired with alarming frequency if the car was driven with any verve. Just about the only thing this car did prove was that the basic Metro chassis was quite good.

METRO 6R4. 1984 (prod: 200 plus). 2-door 2-seater saloon. M/4×4, 2991cc (V6 DOC). Max speed 120mph, 0-60mph 4.3sec. Subtle is not a word you'd use when describing the 6R4. Built for the short-lived Group B rally scene, the 6R4 had a 3.0 litre non-turbo V6 engine giving 250bhp in clubman guise or 380 for the international heros. Williams Grand Prix Engineering, led by Patrick Head, did much of the development work. The 4wd system used Ferguson technology, with the front-rear prop shafts lying to the right of the mid-mounted engine. There were some Metro body panels lurking beneath the huge wings and spoilers. After Group B was outlawed, most of the spare engines were acquired by Tom Walkinshaw Racing. Was it sheer chance that the Le Mans-winning Jaguar engines had very similar dimensions?

MG MAESTRO 1600. 1983-84 (prod: 2,500). 5-door 5-seater hatchback. F/F, 1598cc (S4 OC). Max speed 111mph, 0-60mph 9.6sec. Rushed into production against development engineers' advice for the Maestro launch, this original MG version was a disaster. Plagued with all sorts of problems with its twin Weber carburettors, the R-series engine ran rough, was difficult to start when hot and never seemed able to deliver its claimed 103bhp. The Maestro body's spaciousness was always impressive, but the voice-synthesised warnings of malfunctions were nauseating. Less than a year after launch, the model was quietly dropped.

MG MAESTRO 2.0 EFi. 1984-91 (prod: 5740) 5-door 5-seater hatchback. F/F, 1994cc (S4 OC). Max speed 113mph, 0-60mph 8.4sec. After a decent interval, Austin Rover relaunched the MG-badged Maestro. This time it took the more sensible option, with a fuel-injected version of the 2.0 O-series engine producing a more believable 115bhp. The all-talking digital facia vanished in 1985, replaced by proper dials. Of all the Maestro variants, this was the nicest to drive, with good handling and performance.

MG MAESTRO TURBO. 1989-91 (prod: 3500). 5-door 5-seater hatchback. F/F, 1994cc (S4 OC). Max speed 128mph, 0-60mph 6.7sec. With the Rover Group a matter of months away, this was the final car from ARG. The 2.0/152bhp turbo engine from the MG Montego, driving through a Honda gearbox, was shoehorned under the Maestro bonnet to make it one of the quickest of the badge-engineered MG models – and the savage torque steer that plagued the Montego Turbo was considerably muted. It was fun to drive, but despite the body kit and alloy wheels it remained nothing more than a Maestro with fire in its belly. It might have earned a better reception had it appeared earlier than six years after the Maestro's launch, but as it was sales were pitiful.

MG MONTEGO 2.O EFi. 1984-91 (prod: 57,900). 4-door 5-seater saloon. F/F, 1994cc (S4 OC). Max speed 115mph, 0-60mph 9.1sec. If ever there was a case of cashing in on a name, this was it. BL was using the same 115bhp injected O-series engine in Austin-badged Montegos like the SI and GTi, with equivalent performance and handling. This was not a bad car, but it was created so cynically. Thankfully, BL never had the nerve to produce an estate version. As with the Metro and Maestro, red seat belts were deemed part of the MG identity.

MG MONTEGO TURBO. 1985-91 (prod: 23,000) 4-door 5-seater saloon. F/F, 1994cc (S4 OC). Max speed 124mph, 0-60mph 7.2sec. Anyone who had never experienced the interesting combination of turbo lag and torque steer on a wet road was in for a shock with early versions. Putting 150bhp through the front wheels produced all sorts of interesting results from a car which, even with wide alloy wheels, had at best mediocre handling. It went very fast and could carry five people, but it's hard to think of any other virtues. When production ceased, the MG badge was next to be seen on a model worthy of wearing those initials – the MGB-derived RV8 launched in 1993.

MIDAS (GB)

The concept for the Midas came from the Mini-Marcos, which ex-Jaguar engineer Harold Dermott took over from Marcos and successfully sold. If not the prettiest looking small car, the Midas quickly found favour with its agile handling and attention to detail. A fire in 1989 forced the company into liquidation.

BRONZE. 1978-88 (prod: 350). 2-door 2-seater sports coupé. F/F, 848/998cc (S4 OHV). Max speed n/a, 0-60mph n/a. Glass-fibre monocoques had been tried before (notably by Lotus with the original Elite), but this one worked. The Mini engine and front suspension was carried on a purpose-built galvanised steel subframe, but at the rear a trailing arm system, with coil springs and adjustable dampers, was used. Unlike any rivals, the interior was not cobbled together from other manufacturers' bits. Handling was brilliant – and it simply improved with more power.

GOLD. 1985-89 (prod: 150 coupé, 15 convertible). 2-door 2-seater coupé/convertible. F/F, 1275cc (S4 OHV). Max speed n/a, 0-60mph n/a. Same basic monocoque, with stylist Richard Oakes giving it longer rear quarter windows and a lower tail. The cabriolet was even better-looking, with a hardtop available for winter comfort. Metro components were used at the front. Brabham/McLaren F1 designer Gordon Murray helped with the under-car aerodynamics, which simply made the handling even better.

MIDDLEBRIDGE (GB)

With Japanese finance, the company bought the rights for the Scimitar GTE from Reliant in 1988. The car appeared at that year's NEC Motor Show, but various production and marketing problems led to the project folding during 1990. The company's assets were auctioned on the very day Mrs Thatcher resigned as PM...

SCIMITAR GTE. 1988-90 (prod: 80 approx). 2-door 4-seater sports estate. F/R, 2933cc (V6 OHV). Max speed n/a, 0-60mph n/a. With all Reliant's experience of the model, it was not surprising that Middlebridge went back to the original manufacturer for assistance with its born-again GTE. The principal mechanical change was the replacement of the 2.8 V6 with the later and more efficient 2.9 version. But the high price and impending recession saw sales slow to a trickle and, in 1990, Middlebridge had to give up. The fact that it cost four times as much as an excellent 'classic' Scimitar always worked against it.

MITSUBISHI (J)

Planes and boats and trains - Mitsubishi Heavy Industries makes the lot. The Automobile Division split away in 1970, with cars being sold in the UK under the Colt name. Early in the 1980s the name reverted to Mitsubishi, although the marketing company is still Colt Cars. During the decade a cluttered range started to make much more sense as it was simplified and improved.

COLT MIRAGE. 1978-84 (prod: n/a). 3/5-door 4-seater hatchback. F/F, 1244/1410cc (S4 OC). Max speed 92mph, 0-60mph 13.2sec. Distinguished as Mitsubishi's first front-drive model – and unique for having dual-range, two-lever, power-or-economy eight-speed transmission, but only on larger 1.4/65bhp versions. Distinctive front, with recessed headlamps and prominent indicators. Shape gave roomy interior for compact size. Few managed to survive ravages of rust.

COLT. 1983-88 (prod: n/a). 3/5-door 4-seater hatchback. F/F, 1198/1468cc (S4 OC), 1795cc diesel (S4 OC). Max speed 93mph, 0-60mph 12.3sec. New engines and conventional five-speed gearboxes in hatchback bodies, on essentially the same floorpan as the saloon Lancers. Mid-term revisions in 1986 saw engine tipped back by 10 degrees to give lower bonnet line, plus new-look interiors. New was the 58bhp 1.8 diesel, but few were sold. Well-equipped, with good handling and competent ride.

COLT TURBO. 1984-88 (prod: n/a). 3-door 4-seater hatchback. F/F, 1597cc (S4 OC). Max speed 114mph, 0-60mph 8.7sec. By adding a turbocharger and petrol injection, power of the 1.6 engine rose to 123bhp. The result was furious acceleration to 100mph, helped by a slick gearchange – but the main drawbacks were the equally furious torque steer under full power and turbo lag that could be counted in seconds. Received the same revisions as mainstream models, and always had outstanding equipment for the price. Replaced by more practical GTi.

COLT 1300/1500. 1988-92 (prod: n/a). 3-door 4-seater hatchback. F/F, 1298/1468cc (S4 OC). Max speed 101mph, 0-60mph 12.0sec. Distinctive 'S-look' to body sides, first seen in new Galant, with sharply cut-off stern and steeply sloping windscreen. Engines carried over from previous Colt range, with more powerful 12-valve versions replacing eight-valvers in 1990. Well-sorted suspension, using McPherson struts at the front and independent rear, gave good handling, although ride tended to be too firm.

COLT 1600 GTI. 1988-90 (prod: n/a). 3-door 4-seater hatchback. F/F, 1596cc (S4 DOC). Max speed 122mph, 0-60mph 8.8sec. New twin-cam 16-valve version of 1.6 engine resulted in a fast-revving, eager 125bhp. New chassis sorted handling, with power steering correctly weighted to give good feel. Very well equipped, with body part galvanised for long life. High price and limited numbers gave this model some rarity value.

TREDIA. 1982-85 (prod: n/a). 4-door 4-seater saloon. F/F, 1401/1597cc (S4 OC). Max speed 110mph, 0-60mph 10.1sec. Product planners were working overtime, with Tredia slotting into already overcrowded range between Lancer and Galant. Both 1.4/68bhp and 1.6/75bhp models had same dual-range four-speed manual gearbox as smaller Colt hatchback. Mild turbo 1.6 version managed just 115bhp, although bonnet air intake, alloy wheels and go-faster front seats suggested rather more.

CORDIA. 1982-89 (prod: n/a). 3-door 4-seater coupé. F/F, 1597/1795cc (S4 OC). Max speed 124mph, 0-60mph 9.8sec. Rather ordinary coupé body carried on Tredia floorpan, initially with 1.6 normally-aspirated or turbo engines, and two-range transmission. In mid-1985, 1.6 turbo replaced by beefier 1.8, with 134bhp and conventional five-speed 'box. Fastback styling made rear seat headroom marginal.

LANCER. 1984-89 (prod: n/a). 4/5-door 4-seater saloon/estate. F/F, 1198/1468cc (S4 OC), 1795cc diesel (S4 OC). Max speed 96mph, 0-60mph 13.2sec. Longer wheelbase – 2.4in more at 96in – four-door saloon version of Colt hatchback, with same 1.2/54bhp and 1.5/75bhp overhead-cam engines and five-speed transmissions. Longer estate version went on well after new Lancer appeared in 1988. 'Economy' version – named with unusual marketing department honesty – had no power steering.

LANCER. 1988-93 (prod: n/a). 4-door 4-seater saloon; 5-door 4-seater liftback coupé. F/F, 1468cc (S4 OC), 1596/1836cc (S4 DOC). Max speed 125mph, 0-60mph 8.3sec. Curvey but bland S-line saloon and liftback bodies, once more on longer wheelbase Colt floorpan. High performance GTI-16V version had twin-cam, 16-valve engines developing 125bhp as 1.6, up to 134bhp with larger 1.8 from 1990. Hot hatch performance, certainly, but European rivals had better dynamics. Untidy handling, excessive torque steer and poor traction combined to erode its value as a sporting machine.

LANCER 1800 4WD. 1989-93 (prod: n/a). 5-door 4-seater liftback. F/4×4, 1755cc (S4 OC). Max speed 105mph, 0-60mph 12.6sec. Rather different concept from the fire-breathing 4wd Galant. With a more modest 95bhp, this was a roomy mid-range hatch-back for country-dwellers who needed to keep going in all weathers. But that was as far as this 4wd installation went: unlike most other 4wd cars, the Lancer's aspirations were neither sporting (it was too slow) nor serious off-roading (ground clearance was not increased). Only fair performance from the smooth engine, but super traction, with centre diff and viscous coupling unit splitting torque in permanent 4wd system. Well equipped with electric windows, mirrors and sunroof, but pricey at £11,499 when launched. A strangely unconvincing package.

SIGMA/SIGMA 2600. 1976-85 (prod: n/a). 4-door 5-seater saloon/estate. F/R, 1597/1995/2555cc (S4 OC). Max speed 107mph, 0-60mph 10.8sec. The Sigma had started life as an upmarket version of the original Galant but outlasted it, production going on into the 1980s. The 1.6 and 2.0 litre versions were Japanese-built but the 2600 (a thumping four-cylinder producing only 102bhp) was built in Australia in order to avoid import restrictions. Chassis innovation was non-existent with a live axle hung from semi-elliptic springs at the rear and McPherson struts and recirculating ball steering (power-assisted on the 2600 only) at the front. Handling, as one can imagine, was the sum of those parts.

SAPPORO 2000/EX. 1980-85 (prod: n/a). 2-door 4-seater coupé. F/R, 1997cc (S4 OC). Max speed 120mph, 0-60mph 8.1sec. Yet another variation on the rapidly-dating rear-drive Galant floorpan, this one with a coupé body. With just 102bhp, the 2000's performance did not match its rakish looks. The EX had 170bhp with turbo and fuel injection added to the single-cam engine. With a relatively unsophisticated chassis, the EX needed a firm hand when getting anywhere near its limits. All models were well equipped, but neither handling nor ride matched the semi-sporting appearance.

GALANT. 1982-84 (prod: n/a). 4-door 4-seater saloon; 5-door 4-seater estate. F/R, 1597/1997cc (S4 OC). Max speed 112mph, 0-60mph 9.6sec. Last of the front-engined, rear-drive Galant range – and the chassis was really starting to show its age. The single-cam engines continued, with the 2.0 version turbocharged to boost power from the standard 102bhp to 170bhp, although handling was not up to the performance in this saloon-only model. Mitsubishi's reputation for reliability and equipment was growing.

GALANT. 1984-88 (prod: n/a). 4-door 5-seater saloon. F/F, 1597/1997cc (S4 OC), 1795cc turbo diesel (S4 OC). Max speed 118mph, 0-60mph 8.6sec. After the worthy but dull rear-drive Galants, the first front-drive model was a revelation. The 102.4in wheelbase gave a spacious interior, with McPherson struts at the front and well-located independent rear suspension giving good handling. As well as the 1.6/75bhp and 2.0/100bhp engines, there was a tamed version of the 2.0 turbo, with 170bhp, plus a new 1.8 turbo diesel.

GALANT SAPPORO. 1987-89 (prod: n/a). 4-door 5-seater saloon. F/F, 2351cc (S4 OC). Max speed 114mph, 0-60mph 10.4sec. Aimed at the luxury end of the market, with huge showroom glitz – electronically-controlled suspension, cruise control, anti-lock brakes and electric everything else. Big 2.4 four-cylinder engine gave 127bhp and gutsy performance. But the variable assistance – and always over-light – steering and first-generation reactive suspension seemed to be in semi-permanent conflict.

GALANT. 1989-93 (prod: n/a). 4-door 5-seater saloon, 3-door 4-seater coupé. F/F, 1755/1997cc (S4 OC), 1795cc diesel (S4 OC). Max speed 114mph, 0-60mph 9.6sec. Essentially the same floorpan as the first front-drive Galant, but with new, curvaceous saloon and coupé bodies, the latter with 2.0/110bhp engine. Well enough equipped, but the facia layout, with curious half-dial instruments, looked dated. Nothing wrong with the handling, with all models having power steering.

GALANT 2000 GTI. 1988-93 (prod: n/a). 4-door 5-seater saloon. F/F, 1997cc (S4 DOC). Max speed 122mph, 0-60mph 8.7sec. Mitsubishi abandoned turbocharging in favour of more sophisticated multi-valve technology. New 16-valve twin-camshaft head on 2.0 engine pushed power to 146bhp, with performance to match. Electronically-controlled speed-variable steering standard, but similarly-controlled suspension was an extra. The result was good handling, although the ride was rather too firm.

GALANT 4WD. 1989-93 (prod: n/a). 4-door 5-seater saloon; 5-door 4-seater coupé. F/4×4, 1997cc (S4 DOC). Max speed 127mph, 0-60mph 9.0sec. Ultimate in technology, with four-wheel drive and four-wheel steering – but it was enough to win the 1989 Lombard-RAC Rally with Pentti Airikkala driving. New semi-trailing rear arm suspension, plus rear-drive diff, meant boot space all but vanished, but the trade-off was amazing handling and grip. But despite alloy wheels, extra side mouldings and colour-coded bumpers, it looked just like most other Galants…

STARION 2000. 1982-89 (prod: n/a). 2-door 2-seater coupé. F/R, 1997cc (S4 OC). Max speed 133mph, 0-60mph 6.9sec. Muscle-flexing coupé mixing old with new. Balancer shaft 2.0 engine was turbo-boosted to 170bhp (177bhp by 1985), giving slingshot performance once lag had been overcome. All-round independent suspension, using McPherson struts, gave great handling, although the ride was too firm. Odd door-mounted seat belts were a gimmick which did not catch on.

STARION 2.6 EX. 1989-90 (prod: n/a). 2-door 2-seater coupé. F/R, 2555cc (S4 OC). Max speed 134mph, 0-60mph 7.0sec. Essentially the same bodyshell as before, with 95.7in wheelbase, but now with 2.6 four-cylinder engine with turbocharger and injection, although power dropped to 153bhp with catalytic converter. Better torque meant that performance did not suffer too much. Same handling, same over-firm ride. Around for just 12 months, with sales fading into oblivion against far more modern rivals.

SPACE WAGON. 1984-91 (prod: n/a). 5-door 7-seater estate. F/F, 1755cc (S4 OC), 1755cc diesel (S4 OC). Max speed 101mph, 0-60mph 11.6sec. Stylists were kept at bay when this utterly practical and very car-like people carrier was on the drawing board. Long 103in wheelbase, five doors and three-tier seating provided plenty of room for seven. With just 88bhp, 1.8 petrol engine struggled a bit when fully laden, while 74bhp turbo diesel was even more sedate. Well-equipped, although velour upholstery on early models was a mistake when sticky-fingered kids were expected to occupy the interior.

SHOGUN. 1983-91 (prod: n/a). 3/5-door 4/7-seater off-road estate. F/4×4, 2555cc (S4 OC), 2972cc (V6 OC), 2346/2477cc diesels (S4 OC). Max speed 99mph, 0-60mph 13.2sec. Well-planned off-roader which was just like a car to drive. Tough box-section chassis, wishbone independent front suspension, live axle rear. Turbo diesels were favourites, although not quick. V6 3.0 petrol was quick – and thirsty. Normally rear drive, with front-drive added when needed. Competent on and off road – and the model which brought about Land Rover's Discovery.

MORGAN (GB)

Technology takes its time to reach Malvern Link. Founded in 1910, the company built its first four-wheeler in 1936. Changes to the bodywork in recent times offer slightly less resistance to the air, although engines have improved immeasurably. Underneath much of the original chassis design remains. People still like them, for the waiting list continues to vanish way over the horizon.

4/4 1600. 1970-82 (prod: 7000 plus). 2-door 2/4-seater convertible. F/R, 1599cc (S4 OHV), 1584cc (S4 DOC). Max speed 107mph, 0-60mph 9.8sec. Morgan's chassis R&D department did not occupy much room, because the sliding pillar front suspension and semi-elliptic layout at the rear were much the same as H.F.S. Morgan had used in the late 1930s. Handling was fine, once you learned to use bumps in the road to help change direction. Ford 1600 'Kent' pushrod engine (70bhp standard, but most buyers chose 96bhp competition version) was joined by Fiat 1600 twin overhead cam (98bhp) unit in 1981 as stop-gap measure before Ford CVH engine took over – only 92 Fiat-powered cars were built.

4/4 1600 CVH. 1982 to date (prod: see above). 2-door 2/4-seater convertible. F/R, 1597cc (S4 OC). Max speed 105mph, 0-60mph 10.5sec. In 1982 Morgan dropped the Fiat and pushrod Ford engines, using just the overhead cam 1.6/95bhp Ford CVH in their place. Major improvements were made to both chassis and body in 1986: the former was powder-coated (or galvanised at extra cost), the ash frame of the latter treated with Cuprinol to keep rot at bay. Otherwise the tooth-loosening ride, scant weather protection and never-ending demand continued unchanged.

PLUS 4. 1985 to date (prod: see above). 2-door 2/4-seater convertible. F/R, 1994/1995cc (S4 DOC). Max speed 109mph, 0-60mph 7.7sec. The Plus 4 name was revived to distinguish the 2.0 models from the smaller-engined versions. The 2.0/122bhp Fiat twin-cam engine and gearbox was used initially, but the model was dropped when supplies ceased in 1987, 122 having been built. It surfaced once more in 1988 with the new Rover M16 unit and five-speed gearbox from the 820, with fuel injection and 138bhp. Much the same character as the 4/4, but with stronger performance.

PLUS 8. 1968 to date (prod: 4154 to mid-1994). 2-door 2-seater convertible. F/R, 3528/3946cc (V8 OHV). Max speed 125mph, 0-60mph 5.4sec. Thankfully, cars like this rarely, if ever, get into the wrong hands, for it needs an heroic streak to cope with even the mildest version: the combination of the 1930s chassis and Rover V8 power can be a recipe for white knuckles. Carburettors on all Plus 8s until 1983 (changing from twin SUs to Strombergs in 1981) gave 155bhp at most, then injected 190bhp version from Rover SD1 Vitesse became available, at first as an option but on all cars from 1987. In 1990, engine size went up from 3.5 to 3.9. If you could survive wind battering and kidney-pulverising ride, you could make the Plus 8 rocket to 60mph in less time than a Ferrari Testarossa.

NAYLOR (GB)

Restoring cars is one thing, but improving on the genuine article is a brave move. This is what Naylor Bros of Shipley, Yorkshire, did in 1985, creating the only authorised replica of the 1950s MG TF. But the price was more than you would pay for a fully restored real TF, and only a year after the first TF 1700 was rolled out, the firm went into liquidation and Alastair Naylor resumed his main business of restoring all T-type models.

TF 1700. 1985-86 (prod: 100 approx). 2-door 2-seater sports car. F/R, 1657cc (S4 OC). Max speed 94mph, 0-60mph 12.0sec. About as close as you could get to the real thing – and in most ways better. The O-series engine developed just 77bhp and the TF stayed with a four-speed gearbox, but the live rear axle ran with coil springs and Panhard rod, rather than the original's semi-elliptics, improving the handling nearly out of recognition. Since it was screwed together by long-time TF restorers, quality was outstanding. Price, however, was the downfall of the TF 1700, because for the £14,950 cost you could also buy a Toyota MR2 and still have £1000 left. Hutson took over the manufacturing rights and still builds a few cars.

NISSAN (J/GB/ I)

During the early 1980s the name changed from Datsun to Nissan, with the UK marketing success headed by Octav Botnar. The Z-cars apart, the Nissan range lacked anything unexpected. For the money you had a car which was totally reliable, easy to drive and not much else. But Nissan made history by being the first Japanese manufacturer to set up in Britain, opening its Tyne & Wear factory in 1986. During the early 1990s, Nissan Japan unilaterally ended its marketing agreement with the original importer, Nissan UK.

LAUREL SIX. 1977-81 (prod: 423,209). 2-door 5-seater coupé, 4-door 5-seater saloon. F/R, 1770/1952cc (S4 OC), 1998/2393/2753cc (S6 OC), 1991cc diesel (S4 OHV). Max speed 99mph, 0-60mph 11.9sec. Datsun saw no reason to break away from the US method of producing 'new' models by putting different bodies over existing floorpans. Roomy saloon-only body for the UK, still with live rear axle. Well-equipped, only with six-cylinder 2.4 engine in UK in 1980s, many with automatics. Any image was spoiled by wallowing handling and galloping rust.

LAUREL MK2. 1981-89 (prod: 670,900). 4-door 5-seater saloon. F/R, 1998/2393cc (S6 OC). Max speed 115mph, 0-60mph 11.4sec. By European standards, the Laurel seemed to be going backwards. Same underpinnings, complete with live rear axle, but now with option of smaller 2.0/96bhp six-cylinder engine, dropped in 1985. The 2.4 received injection at the same time, power going up from 113bhp to 128bhp. Masses of equipment, including verbal warning facia, but both handling and ride owed more to Detroit than anywhere on this side of the Atlantic.

SKYLINE 240K. 1977-81 (prod: 576,797). 2-door 5-seater coupé, 4-door 5-seater saloon/estate. F/R, 1595/1770cc (S4 OC), 1998/2393cc (S6 OC). Max

speed 112mph, 0-60mph 11.3sec. Planned to bridge the gap between the Laurel and curiously-named Cedric. In its last form, it had a fuel-injected version of the famous 240Z engine, in a committee-designed coupé body for the UK. Someone had also thought about the suspension, with a trailing-arm independent layout at the rear, plus power steering. Few sold, even fewer remain.

VIOLET 140J/160J. 1977-81 (prod: 610,614). 2/4-door 4-seater saloon/estate; 2-door 4-seater coupé. F/R, 1397/1595/1770cc (S4 OC). Max speed 98mph, 0-60mph 14.5sec. Someone at Datsun had an odd sense of humour when it came to names. Sold here with just the 1.4 and 1.6 engines, but higher performance SSS versions, with 1.8, seen in rallying – and nicknamed 'Violent'. Live-axle rear suspension plus struts at front meant utterly uninspired handling, but ease of driving and reliability assured sales success.

280ZX. 1978-83 (prod: 446,059). 2-door 2+2-seater coupé/targa coupé. F/R, 1998/2753cc (S6 OC). Max speed 114mph, 0-60mph 10.3sec. Sad successor to the original 240/260 'Z-Cars', putting on both weight and girth, with sales targeted more towards the US than European markets. Fuel-injected version of 2.8 six for UK market, with revised semi-trailing arm rear suspension. Size and weight took the edge off performance. In Japan it was still being called the Fairlady...

CHERRY N10. 1978-82 (prod: 1,001,508). 2/3-door 4-seater saloon/estate; 3-door 4-seater coupé; 5-door 4-seater hatchback. F/F, 988/1171cc (S4 OHV), 988/1270cc (S4 OC). Max speed 76mph, 0-60mph 21.0sec. Variations on the same theme seemed never-ending, this being the third Cherry since 1970. Same floorpan and wheelbase as previous version, with strut front suspension and transverse pushrod engines until arrival of overhead cam units in the final year. Equipment was sufficient rather than generous – and much the same could be said about both handling and performance.

CHERRY. 1983-86 (prod: 1,450,300). 3/5-door 4-seater hatchback. F/F, 988/1186/1270/1488cc (S4 OC). Max speed 112mph, 0-60mph 8.6sec. Last of the line, this time with bigger engine range but in UK just three five-door hatchback body styles. New was the 1488cc engine, with the 1.5 GL available only with a three-speed auto. The 1.5 Turbo produced a hectic and lag-prone 114bhp, but ran far too short on both handling and grip to be classified as a hot hatch.

CHERRY GTI EUROPE. 1983-84 (prod: 27,900). 3-door 4-seater hatchback. F/F, 1490cc (HO4 OC). Max speed 108mph, 0-60mph 10.2sec. Distinguished as being the first Japanese car to be built in Europe – and the one that all concerned wished had never happened. Nissan sent trimmed Cherry bodyshells to Alfa Romeo's Alfasud plant near Naples, where 1.5/75bhp flat-four boxer engines were installed. Nissan buyers were suspicious of Alfa build quality, Alfa customers even more so of Nissan handling. The idea was thankfully laid to rest after just 18 months.

SUNNY 120Y. 1977-82 (prod: 1,770,814). 2-door 4-seater coupé/saloon/estate; 4-door 4-seater saloon/estate. F/R, 1171/1397cc (S4 OHV). Max speed n/a, 0-60mph n/a. The name carried on, but on top of the previous model's utterly conventional floorpan was a new range of bodies. This was to be the last front-engined, rear-drive Sunny, with strut front suspension and live rear axle. Mechanically reliable, powertrains usually outlasting the rust-prone bodywork.

SUNNY. 1982-86 (prod: 1,857,200). 2/4-door 4-seater saloon, 4-door 4-seater estate; 3-door 4-seater coupé. F/F, 1270/1488cc (S4 OC). Max speed 83mph, 0-60mph 19.1sec. Nissan finally made the move to front-drive and transverse engines for the big-selling Sunny, with neat if somewhat undistinguished range. The 1.3/60bhp and 1.5/75bhp engine had been launched earlier in the Cherry range. Textbook front-drive suspension, using struts at the front and trailing arms at the rear, gave utterly predictable handling. What the Sunny lacked in character was more than compensated in reliability.

SUNNY. 1986-91 (prod: n/a). 3/5-door 4-seater hatchback; 4-door 4-seater saloon; 5-door 4-seater estate; 3-door 4-seater coupé. F/F, 1270/1597cc (S4 OC), 1681cc diesel (S4 OC). Max speed 110mph, 0-60mph 11.0sec. Seemingly endless choice of engine/body combinations, but the result was always a car which you could live with but never learn to love. The 1.3 engine was replaced by new 12-valve 1.4 with 83bhp in 1989, while 1.6 power, with new head, went to 94bhp. Diesel economy came to the Sunny for the first time too. But the cars fell down on shortage of space and unrefined ride.

SUNNY ZX. 1987-91 (prod: 1,990,000). 3-door 4-seater coupé. F/F, 1598cc (S4 DOC), 1809cc (S4 OC). Max speed 128mph, 0-60mph 8.3sec. Ultimate 'Showroom Special', plastered with awful tacked-on spoilers and side skirts, plus too-obvious alloy wheels. Started with 16-valve twin-cam version of 1.6 with 122bhp, going to 1.8 16-valve single-cam with 128bhp in 1989. Fast and furious performance was backed by reasonable handling, but then let down by appalling ride. For the money you could have bought a Peugeot 205 GTi or a VW Golf GTi...

280C. 1980-84 (prod: 975,500). 4/5-door 5-seater saloon/estate. F/R, 2753cc (S6 OC). Max speed 100mph, 0-60mph 13.8sec. Big, blundering saloons and estates that cried out for the wide open spaces of the USA. Granada-sized, with in-line six-cylinder engines and choice of five-speed manual or three-speed auto transmissions. Masses of equipment, including air conditioning, set off with acres of increasingly unfashionable chromium plating.

300C. 1984-87 (prod: 640,470). 4/5-door 5-seater saloon/estate. F/R, 2960cc (S6 OC). Max speed 116mph, 0-60mph 11.6sec. Same platform as the 280C and still with live rear axle, but the single-cam engine size was increased to 2960cc, automatic-only saloon having 155bhp, manual gearbox estate 150bhp. At a time when the European liking for bright trim was fading, the amount adorning the outside of these transatlantic transplants stood out like a sore thumb.

PRAIRIE. 1983-89 (prod: 1,079,000). 5-door 5-seater estate. F/F, 1488/1809cc (S4 OC). Max speed 99mph, 0-60mph 12.4sec. Space-efficient 'people carrier', but hardly the world's most elegant car. Boxy, tall bodywork, with sliding rear doors, on 99in wheelbase, with strut front suspension and independent trailing arms at the rear. Original 1.5/75bhp engine gave gutless performance, so 1.8/88bhp was rather better. Shape dictated rather top-heavy handling, but the idea caught on.

PRAIRIE. 1989-91 (prod: 750,000). 5-door 5-seater estate. F/F or F/4×4, 1974cc (S4 OC). Max speed 100mph, 0-60mph 10.8sec. As elegant as the original was downright ugly, smooth bonnet line blending with spacious, airy cabin. The interesting sliding rear door arrangement was retained, but now without a fixed B-pillar. Larger 2.0/98bhp engine gave goodish performance, while handling, now with power steering, felt more stable. Rare 4wd version was slower and, for what it was, very over-priced.

MICRA. 1983-92 (prod: 2,079,900). 3/5-door 4-seater hatchback. F/F, 988/1235cc (S4 OC). Max speed 93mph, 0-60mph 13.3sec. Unlike Nissan's normal policy, ephemeral is not an adjective which applies here. Nondescript bodyshell served for nine years, with same 1.0/50-55bhp and 1.3/60bhp single-cam transverse engines. Textbook chassis, with struts and disc brakes at the front, semi-independent and drums at the back. A forgiving nature plus seemingly indestructible transmissions made the Micra the driving schools' favourite.

STANZA. 1983-86 (prod: 720,830). 3/5-door 4-seater hatchback, 4-door 4-seater saloon. F/F, 1588/1809cc (S4 OC). Max speed 103mph, 0-60mph 11.9sec. Short-lived mid-range model, slotting between the Sunny and Bluebird, on 97in wheelbase. Assembled from the Nissan parts bin, with strut suspension front and rear, and choice of 1.6 or 1.8 engines. Mediocre sales, which matched both handling and performance, saw the Stanza range pruned back and finally dropped after just three years.

BLUEBIRD. 1980-84 (prod: 1,850,700). 4/5-door 5-seater saloon/estate. F/R, 1598/1809/1973cc (S4 OC). Max speed 100mph, 0-60mph 11.9sec. After the 'Coke Bottle' styling of earlier 180s, the last rear-drive model had simple, clean-cut lines. But underneath it was much the story as before, with the same engine range and McPherson strut suspension, on the same 99in wheelbase. What its handling lacked in flair the Bluebird more than made up for in reliability.

BLUEBIRD. 1984-86 (prod: 1,250,500). 4/5-door 5-seater saloon/hatchback. F/F, 1809/1973cc (S4 OC). Max speed 121mph, 0-60mph 8.8sec. Shades of things to come, with Nissan switching to transverse engines and front-drive for its big-selling mid-sized saloon and estate. Both the 1.8/88-90bhp and 2.0/105bhp engines were carried over from the 180B models, with five-speed gearboxes. New was the 1.8 turbo, which produced a coarsely-delivered 135bhp. Unforgiving body shape did nothing for aerodynamics, but the handling, if not the ride, was a great improvement. Not a car for the discerning driver...

BLUEBIRD. 1986-90 (prod: 167,671). 4/5-door 5-seater saloon/hatchback/estate. F/F, 1598/1809/1973cc (S4 OC), 1952cc diesel (S4 OC). Max speed 112mph, 0-60mph 9.3sec. July 1986 saw the first Sunderland-built Bluebird go on sale. But it was not the smooth new model being made in Japan, but the old, boxy version. New were the 1.6/84bhp engine and the 2.0/67bhp diesel. All but the base version had power steering. Local content – which excluded diesel engines and all transmissions – increased until cars qualified as 'European'. Nissan's build quality lesson was being learned fast at rival factories further south...

PATROL. 1982-91 (prod: 850,900). 3/5-door 5-seater off-road estate. F/4×4, 2753/2962cc (S6 OC), 2826/2828/3246cc diesels (S6 OC). Max speed 86mph, 0-60mph 19.4sec. Nissan stayed with the rugged, traditional recipe as rivals moved upmarket. Massive chassis, with live axles riding on semi-elliptic springs, gave lorry-like ride, while limited axle travel restricted off-road abilities. Short and long wheelbase bodies had workmanlike air, with few frills. Lumbering, lugging 3.2 diesel was finally replaced by turbo diesel 2.8. What the diesels lacked in performance they gained in much better fuel economy than petrol versions. The 1990s replacements were very different in every respect.

300ZX. 1984-90 (prod: 798,450). 2-door 2+2-seater sports coupé. F/R, 2960cc (S6 OC). Max speed 149mph, 0-60mph 6.7sec. Final and rather sad expression of the 1970s Z-car concept, overweight and rapidly losing its looks. Turbo 3.0, with 228bhp was potent and smooth, while the handling was acceptable, with struts at the front and trailing links at the rear. Well-equipped in a suburban manner, with final version, from mid-1987, losing boy racer bonnet intake but gaining new spoilers. Its replacement in 1990 was a high-tech, high-performing, four-wheel-steered wonder.

SILVIA ZX. 1984-1989 (prod: 524,680). 3-door 2+2-seater coupé. F/R, 1809cc (S4 OC), 1990cc (S4 DOC). Max speed 132mph, 0-60mph 7.9sec. With styling apparently originating from somewhere in the mid-Pacific, the Silvia was Nissan's idea of a sports coupé. Between the pop-up headlamps sat an overstated egg-box grille, while the spoilers front and rear appeared to have been added as afterthoughts. But even the smaller 1.8 turbo engine packed a huge 135bhp punch, while the twin-cam 2.0, dropped in 1986, claimed 144bhp. Independent strut suspension was used all round, but this did not guarantee either predictable handling or good ride. But it could get the power down on the road, with some fearsome dry-surface performance. In the wet, it was a different matter...

200SX. 1989 to date (prod: 1,081,200). 3-door 2-seater sports coupé. F/R, 1809cc (S4 OC). Max speed 137mph, 0-60mph 6.8sec. Classic simplicity, with front-engined, rear-drive layout in graceful shape. With 16-valve twin-camshaft head and intercooled turbo, power of 1.8 was boosted to a smooth, gorgeous-sounding 169bhp. Outstanding performance, with good economy too. Beautifully-balanced handling let down by over-light power steering. Interior a bit bleak, with acres of plastic facia and indifferent seats.

MAXIMA. 1989-91 (prod: 758,720). 4-door 5-seater saloon. F/F, 2960cc (V6 OC). Max speed 125mph, 0-60mph 8.9sec. Luxury saloon aimed very much as the US market, with endless equipment and reasonable looks. Considering it was 15ft 8in long, it did not have much leg-stretching room in the back. Sweetly smooth 3.0/160bhp V6 engine matched to four-speed dual-range automatic gave seamless performance. Handling, with struts front and rear, plus US-style dampers, came apart when pushed.

OPEL (D)

For years Opel and Vauxhall ignored each other's existence, even though both were owned by General Motors. In the late 1960s, though, more and more Vauxhalls were designed in Russelsheim, with the full range German-designed from the mid-1970s. The Opel name was gradually dropped in the UK as the Vauxhall brand developed its own impressive image, but the Manta hung on into the late 1980s.

KADETT. 1979-84 (prod: 2,092,140). 2/3/4/5-door 4-seater saloon/hatchback/estate. F/F, 993/1196cc (S4 OHV), 1297/1598/1796cc (S4 OC). Max speed 92mph, 0-60mph 15.4sec. In a slightly tentative manner, GM Europe's first front-drive car came to Britain wearing an Opel badge, eventually to become the Vauxhall Astra. The new overhead-cam 'Family I' engine puts rivals into deep shade, while mix of sharply-styled hatchback, saloon and estate bodies gave plenty of choice. Diesel, from 1982, was first real rival for Volkswagen's oil-burning Golf. Crisp handling matched the sharp looks, which were to set Vauxhall on the path to real success.

ASCONA. 1975-81 (prod: 1,512,971). 2/4-door 5-seater saloon. F/R, 1196 cc (S4 OHV), 1584/1879/1979cc (S4 OC). Max speed 103mph, 0-60mph 11.6 sec. In continental Europe, this was one of the main rivals to Ford's Taunus. But while the Cavalier clone was challenging the Cortina in the UK, the Ascona was still something of an unknown quantity. Utterly conventional in every way. The smallest-engined 1.2 was never sold in the UK.

MANTA. 1975-88 (prod: 603,000). 2/3-door 5-seater coupé/hatchback. F/R, 1196cc (S4 OHV), 1584/1796/1897/1979cc (S4 OC). Max speed 121mph, 0-60mph 8.5sec. Handsome fastback version of the Ascona, using the same floorpan and engine range. With the impending arrival of the new front-drive Ascona/Cavalier in 1981, it was, wrongly, assumed to be for the axe. Instead, it was given an extra lease of life with the new overhead-cam 'Family II' engines. Time then stood still for the Manta, which was left behind by newer, better-handling designs.

MANTA 400. 1981-83 (prod: 236). 2-door 4-seater coupé. F/R, 2410cc (S4 DOC). Max speed 125mph, 0-60mph 6.9sec. Although the number of genuine Manta 400s sold in the UK was tiny, more than a few 'replicar' versions with spoilers, side skirts and black/white/yellow colour schemes were produced. Genuine 400s had twin-cam 16-valve engines, with 144bhp in standard trim, rising to 275bhp for rally use as developed by Cosworth.

REKORD. 1977-86 (prod: 1,362,000). 2/4-door 5-seater saloon/estate. F/R, 1979cc (S4 OC), 2260cc diesel (S4 OC). Max speed 118mph, 0-60mph 10.2sec. For a year the Rekord continued to be sold alongside Vauxhall's 'new' Carlton – which was nothing more than a rebadged German-built Rekord. Opel versions had choice of petrol 2.0/100bhp or diesel 2.2/65bhp cam-in-head engines, with saloon or estate bodies. Sales in the UK were wound up in 1983, leaving the field clear for Vauxhall.

COMMODORE. 1980-83 (prod: 107,350). 4-door 5-seater saloon. F/R, 2490cc (S6 OC). Max speed 118mph, 0-60mph 10.2sec. Based on the Rekord shell, but with the bonnet stretched a little to accommodate the 2.5/136bhp six-cylinder engine, the Commodore was in effect the 'Senator in Waiting' before the new model came to the UK in 1983. The up-market CD version gave a hint of things to come in GM Europe's top models, with electric windows, central locking, alloy wheels and sunroof, features still rare in the early 1980s.

SENATOR/MONZA. 1978-87 (118,500/43,500). 2/4-door 5-seater saloon/coupé. F/R, 2490/2968cc (S6 OC). Max speed 128mph, 0-60mph 10.6sec. Conventional in both looks and engineering, these big Opels simply got better with the years. Only sold in the UK with the 2.5/136bhp and, later, 3.0/180bhp in-line sixes, with the unusual cam-in-head valve operation. It had been intended to use the Opel badge on the upmarket models, but then policy changed, so we had the Vauxhall Senator and Royale, alias the Monza...

PANTHER (GB)

Originally Panther Westwinds, Robert Jankel's company produced beautifully-built 'replicars' recalling the 1930s, with creations like the J72, De Ville and the Lima. Less successful were the Rio, a 'coachbuilt' Triumph Dolomite, and the open-topped Lazer. Bought by Jindo Industries of South Korea in 1981. Largely revamped Lima emerged under its new Kallista title.

J72/BROOKLANDS. 1972-80 (prod: 300 approx). 2-door 2-seater convertible. F/R, 4235cc (S6 DOC), 5343cc (V12 OC). Max speed 125mph, 0-60mph 9.6sec. William Lyons' SS100 looked so right, but the over-bulky J72 'replicar' managed to miss the mark in almost every respect. The tubular frame carried a vaguely 1930s body, with later cars having Jaguar independent front suspension in place of the original beam axle. Jaguar power too: 3.8 XK at first, then 4.2, finally 5.3 V12. Barely concealed under bonnet bulges, the V12 blew away any remaining illusions about provenance. Handling, despite power steering and automatic transmissions, needed a degree of courage. Brooklands name superseded J72 in final year of production.

DE VILLE. 1974-85 (prod: 60). 4-door 5-seater saloon, 2-door 5-seater convertible. F/R, 4235cc (DOC), 5343cc (V12 OC). Max speed 135mph, 0-

60mph 10.5sec. This time Jankel picked Ettore Bugatti's vast Royale as his inspiration, although what *Le Patron* might have thought, thankfully, could never be known. Jaguar in-line six and V12 powertrains were used once more, with independent suspension and disc brakes front and rear. Barrel-sided bodywork, in 'co-respondent' colour schemes and beautifully detailed, was carried on a tubular frame. Barn-door aerodynamics meant wallet-withering fuel bills.

LIMA. 1976-81 (prod: 897). 2-door 2-seater convertible. F/R, 2279cc (S4 OC). Max speed 98mph, 0-60mph 9.9sec. With customers for the hugely expensive J72 and de Ville models few and far between, the Lima represented the closest the Oyster Lane works ever came to mass production. Basis for the original Lima was nothing more thrilling than a Vauxhall Magnum floorpan, suspension and 2.3/108bhp engine, although from 1979 a tubular frame was used. Chassis flexing on early cars led to interesting handling.

KALLISTA. 1982-90 (prod: n/a). 2-door 2-seater convertible. F/R, 1597cc (S4 OC), 2792/2933cc (V6 OHV). Max speed 112mph, 0-60mph 7.7sec. Similar looks to the Lima, but major changes underneath. Bodyshell, in aluminium, was made in South Korea and shipped in the cargo containers which were proprietor Kim's main business. Ford power ranged from 1.6/96bhp CHV 'four' to 2.9/150bhp V6, the former providing feeble 12.5sec 0-60mph acceleration. Well-located rear axle and Cortina double wishbone front suspension resulted in reasonable handling. Nicely built, although cockpit was far too narrow for comfort.

SOLO. 1989-90 (prod: 12). 2-door 2+2-seater sports coupe. F/4×4, 1993cc (S4 DOC). Max speed 144mph, 0-60mph 6.8sec. With more time and more money, could Solo have succeeded? The million-dollar looks, penned by Ken Greenley, were created in aluminium honeycomb, composites and carbon-fibre, while underneath lay Ford Cosworth 204bhp power and Ferguson Formula four-wheel drive. But despite its brilliant handling, Solo suffered from noise, lack of performance, tiny luggage space and a massive price tag of £39,850. Panther promised to make just 100 Solos, all individually numbered. In the event, it made just a dozen...

PEUGEOT (F)

In at the beginning of motoring, under the wonderful title of 'The Sons of the Brothers Peugeot'. Solid engineering paid off, with a reputation for reliability. Peugeot SA, today's company, was founded in 1965, taking over Citroën and Chrysler Europe during the 1970s. At the same time PSA took over the marketing operation in the UK, with assembly of the 309 and latterly 405 starting at Ryton.

504. 1968-83 (prod: 979,800). 4-door 5-seater saloon/estate/cabriolet. F/R, 1796/1971cc (S4 OHV), 1948/2112/2304cc diesel (S4 OHV). Max speed 104mph, 0-60mph 12.0sec. After the slab-sided 404, styled by Pinin Farina, the 504 had far fresher looks with plenty of space within. The 2.0

petrol engine was one of the first to use fuel injection (by Kugelfischer), with 100mph plus performance, but diesels were rare on UK market. All but the cheapest saloons had independent rear suspension, while all the vast-capacity estates used a live rear axle. The four-cylinder cabriolets were never officially imported, so are very rare.

504 V6 COUPE/CABRIOLET. 1974-83 (prod: n/a). 2-door 4-seater coupé/cabriolet. F/R, 2664cc (V6 OC). Max speed 117mph, 0-60mph 9.9sec. Rare and very elegant design from Pininfarina, based on the standard 504 floorpan. This was the first Peugeot to use the PRV – Peugeot-Renault-Volvo – V6 engine. From 1977, and with fuel injection, power increased from 136bhp to 144bhp, many with automatic. Extremely rare in the UK, and always personal imports in the 1980s. Those which have survived the ravages of rust are gaining collector status.

304. Above: Cabriolet. Below: Coupé. Top right: Saloon.

304. 1969-80 (prod: 1,178,425). 2/4/5-door 4-seater saloon/estate/coupé/cabriolet. F/F, 1127/1288/1290/1357cc (S4 OC). Max speed 96mph, 0-60mph 13.0sec. A new front for the Plain Jane 204 bodyshell did little for the appearance. But with a range of larger engines (all with a single overhead camshaft), all-round independent suspension and discs at the front, the 304 made many rivals look technically old-fashioned. The two-door versions simply picked up where the 204s left off. Quickest of the saloons was the 1.3/69bhp 304S, with a 90mph maximum.

104. 1972-88 (prod: n/a). 3/5-door 4-seater hatchback. F/F, 954/1124/1219/1360cc (S4 OC). Max speed 102mph, 0-60mph 13.2sec. Not one of Peugeot's greatest styling successes, but a milestone car nevertheless. Not only its first supermini, but the body was also used in the Citroën LN/LNA and the powertrain was adopted for the Visa. Short – 87in – wheelbase Z version had a more sporting image. The same body was used for the Talbot Samba. Under that high bonnet, the new light-alloy engine was tilted back at 72 degrees. Despite worthiness, dropped like a hot brick in the UK with the arrival of the 205, but soldiered on until 1988 in France.

604. 1975-84 (prod: 240,100). 4-door 5-seater saloon. F/R, 2664/2849cc (V6 OC), 2304/2498cc diesels (S4 OHV). Max speed 113mph, 0-60mph 9.4sec. A strong contender in the dull car stakes, with looks which would never rate a second glance. But despite all its space and increasingly extensive equipment, it remained in a luxury car limbo. V6 engine capacity increased from 2.7 to 2.85 in 1984, with 155bhp. Many turbo diesels seemed destined to become taxis. All-independent suspension gave reasonable if slightly ponderous handling.

505. 1979-92 (prod: 1,743,650). 4/5-door 5-seater saloon/estate. F/R, 1796/1971cc (S4 OHV), 1995/2156/2165cc (S4 OC), 2849cc (V6 OC), 2304/2498cc diesels (S4 OHV). Max speed 123mph, 0-60mph 8.4sec. If the 604 failed on its looks, the 505 was a winner with its clean, unpretentious styling. It was also to be Peugeot's last rear-drive model. Roomy, comfortable saloons joined by pantechnicon-capacity estates in 1982. Saloons, except very cheapest, had independent rear suspension, but all estates had live rear axles. Pleasant and predictable handling, good ride. Quick turbo diesel estate versions lived on until the very end.

305. 1977-88 (prod: 1,740,300). 4/5-door 4-seater saloon/estate. F/F, 1290/1472/1580/1905cc (S4 OC), 1905cc diesel (S4 OC). Max speed 113mph, 0-60mph 10.2sec. Peugeot never waved any flags for the unassuming 305. Much of the front-drive engineering and design was 304-based, with a major facelift in 1983. Performance was boosted with the 1.9/105bhp engine, giving 113mph top speed in the GTX saloon and estate. But the 1905cc diesel was the real milestone, proving that oil-burners need not be noisy or smokey. Estate was brilliant too, with 'lay-flat' rear suspension which took up no load space.

205. 1983 to date (prod: 2,740,000). 3/5-door 4-seater hatchback. F/F, 954/1124/1360cc (S4 OC), 1769cc diesel (S4 OC). Max speed 104mph, 0-60mph 11.3sec. After a succession of technically sound but visually dull models, the 205 arrived like a whirlwind. Superb Pininfarina shape, outstanding handling, supple ride – and all in a hatchback 12ft 2in long. Original petrol engines replaced by punchy TU series in 1988, along with the first – and only – major trim revisions, with revised facia. Excellent diesel versions quickly caught on, with the availability of turbocharging from 1990 pushing power up from 59bhp to 78bhp. Peugeot's only problem was how to phase out the 205 without causing a riot...

205 GTi. 1984-94 (prod: see above). 3-door 4-seater hatchback. F/F, 1580/1905cc (S4 OC). Max speed 121mph, 0-60mph 8.1sec. After a slightly luke-warm start, with the 1.6 engine giving just 105bhp, the GTi joined the Hot Hatchback Club in 1986. Power for the 1.6 went up to 115bhp, while the new 1.9 version produced 130bhp, dropping to 122bhp when a catalyst was fitted in 1990. Original suspension gave skateboard ride, but improved with softening. But as many drivers found, the 1.9 could test skills when pushed towards its considerable limits.

205 CABRIOLET. 1986 to date (prod: see above). 2-door 4-seater convertible. F/F, 1360/1580/1905cc (S4 OC). Max speed 115mph, 0-60mph 10.6sec. Hard on the heels of the success of the 115bhp GTi came the Cabriolet, designed and part-built by Pininfarina. And two years later, in 1988, came the CJ version with only 1360cc/65bhp but just as much fresh-air appeal. Pininfarina lopped off the tops and reinforced the shells before returning them to Peugeot for final trim and assembly.

205 T16. 1983-84 (prod: 200 plus competition cars). 3-door 2-seater hatchback. M/4×4, 1774cc (S4 DOC). Max speed n/a, 0-60mph n/a. Best-looking and easiest to drive of the Group B supercars. Transverse 1.8 turbo engine sat behind the passenger seat, with gearbox behind the driver. Centre body section and front grille were from production 205 – the rest was very special. Road cars had 200bhp, rally cars up to 450bhp. Production cars were all finished in gunmetal grey. Handling and grip meant that the outer limits were rarely reached. This has to be one for the collection.

309. 1986-93 (prod: 837,520). 3/5-door 4-seater hatchback. F/F, 1118/1290/1360/1472/1580cc (S4 OC), 1905cc diesel (S4 OC). Max speed 113mph, 0-60mph 9.9sec. Something of a diversion in the Peugeot story. The UK-led design, based on the Horizon floorpan, was inherited during the takeover of Talbot. Looks did nothing for its appeal, which was always underrated. Agile handling, smooth ride, a roomy interior and a wide range of engines were main selling points. And it must never be forgotten that the 309 was built in Britain.

309 GTi. 1987-93 (prod: see above). 3/5-door 4-seater hatchback. F/F, 1905cc (S4 OC). Max speed 120mph, 0-60mph 8.3sec. This was the first time we had seen the 1905cc 130bhp TU engine, pre-dating the 205 version. The GTi started life as a three-door, gaining a five-door version in 1988. Lacking the 205 GTi's chic appearance, it tended to be unfairly overlooked. But the chassis proved to be more than equal to the extra power, with the towards-the-limit handling much more manageable.

405. 1988 to date (prod: 1,843,500). 4/5-door 5-seater saloon/estate. F/F or F/4×4, 1580/1905cc (S4 OC), 1769/1905cc diesels (S4 OC). Max speed 120mph, 0-60mph 9.1sec. Second of the Ryton-built models, although estates were made in France. Another elegant Pininfarina design made it one of the best-looking saloons of the 1980s. Peugeot wanted the stiffest possible bodyshell for best handling, so there was a high boot sill and no folding rear seat. But it worked, with outstanding manners and ride. The 1.9/115bhp engine would outrun most rivals, the 1.8/90bhp turbo diesel was also swift. Four-wheel drive estate was rare.

405 Mi16. 1988 to date (prod: see above). 4-door 5-seater saloon. F/F or F/4×4, 1905cc (S4 DOC). Max speed 132mph, 0-60mph 8.2sec. Twin-cam 166bhp version of the 1905cc engine proved just how good the 405 chassis was – and the 4wd version simply confirmed it. Unusual Bendix high-pressure anti-lock brakes spoiled otherwise superb driveability, lacking sensitivity. Despite spoilers, side skirts and alloy wheels, they never made much of an impression visually.

605. 1989 to date (prod: n/a). 4-door 5-seat saloon. F/F, 1998cc (S4 OC), 2975cc (V6 OC), 2088cc turbo diesel (S4 OC), 2138cc diesel (S4 OC). Max speed 145mph, 0-60mph 8.3sec. As the much-loved 505 range dwindled into near-oblivion, the 605 couldn't be far away. Although the new car marked the final switch from rear to front wheel drive, its looks were rather too similar to the 405 to make its appearance that different. PSA's good XU 2.0 engines in the high-volume models were backed by two V6 versions, the hottest with 24 valves and 200bhp. New for the 605 and Citroën XM was the 12-valve 2.1 diesel. Although both ride and handling were fine, neither was inspirational.

PORSCHE (D)

The theory, if not exactly the practice, of Ferdinand Porsche Snr's original design for the VW Beetle lives on in today's Carrera 2/4 models. The first Porsche was sold in 1948, with the almost everlasting 911 appearing in 1963. The 928 was meant to displace it, but the buying public had other ideas. Sales success - until the early 1990s recession at least - was ensured by Porsche's image and a seemingly endless string of impressive wins at Le Mans during the 1970s and 1980s.

911 SC. 1978-83 (prod: 108,081). 2-door 2+2-seater coupé/targa/cabriolet. R/R, 2687/2994cc (HO6 OC). Max speed 141mph, 0-60mph 6.5sec. The Triumph of Engineering Over Design was almost at its peak, with the air-cooled flat-six engine still hung aft of the rear axle line. By 1980s, engine had grown to 3.0/204bhp. Beneath the assorted flared wheel arches and spoilers, the basic 911 shape remained. Any wayward handling tendencies were well tamed – but lift-off oversteer still lay in waiting for the foolhardy. Cabriolet arrived in 1982, but targa style (with fixed rear window and roll hoop) lived on.

911 CARRERA. 1983-89 (prod: 21,740). 2-door 2+2-seater coupé/targa/cabriolet. R/R, 3164cc (HO6 OC). Max speed 152mph, 0-60mph 6.1sec.

The final expression of the original 901 concept – Peugeot made Porsche change the title to 911 – was now in its 19th year. Engine size increased to 3.2, with new management system and increased compression helping to push power to 231bhp. Ultimate was the lightweight, stripped-out Club Sport, with rock hard suspension and 'rubber band' low-profile tyres.

911 TURBO. 1977 to date (prod: 36,876). 2-door 2+2-seater coupé, targa/cabriolet. R/R, 3299cc (HO6 OC). Max speed 168mph, 0-60mph 5.0sec. The ultimate 911, with 300bhp and, until 1988, only a four-speed gearbox. But with that sort of power and 332lb ft torque, it did not really matter. Shatteringly quick, backed by a soul-stirring, clattering howl. In 1990 it was rebodied with Carrera 2 shell, but facia layout remained cluttered. Despite those wide, wide rear wheels under Partonesque wheel arches, even the later Turbos needed to be treated with respect, especially in the wet.

911 CARRERA 2/CARRERA 4. 1989 to date (prod: 23,295). 2-door 2+2-seater coupé/targa/cabriolet. R/R or R/4×4, 3600cc (HO6 OC). Max speed 162mph, 0-60mph 5.7sec. The lines looked familiar, but the body was in fact entirely new, although the engine remained resolutely bringing up the rear. The Carrera 4, with its 4wd system based on that developed for the 959, came first, the rear-drive Carrera 2 following a few months later. New, too, was the expensive manual-or-automatic Tiptronic transmission, which made the Carrera 2 even quicker. Handling? Well, it never let you forget that once a 911, always a 911…

928/928S. 1977-84 (prod: 17,710). 2-door 2+2-seater coupé. F/R, 4474/4664cc (V8 OC). Max speed 152mph, 0-60mph 6.2sec. This was the car which was meant to replace the 911 – except that traditionalists had other ideas. Big, almost too comfortable and beautifully made, the bulky 928 used a new single overhead cam V8. The original 4.5 gave 240bhp, the 4.7 S version 300bhp. Manual transmission was standard, although many were sold with a three-speed automatic. Suspension used double wishbones at the front, trailing arms at the rear, giving outstanding handling. But lack of character ensured that the 911's future was safe.

928 S4. 1986 to date (prod: 14,830). 2-door 2+2-seater coupé. F/R, 4957cc (V8 DOC). Max speed 168mph, 0-60mph 5.6sec. A smoother nose section with electrically-controlled air intakes gave a distinctive look, while the V8 had grown to a 5.0 with twin-cam heads and 32 valves. Power went up to 320bhp, with automatic option now a Mercedes-Benz four-speed. GT version had 330bhp, with five-speed close-ratio manual gearbox, electronically-operated limited slip diff and sports suspension. Handling became even better, but ride comfort suffered.

924/924S. 1976-85 (prod: 122,304). 2-door 2+2-seater coupé. F/R, 1984/2479cc (S4 OC). Max speed 134mph, 0-60mph 8.0sec. Had this been a Porsche from the outset, the layout of the front-mounted water-cooled engine with rear-drive would have been revolutionary for Porsche. But it was a Porsche design for Audi, which went on to build the 924 for Porsche after original marketing plans were dropped. Ex-van 2.0 engine gave 125bhp, which provided merely acceptable performance, but putting the 944's 2.4/163bhp engine in the 924S improved things. VW-sourced strut front suspension, with trailing arms and torsion bars at the rear, gave safe handling. Despite Porsche badges and reasonable price, the 924 was never really regarded as a 'real' Porsche.

924 TURBO. 1978-83 (prod: 12,365). 2-door 2+2-seater coupé. F/R, 1984cc (S4 OC). Max speed 141mph, 0-60mph 6.9sec. With some far less expensive hot hatchbacks starting to run rings round the ordinary 924, the image-boosting Turbo was added. Now with 170bhp thanks to a KKK turbocharger, plus stiffer suspension, wider alloy wheels and rear disc brakes, the 924 came to life – and showed that the chassis could certainly accept more power. The rather narrow, dated appearance was lifted by the neat rear spoiler, while cooling slots in the top of the nose were another recognition point.

944/944S. 1982-92 (prod: 93,430). 2-door 2+2-seater coupé/cabriolet. F/R, 2479/2681cc (S4 OC/DOC). Max speed 134mph, 0-60mph 7.1sec. Similar in profile to the 924, but otherwise very different. Porsche-designed 2.5/163bhp four-cylinder balancer-shaft engine was based on half the 928's V8. S version, from 1986, had 16-valve twin-cam head and 190bhp. Size of 'basic' version rose to 2.7/165bhp in 1988, but S was soon to metamorphose into 3.0 S2. Lower, wider stance gave far more purposeful appearance which was reflected in the very competent handling. Power steering standard from 1984.

944 TURBO. 1985-91 (prod: 51,270). 2-door 2+2-seater coupé. F/R, 2497cc (S4 OC). Max speed 157mph, 0-60mph 5.6sec. With power pushed to 220bhp with the aid of a KKK turbo and Bosch engine management system, the 944 finally got the performance the chassis needed. Wider alloy wheels – 7in front, 8in rear – and stiffened suspension polished the already good handling. In 1988, this 944 flagship S2 chassis received a larger turbo (taking power to 250bhp), a limited slip diff and 1in wider rear wheels.

944 S2. 1989-93 (prod: 19,120). 2-door 2+2-seater coupé/cabriolet. F/R, 2990cc (S4 OC). Max speed 149mph, 0-60mph 6.5sec. New, sleeker nose, still with pop-up headlamps, clad subtley revised chassis, which had to handle even more power with engine, still with just four cylinders, now up to 3.0/211bhp. Internal changes included 'port holes' between cylinders to increase block stiffness as well as smaller water jackets to improve fuel efficiency – these lessons were learned from experience. From the rear, the Turbo-style under-bumper spoiler added to the car's purposeful stance.

959. 1987-88 (prod: 200). 2-door 2-seater coupé. R/4×4, 2994cc (HO6 DOC). Max speed 190mph, 0-60mph 3.7sec. Very much a 'Weissach special', built with Group B competition in mind. Twin-turbo flat-six engine with water-cooled four-valve heads gave 405bhp and massive 369lb ft torque. Four-wheel-drive was through a six-speed gearbox, with front-to-rear torque sensing. Competition thoughts meant wishbone and coil suspension fore and aft, backed by electronic ride height control. Performance was little short of incredible, but the sophisticated chassis was well able to handle it and this car was always surprisingly easy to drive.

PROTON (MAL)

Malaysia's move into the technological age started with electronics, but the government's ambition was to join the world's car producers. In the mid-1980s, Mitsubishi supplied both the know-how and the car - originally to be called the Saga - in the form of the old-model Lancer. Dedicated marketing, reliability and low prices ensured instant success in the UK.

PROTON. 1989 to date (prod: 484,600). 4/5-door 5-seater saloon/hatchback. F/R, 1298/1468cc (S4 OC). Max speed 103mph, 0-60mph 12.4sec. The badge on the grille is the most lurid thing about these cars. With a model as competent as the mid-1980s Lancer, nothing was lost when production started in Malaysia. The eight-valve 1.3 and 1.5 engines produced 68bhp and 75bhp respectively; a 12-valve design with more power came in 1991. Inexpensive (but not cheap) to buy, easy to drive, reasonable handling and ride, long warranties – all this gave Proton an eager market in the UK.

RELIANT (GB)

While the three-wheelers brought in the money, Reliant ventured into the sports car field in 1961 with the Sabre, the first Scimitar following three years later. Simple construction used separate chassis, glass-fibre bodywork and Ford power.

KITTEN. 1975-82 (prod: 4074). 2-door 4-seater saloon/estate. F/R, 848cc (S4 OHV). Max speed 81mph, 0-60mph 17.2sec. While a quirk in the British vehicle tax system made the three-wheelers financially attractive, the four-wheel Kitten had far tougher opposition. A simple chassis carried an Ogle-designed body in glass-fibre, with power coming from a larger 848cc version of Reliant's own all-alloy engine, with 40bhp. Economy (45mpg plus) and tiny 23ft turning circle were no match for the price advantage of cars like the Mini and Renault 4.

SCIMITAR GTE (SE6). 1975 -82 (prod: 4420). 3-door 4-seater hatchback coupé. F/R, 2994cc (V6 OHV). Max speed 118mph, 0-60mph 8.6sec. With a separate chassis – galvanised in the final year of production – and glass-fibre body, making the GTE larger was simply a matter of splitting the moulds and adding 4in to the wheelbase and 3in to the width. Long-legged cruising ability and well-mannered handling made this a great touring car as well as a practical load carrier. Later SE6a version had a stiffer scuttle to eliminate door rattle.

SCIMITAR GTE (SE6b). 1982-86 (prod: n/a). 3-door 4-seater hatchback coupé. F/R, 2792cc (V6 OHV). Max speed 122mph, 0-60mph 8.8sec. The separate chassis and body made improvements relatively easy, so Tamworth-based Reliant was able to make the scuttle torsionally stiffer still, and lop 50lb off the car's weight. Ford's new 2.8/150bhp V6 provided the power, while fuel economy improved to around 23-25mpg. With demand slackening during the mid-1980s, production finally ceased in 1986. Manufacturing rights were sold to Middlebridge (see page 92), which gave the Scimitar a short-lived revival between 1988-90.

SCIMITAR GTC (SE6b). 1980-86 (prod: 443). 2-door 4-seater convertible. F/R, 2792cc (V6 OHV). Max speed 119mph, 0-60mph 8.9sec. Interest in soft-tops was on the increase, so Reliant called in Ogle to develop the open version of the GTE. With the roll-over bar doubling as a body stiffener, the new four-seater convertible looked ready for success. The handling was a little softer than that of the GTE, but this disadvantage was far outweighed by the fresh-air appeal. Disappointing sales, however, saw an end to production.

SCIMITAR SS1. 1984-89 (prod: n/a). 2-door 2-seater convertible. F/R, 1296/1392/1596cc (S4 OC). Max speed 108mph, 0-60mph 11.5sec. With the MG Midget and Triumph Spitfire long gone, the market was wide open once more for a simple, fun sports car. Italian stylist Michelotti was hired to design the body, but he died before completion. The gawky, unhappy result, with ill-fitting panels, had few admirers. The Ford 1.3 version could be outrun by very ordinary hatchbacks, while insufficient under-bonnet space for Ford's injection XR3i engine forced Reliant to use the carburettor 1.6 version.

SCIMITAR SS1 1800Ti. 1986-89 (prod: n/a). 2-door 2-seater convertible. F/R, 1809cc (S4 OC). Max speed 126mph, 0-60mph 6.9sec. In an urgent search for more power, Reliant found that Nissan was prepared to supply the engine it so desperately needed. The Silvia's 1.8 turbo, a rather coarse unit with 135bhp, slotted in neatly – and proved that the Scimitar's chassis was indeed as good as everyone said. Sales picked up, with the SS1 title being dropped in continental European markets. The black boot spoiler and alloy wheels marked out the turbo models from lesser Ford-powered versions. Sales were always sluggish, but two facelifts helped the model to survive the early 1990s recession.

RENAULT (F)

In at the dawn of the motor car, Louis Renault having founded the company in 1898. It was nationalised in 1945 to become the dominant French manufacturer until it was challenged by Peugeot SA towards the end of the 1980s. Immediate post-war models were rear-engined, with the mould being broken in 1961 by the R4. The inevitable move to front-drive continued, the R16 being a landmark model with its modern looks and hatchback design.

4. 1961-91 (prod: 8,000,000 approx). 4-door 4-seater estate. F/F, 603/747/848/956/1108cc (S4 OHV). Max speed 82mph, 0-60mph 18.2sec. Renault's answer to the Citroën 2CV. It may have lacked the 2CV's charisma, but it was a far more practical car – and so much better to drive. Renault's first front-drive model, with gearbox ahead of the engine, operated through facia-mounted gear lever. Supple torsion bar suspension was designed with now-forgotten village street pavé in mind. Best version was the final incarnation, with 1.1/34bhp engine and long-legged gearing which made motorway cruising tolerable. Production was continued until 1991 in Argentina.

12. 1969-80 (prod: 2,865,079). 4-door 4-seater saloon/estate. F/F, 1289/1565/1674cc (S4 OHV). Max speed 94mph, 0-60mph 12.9sec. Despite the success of the hatchback 16, Renault played it safe by building the 12 only as a saloon and estate. Fore-and-aft engine was ahead of transmission. Renault sold only 1289cc versions in the UK, quickest being the 60bhp TS. A few 1.6/110bhp Gordini versions found their way into the country. Gawky rear styling gave distinctive appearance, and ride quality was from the Renault textbook. But have any survived the ravages of rust?

5. 1972-84 (prod: 5,471,709). 3/5-door 4-seater hatchback. F/F, 782/845/956/1108/1289/1397cc (S4 OHV). Max speed 96mph, 0-60mph 12.2sec. The secret of the 5's huge success lay in its ageless, charming, classless looks. Smallest-engined versions were French 'tax specials', 956cc TL and 1289cc GTL being the best-sellers in the UK. Engine layout was north-south, with gearbox ahead. Torsion bar independent suspension gave outstanding ride and, when pushed hard, almost door-handle cornering. The shape made use of every cubic centimetre of interior space.

5 GORDINI. 1976-81 (prod: see above). 3-door 4-seater hatchback. F/F, 1397cc (S4 OHV). Max speed 111mph, 0-60mph 10.9sec. In France they wore Alpine badges, but for copyright reasons (Chrysler had the Alpine name in the UK) they had to be called Gordinis here. Relatively mild tuning produced 93bhp from the 1397cc pushrod engine, but 100bhp was not too difficult to squeeze out. Five-speed gearbox with floor change, plus tuned suspension, alloy wheels and 110mph plus top speed, let plenty of continental drivers cut their competition teeth without breaking the bank.

5 GORDINI TURBO. 1982-84 (prod: see above). 3-door 4-seater hatchback. F/F, 1397cc (S4 OHV). Max speed 112mph, 0-60mph 9.8sec. Cashing in on its success in F1, Renault replaced the naturally-aspirated 5 Gordini with the turbo version. The chassis needed few changes to handle the extra power, but alloy wheels were wider. The existing 1397cc engine was modestly boosted to give 110bhp, but turbo lag was always a handicap. In spring 1984 it was renamed Le Car 2 Turbo, with pruned-back spec, to be replaced by the Supercinque that autumn.

5 SUPERCINQUE. 1984 to date. (prod: 4,943,629). 3/5-door 4-seater hatchback. F/F, 956/1237/1721cc (S4 OHV), 1108/1390cc (S4 OC), 1595cc diesel (S4 OHV). Max speed 105mph, 0-60mph 9.3sec. Sensibly, Renault simply made the much-loved 5 even better. The biggest change was under the bonnet, with the engine finally being turned through 90 degrees, copying most rivals. Appearance was carefully restyled, and the new facia – with an odd 'canopy' design – was the basis for a corporate theme. Smaller engines unchanged, but 1595cc/55bhp diesel added in June 1986. Biggest-engined 5 so far was the GTX, with 1721cc/90bhp giving 100mph plus performance. Despite the all-round improvements, the 'Supercinque' never quite matched the original 5's sales success.

5 CONVERTIBLE. 1985-89 (prod: n/a). 2-door 4-seater convertible. 957/1237/1721cc (S4 OHV), 1108/1309cc (S4 OC), 1595cc diesel (S4 OHV). Max speed 105mph, 0-60mph 9.3sec. Rather than pick a major coachbuilder, Renault chose EBS, based near Brussels Airport, to produce the rag-top Supercinque. Bodyshells were produced on special jigs at Renault's nearby factory, with final trim and assembly done by EBS, who also made the frameless doors. Renault, however, were never satisfied by quality and pulled out of the project at the last moment. So it was left to EBS to make what they could of it, carrying out conversions on customer's existing cars. Very rare in the UK – or anywhere else for that matter.

5 GT TURBO. 1986-91 (prod: see above). 3-door 4-seater hatchback. F/F, 1397cc (S4 OHV). Max speed 120mph, 0-60mph 7.3sec. By far the quickest front-drive 5 model yet. With an intercooler and more boost, power from the 1397cc engine was pushed to 115bhp, rising to 120bhp in summer 1987. Renault produced endless modification kits to overcome notorious hot starting problems, caused by fuel vaporisation. Hugely responsive engine, with massive low-down torque, and outstanding chassis dynamics made this one of the greatest handling hot hatchbacks – although hard-charging drivers found wheelspin almost ever-present. Flimsy build and expensive maintenance have sent many to an early grave.

5 TURBO 2. 1983-86 (prod: 3576). 2-door 2-seater hatchback. M/R, 1297cc (S4 OHV). Max speed 124mph, 0-60mph 7.0sec. Created as an 'homologation' special for competition use. The 1297cc/160bhp turbo engine was moved between the rear wheels, with wishbone and coil spring suspension. Huge, flared wheel arches and distinctive air intakes behind the doors gave the Turbo 2 a very special look. Aluminium-bodied versions had power boosted dramatically to 240bhp. Despite rear weight bias, handling was sure-footed and agile, but the ride could put fillings at risk. Never officially sold in the UK – and beware the phoney front-engined 'replicar' versions.

30. 1975-84 (prod: 160,165). 5-door 5-seater hatchback. F/F, 2664cc (V6 OC). Max speed 117mph, 0-60mph 9.8sec. Developing the hatchback theme begun by the 'electric razor' styled 16, the 30 had rather less head-turning ability. A big, comfortable load carrier, with all-round independent suspension, and coils rather than torsion bars at the rear. Power came from the then-new V6 developed jointly with Peugeot and Volvo. Plenty of performance and essentially a nice car to drive, even though the handling did tend towards ultimate tyre-scrubbing understeer.

20. 1975-84 (prod: 622,314). 5-door 5-seater hatchback. F/F, 1647cc (S4 OHV), 1995/2165cc (S4 OC). Max speed 106mph, 0-60mph 10.5sec. With the same bodyshell as the 30, the 20 was aimed more at the high-volume end of the market. North-south engine layout, with engine ahead of transaxle, meant a long bonnet line. In the early 1980s, the 1.6 version was dropped, replaced with a new 2.2 unit. Despite rivalry, the 2.0 was a Peugeot design, used also in the 505. And despite its practicality, the 20 never quite managed to outsell Peugeot rivals.

14. 1976-82 (prod: 999,093). 5-door 4-seater hatchback. F/F, 1218/1360cc (S4 OC). Max speed 96mph, 0-60mph 12.6sec. Renault's first transverse-engined car – but only because it used the Peugeot-sourced on-its-back engine from the 104 and Citroën Visa. Unusual styling led to one being exhibited in Paris's Pompidou Centre – but the remainder were mainly claimed by rust. Usual off-beat Renault character inside, but the handling made it a pleasant enough car to drive, with a supple ride and light controls.

18. 1978-86 (prod: 2,173,100). 4-door 5-seater saloon/estate. F/F, 1397/1647cc (S4 OHV), 1995cc (S4 OC), 2068cc diesel (S4 OC). Max speed

96mph, 0-60mph 13.2sec. With styling coming from the same drawing board as the smaller 12, the 18 saloon and estate complemented the bigger 20 hatchback. The first model to use Renault's new wet-liner 1.4/64bhp pushrod engine, but it hardly had a chance to shine in this rather unremarkable car. The 18 sold well enough, with the estate version proving to be a useful load carrier.

18 TURBO. 1980-85 (prod: see above). 4-door 5-seater saloon. F/F, 1565cc (S4 OHV). Max speed 121mph, 0-60mph 10.1sec. In 1977 Renault had brought turbocharging to F1 motor racing – and just three years later announced its first turbo production model. The 1.6 engine with Garrett T3 turbo developed 125bhp at 5500rpm, but putting even that amount of savagely-delivered power through the front wheels needed careful pedal balance. But the chassis was well able to handle the performance, and standard power steering helped. Grip was improved with wider wheels in the last year.

FUEGO. 1980-86 (prod: 83,725). 3-door 4-seater coupé. F/F, 1397/1565/1647cc (S4 OHV), 1995cc (S4 OC). Max speed 118mph, 0-60mph 9.3sec. Out of the blue Renault adopted a name rather than a number for its new model. Sporting coupé body used a modified 18 floorpan, with similar engine line-up. The 1.4/64bhp hardly had sporting performance, but the 2.0/110bhp and fiercely wheelspinning 1.6/132bhp turbo were quick. Rear seat room was limited, but equipment got better higher up the price scale. Power steering on GTX and Turbo models, the latter having the word Turbo written in large letters down both sides.

9. 1982-89 (prod: 1,109,300). 4-door 4-seater saloon. F/F, 1108/1237/1397cc (S4 OHV), 1721cc (S4 OC), 1595cc diesel (S4 OHV). Max speed 112mph, 0-60mph 10.8sec. Renault was not looking for any design awards with the ultra-conservative three-box styling and equally uninspiring interior, but this was nevertheless a 'Car of the Year'. The 98in wheelbase provided reasonable space, with MacPherson strut front suspension and torsion bars at the rear. Transverse engine layout, with end-on transmission, included 1.7/82bhp overhead-cam unit for the first time. Mid-term facelift did little for the dull image.

9 TURBO. 1984-87 (prod: see above). 4-door 4-seater saloon. F/F, 1397cc (S4 OHV). Max speed 116mph, 0-60mph 8.9sec. Although it was launched in France in 1984, the Turbo was short-lived on the UK market. It went on sale in March 1986 and vanished in the winter of 1987. The mildly-boosted 1.4 engine initially managed just 105bhp, rising to 115bhp with the facelift of 1987, when the body gained side skirts. Despite all its equipment and reasonable handling, this car, like the rest of the 9 range, has faded from everyone's memories.

11. 1983-89 (prod: 973,740). 3/5-door 4-seater hatchback. F/F, 1108/1237/1397cc (S4 OHV), 1721cc (S4 OC), 1595cc diesel (S4 OHV). Max

speed 96mph, 0-60mph 12.6sec. On the same 98in wheelbase as the 9, the 11 had slightly more appeal thanks to its more practical hatchback body. Same engine line-up as the 9 saloon, with the TXE Electronic having the then-fashionable bar-graph instrument display and voice synthesizer.

11 TURBO. 1984-89 (prod: see above). 3-door 4-seater hatchback. F/F, 1397cc (S4 OHV). Max speed 116mph, 0-60mph 8.7sec. The hatchback lines suited the turbo image rather better than the dull 9's saloon body did. It used the same 1.4 engine, power rising from 105bhp to 115bhp in autumn 1986. At the same time it was given a new, more sporty look, with four headlamps, red inserts on the bumpers and side mouldings, and a rear spoiler. Firmer suspension gave the handling the edge it always needed.

25. 1984-92 (prod: 173,685). 5-door 5-seater hatchback. F/F, 1995/2165cc (S4 OC), 2458/2664/2849cc (V6 OC). Max speed 134mph, 0-60mph 7.5sec. After the practical 30/20 hatchbacks, the 25 had a more upmarket image and sleek lines with glassy tailgate. The 107in wheelbase meant plenty of space for passengers, especially in the back – and the long-wheelbase V6-powered Limousine was even roomier. Power of the 2.0 ranged between 102bhp and 140bhp, latterly with 12-valve head and injection. Top versions used PRV (Peugeot-Renault-Volvo) V6 engine, with smallest 2.5 giving 182bhp with turbocharging. Long-legged feel, with poised handling and good ride.

ESPACE. 1985-91 (prod: 147,960). 5-door 5/7-seater estate. F/F or F/4×4, 1995cc (S4 OC). Max speed 109mph, 0-60mph 9.9sec. Matra's space age technology was used to develop the composite-clad steel skeleton body frame for Europe's first purpose-built people carrier. North-south engine layout meant a long, steeply-sloped bonnet, with windscreen a long way ahead of the driver. Highly adaptable seating, although the rearmost pair of seats was optional on most trim levels. The 2.0 engines ranged from 103bhp carburettor to 120bhp injection, with slow-selling four-wheel drive Quadra versions available from 1989. Smoother post-1988 nose styling looked neater. Despite size, handling was almost car-like, with performance to match. From the start, a definitive people-carrier which others tried in vain to match.

GTA. 1986-93 (prod: 17,450). 2-door 2+2-seater sports coupé. R/R, 2458/2849cc (V6 OC). Max speed 165mph, 0-60mph 5.7sec. It may have lacked Ferrari-challenging image, but the Dieppe-built A610 in turbo form could show a clean pair of tyres when it came to performance. The normally-aspirated 2.8 V6 gave 160bhp, the 2.5 turbo 200bhp in non-catalyst form. There was even room for two in the back of the sleek-all-plastic body. Outstanding handling and massive grip made this unusual sports coupé a hugely rewarding driving experience. But despite numerous rave reviews, UK sales were always slow.

21. 1986-94 (prod: 2,743,100). 4/5-door 5-seater saloon/hatchback/estate. F/F or F/4×4, 1721cc (S4 OC), 1995cc (S4 OC), 1870cc diesel (S4 OHV), 2068cc diesel (S4 OC). Max speed 124mph, 0-60mph 8.6sec. In time the 21 developed into a complete package, with estate (badged Savanna in the UK) and hatchback following original saloon. Uniquely, Renault mixed east-west 1.7 engine layout with north-south 2.0, with front axle line moved within same wheelarch opening. Power of the 2.0 engines ranged from 120bhp to multi-valve 140bhp. Facelift in 1989 inside and out helped boost otherwise unremarkable image, which concealed outstanding ride and, with top engines, great performance. Longer wheelbase estates were huge load-carriers, with part-time 4wd available for country-dwellers.

21 TURBO. 1988-92 (prod: see above). 4-door 5-seater saloon. F/F or F/4×4, 1995cc (S4 OC). Max speed 139mph, 0-60mph 7.3sec. It was almost as if Renault was telling us just how well the 21 chassis had been developed. With a turbocharger, the 2.0 engine put out 175bhp, giving close to 140mph top speed. Lowered, stiffened suspension and wide, low-profile tyres gave outstanding handling – but could not conquer furious front-drive wheelspin and torque steer. But the full-time Quadra 4wd system, first used on the Espace, solved that problem in 1990. Luxury included leather upholstery and multiple instruments.

19. 1988 to date (prod: 1,179,600). 3/5-door 4-seater hatchback; 4-door 4-seater saloon. F/F, 1397cc (S4 OHV), 1390/1721cc (S4 OC), 1870cc diesel (S4 OHV). Max speed 109mph, 0-60mph 10.6sec. The first indication of changes to come, with the 19 fitting between the soon-to-be replaced 5 and 21. Launched as a hatchback, with 1.4/60bhp and 1.7/92bhp transverse engines, plus 1.9/65bhp diesel. The saloon version was briefly called. Chamade before getting a 19 badge on the boot. Beneath the faceless look lurked well-mannered handling and a good ride.

ROLLS-ROYCE (GB)

The Hon Charles Rolls met Henry Royce in March 1904 at the Midland Hotel in Manchester - and the rest is history. After serious financial troubles in 1972, Rolls-Royce Motors Ltd was formed to take over the assets of the automotive part of the original company, to become part of Vickers in 1980. Despite the essentially conservative designs, the appeal of the 'Best Car In The World' seemed unbeatable, although sales dropped sharply in the recession of the early 1990s.

PHANTOM VI. 1968-90 (prod: 409). 4-door 7/9-seater limousine. F/R, 6750cc (V8 OHV). Max speed 112mph, 0-60mph 11.5sec. Majestic in every possible sense. As coachbuilding tradition demanded, there was a separate chassis with a 145in wheelbase, clad in imposing Mulliner Park

Ward bodywork. The 6.7 V8 engine could cope with everything from processional crawling to a top speed of over 110mph, its effortless progress aided by a GM Hydramatic three-speed automatic 'box. Drum brakes were used right up to the end – but they gave super-smooth stopping at very low speed. Prices started in six figures and continued upwards.

SILVER SHADOW II. 1977-80 (prod: 8422). 4-door 5-seater saloon. F/R, 6750cc (V8 OHV). Max speed 118mph, 0-60mph 10.9sec. A carefully planned freshening of the Silver Shadow to maintain interest in its closing years. A discreet air dam appeared beneath the front bumper, while inside the facia was altered, featuring dual-level air conditioning. Discerning drivers would have noticed the more precise rack and pinion steering. As ever, power output remained 'adequate', with fuel injection finally replacing the SU carburettors – but only for cars going to California.

SILVER WRAITH II. 1977-80 (prod: 2144). 4-door 5/7-seater saloon/limousine. F/R, 6750cc (V8 OHV). Max speed 116mph, 0-60mph 11.4sec. With the Silver Shadow II facelift, the long wheelbase Shadow I was renamed Silver Wraith. The same 6.7 V8, with GM three-speed automatic, was used, but the body was stretched by 4in in the rear. Limousine version had glass division between front and rear seats. Despite the size, the handling was surprisingly agile, although road noise at speed could be rather more intrusive than expected.

CORNICHE. 1972 to date (prod: 6110). 2-door 5-seater saloon/convertible. F/R, 6750cc (V8 OHV). Max speed 119mph, 0-60mph 10.9sec. Bridging the Silver Shadow II and Silver Spirit periods, the Corniche was built with all their mechanical and trim changes. The two-door saloon was dropped in spring 1981. The Corniche II was launched in autumn 1987, shortly after the V8 engine had received fuel injection – and with it came the revelation that power output was just 225bhp. When Mulliner Park Ward closed, assembly was transferred to Crewe.

CAMARGUE. 1975-86 (prod: 530). 2-door 5-seater saloon. F/R, 6750cc (V8 OHV). Max speed 115mph, 0-60mph 11.3sec. With an eye on lucrative export markets, Rolls-Royce unusually went to Pininfarina in Italy to design the Camargue. Unusually, too, Pininfarina missed the target: the bulky two-door body, built by Mulliner Park Ward on a Silver Shadow platform, lacked the elegance of the Corniche. To cope with the extra weight, the undisclosed power output was made even more 'adequate' with a four-barrel Solex carburettor replacing the usual twin SUs.

SILVER SPIRIT/SILVER SPUR. 1980-89 (prod: 14,366). 4-door 5-seater saloon. F/R, 6750cc (V8 OVH). Max speed 119mph, 0-60mph 9.5sec. Longer, lower and heavier successor to the Silver Shadow, with the Spur having an extra 4in in the wheelbase to provide even more rear legroom. Output of the venerable all-alloy V8 engine was improved from its undisclosed figure in carburettor form by fuel injection in 1986, when anti-lock brakes and improved air conditioning became standard. Suspension offered silence and sublime ride quality, the rear using Citroën oleo-pneumatic units to control level. Inelegant styling compared with the graceful Silver Shadow did nothing to disguise the car's bulk, but peerless leather/walnut/woolcloth interior remained.

SILVER SPIRIT II/SILVER SPUR II. 1989 to date (prod: 2810). 4-door 5-seater saloon. F/R, 6750cc (V8 OHV). Max speed 119mph, 0-60mph 9.9sec. Same basic bodyshell as the original, but with many under-the skin changes. Bosch Motronic engine management was fitted, plus automatic ride control. The rather fussy facia design was revised, with the driver getting a nice leather-bound steering wheel in place of the traditional thin-rimmed item. The motoring press was not too sure about the handling – but when did you last see a Rolls-Royce cornering anywhere near its expensive door handles? The 'Best Car in the World' tag was now under attack, but nothing else in the world could match this R-R's ability to instil a sense of well-being and calm.

ROVER (GB)

Sewing machines, bicycles and motorcycles - and, in 1904, the first Rover car. Rover stayed independent until 1967, when it became part of Standard Triumph, and a year later British Leyland. During the 1980s the Rover name started to become dominant, first linked with Austin and finally alone, using its image - and technical collaboration with Honda - to rebuild its battered reputation for poor build quality and indifferent design. A terrific success story in recent years, ownership passing from British Aerospace to BMW in January 1994.

3500 (SD1). 1976-86 (prod: 37,900). 5-door 5-seater hatchback. F/R, 3528cc (V8 OHV). Max speed 135mph, 0-60mph 9.8sec. In the wake of the P6 models, the low, fastback design of the SD1 – Specialist Division No 1 – was a revolution. The only carry-over was the V8 engine, with 155bhp for most models, but 190bhp in the Vitesse (from 1982). After the complex P6 chassis, the SD1 was simplicity itself, with McPherson struts at the front, live axle and drum brakes at the rear. Nevertheless, the handling was sound and the ride good. Despite questionable build quality at first, the SD1 proved itself to be as tough as they come.

2000/2300/2400SD/2600 (SD1). 1977-86 (prod: 57,980). 5-door 5-seater hatchback. F/R, 1996cc (S4 OC), 2351/2567cc (S6 OC), 2393cc (S4 OHV). Max speed 116mph, 0-60mph 11.5sec. Initially this additional SD1 model appeared with the 'Innsbruck' versions of the Triumph 2500 engine, with a single overhead-cam cylinder head. Later the 2.0/100bhp O-series engine and the four-cylinder turbocharged Italian-made VM diesel (with just 93bhp) were added, with an eye on the tax-conscious European export market. Despite the apparent size, the SD1 cabin did not have anywhere near as much room as you might expect.

213/216. 1984-89 (prod: 408,521). 4-door 4-seater saloon. F/F, 1342/1598cc (S4 OC). Max speed 109mph, 0-60mph 9.4sec. The car which really set Rover on the road to success. Developed jointly with Honda, using 1.3/71bhp Honda engine in the 213 and Rover's own S-series in the 216, with injection version giving 103bhp. Not a huge amount of room inside, and the ride could get a bit edgy. The 200's predecessor, the Ballade 'box of bits' which became the Triumph Acclaim, proved that the Brits could put cars together properly – and they did it again with the new Rover. So well, indeed, that Rover finished by making Honda Ballades on the same assembly line.

214/216. 1989 to date (prod: 384,379). 5-door 5-seater hatchback. F/F, 1396/1590cc (S4 OC). Max speed 120mph, 0-60mph 9.2sec. Rover's secret weapon for its new car was the brilliant K-series engine. In its twin-cam 16-valve form the 1.4 gave 95bhp, while the 216 used the Swindon-built Honda twin-cam 16-valve unit with 116bhp. Base 214s had eight-valve 76bhp engines. The 16-valve 1.4 was quick, with a 106mph maximum and 0-60mph in 11.0sec. Precise handling, but the ride could suffer on any but the best surfaces. More interior room than before, but Honda's better-equipped Concerto, built on the same line, was better value – but nowhere near as popular.

820. 1986-92 (prod: 128,951). 4/5-door 5-seater saloon/hatchback. F/F, 1994cc (S4 OC), 1994cc (S4 DOC). Max speed 126mph, 0-60mph 8.9sec. Honda's role in the partnership seemed rather too dominant, especially as far as handling feel went. But Rover's new M16 twin-cam 16-valve engine, based around the O-series, proved to be a winner, despite some teething problems which lasted into adolescence. Single-point injection version gave 120bhp, multi-point 140bhp. From 1988, a new entry-level model had the 100bhp O-series single-cam unit. Saloon body was joined by fastback at the same time. Handling always a little tip-toe, with over-light power steering. Reskinned version with traditional Rover grille took over in 1992.

825. 1986-88 (prod: 42,780). 4-door 5-seater saloon. F/F, 2594cc (V6 OC). Max speed 125mph, 0-60mph 8.4sec. The best laid plans...on paper Honda's 24-valve V6 engine appeared just right for the new Rover. But even with 167bhp – or 173bhp when the four-speed automatic was fitted – the peaky torque curve simply did not dovetail with the quasi-limo intentions. Rover was only too aware of the shortcomings, but Honda wanted the car in the showrooms. Despite the problems, the speed-related power steering gave the V6 a nicer road feel than smaller versions. After just 18 months, the 2.5 was superseded by the 2.7. In top-of-the-range Sterling guise, equipment and luxury were lavish – but police versions were spartan.

827. 1988-92 (prod: 49,496). 4/5-door 5-seater saloon/hatchback. F/F, 2675cc (V6 OC). Max speed 131mph, 0-60mph 9.0sec. Now with the engine it always needed, Rover was faced with the task of rebuilding the image of its new big model. The 2.7 V6 had 177bhp, but a much flatter, meatier torque curve. The dual-range, four-speed automatic became standard, with a five-speed, Honda-sourced manual gearbox a no-cost option. Smooth engine and refined transmission went well with the up-market level of equipment, and appeal was widened with the arrival of the hatchback (designated Fastback) in spring 1988.

VITESSE. 1988-92 (prod: see above). 5-door 5-seater hatchback. F/F, 2675cc (V6 OC). Max speed 131mph, 0-60mph 9.0sec. Unlike the original SD1 version, with its higher-output engine, the new Vitesse kept the same 177bhp Honda V6 as the 827, but with the five-speed manual gearbox standard and the automatic the no-cost extra. But while it was no quicker, its lowered suspension, 15in alloy wheels and rear spoiler did improve the handling. As with the 827, power dropped to 169bhp in 1989 when a catalytic converter became standard.

STERLING. 1988-91 (prod: see above). 4-door 5-seater saloon. F/F, 2675cc (V6 OC). Max speed 130mph, 0-60mph 9.3sec. Mechanically the Sterling was nothing more than an 827 saloon, with the vast majority being sold with the super-smooth dual-range four-speed automatic transmission. Where it excelled was in the equipment, which ran to Connolly leather trim, air conditioning, cruise control, electrically-adjusted and heated front seats, and, like the Vitesse, anti-lock brakes. The price, however, put it up against the might of BMW and Mercedes-Benz.

SAAB (S)

Ugly it may have been, but Saab's first car, the 92, reflected its parent company's aircraft interests. During the 1960s, four-stroke engines replaced the two-strokes, with the Triumph Dolomite-engined 99 appearing in 1967. Turbos, initially with spectacular turbo lag, arrived ten years later. At the end of the 1980s, General Motors took a major stake in Saab.

99/90. 1967-85 (prod: 588,643/25,378). 2/3/4/5-door 4-seater saloon/hatchback. F/F, 1709/1854/1985cc (S4 OC). Max speed 101mph, 0-60mph 13.6sec. After its 'single model' image, Saab took off with the 99, with a variety of saloon and hatchback body styles. The overhead cam engine was initially supplied by Triumph – so delaying the launch of the Dolomite for a few months – with the gearbox located beneath (but not in) the sump. Fuel injection in the 2.0 EMS brought power to 110bhp, but this in no way stretched the abilities of the chassis. Designation changed to 90 in 1984 to tie in with imminent arrival of the new 9000.

99 TURBO. 1977-80 (prod: 10,607). 2/3/4/5-door 4-seater saloon/hatchback. F/F, 1985cc (S4 OC). Max speed 125mph, 0-60mph 9.0sec. Saab took the plunge into turbocharging when others had not even stuck a toe in the water. Power of the 1985cc engine was pushed from 118bhp to 145bhp, helped by fuel injection. The basic soundness of the front-drive chassis proved equal to the extra performance, although fierce take-offs could result in hectic torque steer for the unwary. With electronic management systems in their infancy, drivers also had to learn their way round a new motoring hazard – turbo lag.

900. 1978-93 (prod: 710,163). 2/3/4/5-door 5-seater saloon/hatchback. F/F, 1985cc (S4 OC). Max speed 107mph, 0-60mph 10.8sec. Archetypal Saab of the 1980s, with the 99's cabin grafted onto a 2in longer wheelbase, which allowed longer, smoother bonnet and boot lines. Power of the 2.0 engine ranged from 100bhp to 118bhp, with five-speed gearbox standard across the range from 1983. Safe, reassuring handling was backed up by a reputation for immense structural safety. Much-loved workhorse mourned by many loyal customers when it passed away in 1993.

900 TURBO. 1979-93 (prod: 202,284). 2/3/4/5-door 5-seater saloon/hatchback. F/F, 1985cc (S4 OC/DOC). Max speed 133mph, 0-60mph 6.9sec. Building on the experience gained with the 99 Turbo, the 900 version was a logical progression. Eight-valve single-cam engine output stayed at 145bhp, but with new 16-valve twin-cam head, from 1984, power jumped to 175bhp, putting performance close to supercar figures. Wider wheels and ventilated front discs helped handling and stopping. Ultimate version was the 1989 whale-tailed Carlsson (named after Saab's famous rally driver, Erik Carlsson), with power notched up to a fierce 185bhp.

900 16V. 1988-92 (prod: 185,767). 2/3/4/5-door 5-seater saloon/hatchback. F/F, 1985cc (S4 DOC) Max speed 112mph, 0-60mph 10.6sec. Yet another variation on the 900 theme, with the 2.0 16-valve engine appearing in non-turbo form. The 133bhp output went down to 128bhp in 1990 when a catalyst, previously fitted on automatics, became standard. Equipment levels grew better with time, but as it went into the 1990s, the 900 was starting to show its age.

900 CONVERTIBLE. 1986 to date (prod: 185,744). 2-door 4-seater convertible. F/F, 1985cc (S4 OC/DOC). Max speed 126mph, 0-60mph 7.5sec. Although it had been launched in the USA back in 1986, it took four more years for the convertible to go on sale in the UK. The turbo engine gave 175bhp, which gave shattering performance. But that lag problem remained... Clever in-house design on two-door shell, with steeply curved windscreen frame retaining a lot of strength – and finally shedding the beetle-browed look. Extra body stiffening put on weight, which took the edge off performance.

9000 TURBO. 1985 to date (prod: 153,469). 5-door 5-seater hatchback. F/F, 1985cc (S4 DOC). Max speed 145mph, 0-60mph 7.4sec. The 'Type Four' design developed jointly with the Fiat group, Saab's rival to BMW and Mercedes-Benz first appeared, unusually, in turbo form, with the 2.0 twin-cam 16-valve engine giving 175bhp. Advanced ignition and injection electronics ensured that turbo lag was no problem, making the new car outstandingly tractable and refined. The black-only Carlsson, with lowered suspension and road-hugging tyres, produced a fierce 204bhp. Refinement, good handling and a huge amount of interior space gave Saab its first Grand Tourer.

9000. 1986 to date (prod: see above). 5-door 5-seater hatchback. F/F, 1985/2290cc (S4 DOC). Max speed 127mph, 0-60mph 10.0sec. A matter of months after the 9000 Turbo came the non-turbo version, initially with the 2.0/130bhp engine. The 2.3/150bhp versions, with twin balancer shafts, came in 1989. MacPherson struts at the front, with well-located dead axle at the rear, plus power steering, gave well-balanced handling and outstanding ride.

CD. 1988 to date (prod: 35,565). 4-door 5-seater saloon. F/F, 1985/2290cc (S4 DOC). Max speed 117mph, 0-60mph 9.8sec. The 9000 part of the title was dropped to distinguish the saloons from the well-established hatchbacks. Appearance apart, Saab also went as far as making the rear seat on the CDs fixed, so that it could not be folded to expand load space. No worry, because boot space was huge. Same engine and trim line-up, with top versions having leather seats and walnut-veneered facia – and no end of equipment.

CD TURBO. 1988 to date (prod: see above). 4-door 5-seater saloon. F/F, 1985/2290cc (S4 DOC). Max speed 143mph, 0-60mph 7.5sec. Chronologically, the CD Turbos arrived a matter of months before the standard saloons. The 2.3 version came late in 1990, when the 220bhp Carlsson supplanted the short-lived 2.0/195bhp model. Equipment levels improved with price, with top versions having sophisticated air conditioning and traction control.

SEAT (E)

Founded in conjunction with Fiat to circumvent Spain's high import duties on cars during the 1950s, Seat ended its financial links with Fiat at the end of the 1970s, although it went on producing Fiat-based cars. Under government control, the Ibiza was developed, going on sale in the UK in 1985. Volkswagen's stake during the latter part of of the 1980s expanded the range and improved quality.

MARBELLA. 1988 to date (prod: 560,900). 3-door 4-seater hatchback. F/F, 843/903cc (S4 OHV). Max speed 83mph, 0-60mph 19.3sec. For a car-hungry domestic market, Seat's version of the Fiat Panda was an ideal entry-level model. However, as the Panda developed and Seat's links with Fiat vanished, the Marbella stood still. So it stayed with the dated, Fiat-based, clattery pushrod engines and the original harsh-riding, simple leaf-spring rear suspension. Minimal equipment was on a par with the feeble performance.

MALAGA. 1985-92 (prod: 247,300). 4-door 5-seater saloon. F/F, 1193/1461cc (S4 OC). Max speed 104mph, 0-60mph 12.9sec. Half-Fiat, half-Seat saloon, based on the Strada but using the System Porsche engines developed for the Ibiza. Dull, old-fashioned looks matched the stodgy ride and heavy steering. Even with the larger 85bhp engine, the Malaga's size and weight meant that acceleration was a bit of a struggle. Even less memorable were the odd facia and poor seats.

IBIZA. 1985-93 (prod: 543,900). 3/5-door 5-seater hatchback. F/F, 903cc (S4 OHV) 1193/ 1461/1714cc (S4 OC). Max speed 107mph, 0-60mph 10.4sec. Even though System Porsche produced the larger overhead-cam engines and Giugiaro the styling, there was still some Fiat left in Seat's new car, with the Strada's suspension living on, as well as the smallest engine. Tidy looks and lots of room, but let down by dead steering, noisy powertrain and, on the original, a weird facia layout. But Seat was learning fast and, under VW influence, quality improved. A revised model, based on the original, appeared in 1989.

SKODA (CS)

Unlike other ex-communist countries, Czechoslovakia's motor industry can be traced back to 1905. But in post-war years, design progress was slow, with the first rear-engined design, the 1000 MB, appearing in 1964. Exports brought in hard currency, with low prices rather than technical expertise attracting sales. After communism collapsed in the 1990s, Volkswagen stepped in, revolutionising build quality and, hopefully, image.

S100/S110. 1970-80 (prod: 1.24 million all models). 2-door 4-seater coupé. R/R, 988/1107cc (S4 OHV). Max speed 90mph, 0-60mph 18.2sec. Underneath the coupé bodywork (the saloon had been replaced by the Estelle in 1977), the original rear-engined, rear-drive layout remained. Combine this with swing axles and the result could be very nerve-racking for the unwary. The larger-engined version, with 52bhp, could be wound up to 90mph if conditions and ear plugs allowed.

ESTELLE. 1977-92 (prod: 1,350,250). 4-door 4-seater saloon. R/R, 1046/1289cc (S4 OHV). Max speed 93mph, 0-60mph 14.2sec. Skoda stayed with its rear-engined layout, which, despite the engine's alloy block, meant that the handling of the original versions remained as wayward as ever. In 1979, following criticisms in the press and from safety organisations, modifications were made to the rear suspension, and wider, alloy wheels became standard. This was the model which inspired all the Skoda jokes.

RAPID. Above: Hatchback. Below: Cabriolet.

RAPID. 1982-90 (prod: 29,500). 2-door 4-seater coupé/cabriolet. R/R, 1289cc (S4 OHV). Max speed 93mph, 0-60mph 14.2sec. If funds could not run to a Porsche 911, you could always pretend – at a tenth of the cost. Power went up from 58bhp to 61bhp, plus a five-speed gearbox in 1988. Tied-down rear suspension made handling much more predictable. Despite its stiffening roll-over bar, the cabriolet suffered from scuttle shake, but nevertheless offered huge fun at a modest price. The laughter was fading…

FAVORIT. 1989 to date (prod: 897,250). 4-door 4-seater hatchback. F/F, 1298cc (S4 OHV). Max speed 85mph, 0-60mph 13.6sec. Overnight Skoda joined the real world, switching to the now-conventional front-engined, front-drive layout in a practical, sensible hatchback. In place of the lurking oversteer was nice, safe understeer, although ride tended to verge on the hectic over poor surfaces. Early models suffered from the ultimate in tacky plastic interiors and scattered facia design. In the 1990s, Volkswagen took control, quality and equipment improvements coming by the dozen.

SUBARU (J)

Part of the massive Fuji Heavy Industries empire, Subaru has been making cars since the mid-1950s. A feature of most models has been the horizontally-opposed 'boxer' cylinder layout and increasingly sophisticated four-wheel drive systems for on-road, rather than off-road, use.

JUSTY. 1986 to date (prod: 398,635). 3/5-door 4-seater hatchback. F/4×4, 1189cc (S3 OC). Max speed 96mph, 0-60mph 13.2sec. Tiny four-wheel drive whizzabouts are common in Japan, but the Justy is a bit more grown up. The three-cylinder engine produced frenzied noises when pushed, but performance was reasonably brisk considering the carrying capacity. Simple 4wd system, but the Justy had no off-road aspirations. The electronically-controlled stepless automatic transmission made rival systems seem slightly basic.

1600/1800. 1980-89 (prod: 3,749,817). 3/4/5-door 4/5-seater hatchback/saloon/coupé/estate. F/F or F/4×4, 1595/1781cc (HO4 OC). Max speed 115mph, 0-60mph 8.9sec. With the flat-four water-cooled 'boxer' engines the common theme, Subaru played every possible mechanical combination.

Smaller 1.6 outputs ranged from 69bhp to 74bhp, but 1.8 varied from 89bhp in carburettor form to 136bhp with turbocharger. Four-wheel drive systems ranged from the simple 'add-on' rear-drive to full-time layouts. Confusing range, but practical, sensible load carriers.

XT COUPE. 1985-90 (prod: 98,911). 2-door 2-seater coupé. F/4×4, 1781cc (HO4 OC) Max speed 119mph, 0-60mph 8.7sec. Just where this styling aberration was meant to fit into the otherwise sensible Subaru line-up is hard to see. Initially with part-time 4wd system, the XT later had more power, 136bhp instead of 134bhp, plus full-time all-wheel drive. Performance was there, but flexibility spoiled by turbo lag. The 'Thunderbirds' interior was an exercise in bad taste, littered with gimmicks, and with poor seats and lurid upholstery. A Subaru to forget.

LEGACY. 1989 to date (prod: 476,980). 4/5-door 5-seater saloon/estate. F/4×4, 1820/1994cc (HO4 OC). Max speed 137mph, 0-60mph 6.4sec. There are not too many motoring conditions which this range cannot cope with. Same flat-four boxer engine layout, but with outstanding dual-range 4wd system that gives sure-footed handling in the worst conditions, plus motorway mile-eating ability. Estates the most practical, with top versions having self-levelling air suspension. Fearsomely quick and thirsty 197bhp turbo versions do not have dual-range facility, but do win rallies.

SUZUKI (J)

Motorcycles were the foundation on which Suzuki built up its four-wheel business. Although car production began 64 years ago, UK sales did not start until the late 1970s. Early cars leaned a great deal on motorcycle engine technology. With a classic piece of niche marketing, Suzuki virtually created the market for small four-wheel drive 'leisure' off-roaders.

SC 100. 1979-82 (prod: 894,000). 2-door 4-seater coupé. R/R, 970cc (S4 OC). Max speed 76mph, 0-60mph 16.4sec. One of the first generation Japanese micro cars, sold domestically as the Fronte, with tiny two- and four-stroke engines. For UK market, larger 1.0 four-stroke slotted between the rear wheels, and produced a frenzied, noisy 47bhp. Neat handling but harsh ride. Rust was a serious problem – and it helped if rear seat passengers did not suffer from claustrophobia.

ALTO. 1981-92 (prod: 743,500). 4/5-door 4-seater saloon/hatchback. F/F, 793cc (S3 OC). Max speed 80mph, 0-60mph 20.0sec. Diminutive saloons and hatchbacks, with four doors making access to what little room there was inside that bit easier. The Alto was the top-selling car in Japan in the mid-1980s, but few found homes in the UK. Low gearing helped fussy little transverse three-cylinder engine give some performance, but the two-speed automatic (available from 1986) needed an hourglass rather than a stopwatch to record acceleration – but at just over £4000 it was the smallest and cheapest automatic sold in Britain. Easy to drive, with agile handling, but the ride was on the nervous side.

SWIFT SA 310. 1984-86 (prod: 675,450). 3-door 4-seater hatchback. F/F, 993cc (S3 OC). Max speed 85mph, 0-60mph 15.2sec. Suzuki's first supermini-sized car, 11ft 9in long but still faithful to the three-cylinder concept, this time with 993cc. The engine's note was offbeat, but at least there were now five gears to spread the 50bhp over a wider range. Reasonable handling, but the Japanese still had to learn about ride. GL version had what was then fashionable electronic digital instrumentation. The SA 310 title was dropped in spring 1985.

SWIFT. 1985 to date (prod: 701,000). 3/5-doors 4-seater hatchback. F/F, 993/1324cc (S4 OC), 1298cc (S4 DOC). Max speed 112mph, 0-60mph 8.6sec. A coming of age for the Swift, now finally with four-cylinder engines. The shorter-wheelbase GTi had a 16-valve engine, punching out a rorty 101bhp and performance to match. Rather more sedate were the three-door (dropped in 1986) and five-door versions with GS, GL or GLX trim, 1.0 or 1.3 engine sizes, plus an Executive model with automatic transmission and air conditioning as standard. With just 50bhp under the bonnet, performance was rather less than adequate. Stylish new body arrived in 1989 and 1.0 engine was dropped: GTi remained an engaging hot mini-hatch, while lesser versions with 1.3/67bhp offered decent value for those who required mere transport.

SJ 410/SANTANA. 1982-90 (prod: 104,310). 3-door 4-seater soft and hard top off-roader. F/4×4, 970cc (S4 OC). Max speed 75mph, 0-60mph n/a. Assorted consumer bodies attacked the SJ for being unstable – and proved it by driving them too fast into bends. What else might you expect? Little four-cylinder engines gave just 45bhp, so, with brick-like aerodynamics, performance hardly sparkled. But the image was everything, despite the noise, draughts and rock-hard ride. Off-road abilities were never meant to be in the Land Rover class. From 1987, made in Spain, so beating import quota restrictions.

SJ 413 SAMURAI. 1985 to date (prod: 256,700). 3-door 4-seater soft and hard top off-roader. F/4×4, 1324cc (S4 OC). Max speed 78mph, 0-60mph 16.0sec. Same concept as the SJ 410, but now with a bigger 63bhp engine. Launched as an estate, with soft top arriving in mid-1989. Long wheelbase added in summer 1990. Same basic suspension, with compromised handling and spine-jarring ride, and below-average refinement in town or motorway driving. But now they were starting to achieve almost cult status, with Suzuki marketing graphics packs, alloy wheels, bull-bars and side rails. Another landmark in Suzuki's pioneering efforts to flog off-roaders as fashion accessories.

VITARA. 1988 to date (prod: 350,800). 3-door 4-seater soft and hard top off-roader. F/4×4, 1590cc (S4 OC). Max speed 96mph, 0-60mph 16.0sec. A brilliant piece of marketing by Suzuki, picking up sales from would-be owners of larger, more expensive 'image' off-roaders. All the creature comforts of a hatchback, with power steering and electric windows available as extras, in a good-looking three-door body. The 75bhp engine gave easy high-speed cruising, while 4wd allowed gentle off-road excursions. The long-wheelbase, 16-valve JLX estate did not arrive until 1991.

TALBOT (F/GB)

In 1978, as Chrysler retreated back across the Atlantic from its foray into Europe, buyer Peugeot had a problem - how to badge the existing cars. The solution was found in the Talbot name, which in France was Simca and in the UK part of what had been the Rootes Group, bought in 1967 by Chrysler. Although the name was kept for light commercials, Peugeot gradually discarded it as new models arrived during the 1980s.

AVENGER. 1970-81 (prod: 187,722). 4/5-door 4-seater saloon/estate. F/R, 1295/1598cc (S4 OHV). Max speed 92mph, 0-60mph 14.1sec. By any standards the Avenger was a long-distance runner, starting life wearing Hillman badges, then becoming a Chrysler, and finally a Talbot. Utterly conventional design – pushrod engines, four-speed gearboxes, McPherson struts at the front, live axle at the rear. Performance certainly did not sparkle – and much the same could be said for both ride and handling.

SUNBEAM. 1977-81 (prod: 105,847 inc Chrysler models). 3-door 4-seater hatchback. F/R, 928cc (S4 OC), 1295/1598cc (S4 OHV). Max speed 95mph, 0-60mph 12.9sec. The final twitch from the Rootes Group, and in its way very successful. Three inches were taken out of the Avenger floorpan, which was topped by a neat three-door hatch body with a glassy tailgate. Smallest engine was a large-capacity Imp single overhead cam unit, the others ex-Avenger pushrod units. Built at the ill-fated Linwood plant near Glasgow, which had been specifically created for the Imp.

SUNBEAM 1600TI. 1979-81 (prod: 10,113 inc Chrysler models). 3-door 4-seater hatchback. F/R, 1598cc (S4 OHV). Max speed 107mph, 0-60mph 10.7sec. The shorter wheelbase gave the Sunbeam good handling, so with the 100bhp twin-Weber Avenger Tiger engine, a rather ordinary car was transformed. Distinguished by a deeper chin spoiler, driving lamps, alloy wheels and a further spoiler across the tailgate, it was a fast but somewhat noisy road car, and more than a few rally drivers cut their competition teeth with it.

SUNBEAM-LOTUS. 1979-81 (prod: 2308). 3-door 4-seater hatchback. F/R, 2174cc (S4 DOC). Max speed 121mph, 0-60mph 7.4sec. The 2.2 Lotus twin-cam engine gave 150bhp, still driving the drum-braked live rear axle, but this time through a five-speed ZF 'box with 'dog-leg' first gear. The suspension was lowered and stiffened, with the car riding on wide-tyred alloy wheels. One great advantage was the simple mechanical layout, which made working on it easy. But with more refined if less quick rivals around, sales remained slow – even though Henri Toivonen added kudos by winning the World Rally Championship in one.

ALPINE. 1975-85 (prod: 185,827 in UK). 5-door 5-seater hatchback. F/F, 1294/1442/1592cc (S4 OHV). Max speed 101mph, 0-60mph 12.6sec. Designed by Chrysler in France, badged as a Simca on the continent, but as Chrysler and finally Talbot here. Transverse engine and front-drive layout was first used on Simca 1100 and brought more up to date for the Alpine. The first 'foreign' car to be assembled at the then-ailing Ryton plant. Roomy and rust-prone body, with torsion bar front suspension. Massive understeer and soft ride made handling interesting.

SOLARA. 1982-84 (prod: 98,150). 4-door 5-seater saloon. F/F, 1294/1592cc (S4 OHV). Max speed 93mph, 0-60mph 13.9sec. Playing tunes on the Alpine theme, with this booted four-door saloon version using the same 103in wheelbase but the extra load space adding 3in to overall length. Same engine range, with 1.3 giving 68bhp, while the 1.6, with standard five-speed gearbox or optional three-speed automatic, had 89bhp. Although all 1.6 models except LE had power steering, it did little except disguise the understeer.

MINX/RAPIER. 1984-86 (prod: 27,250). 5-door 5-seater hatchback; 4-door 4-seater saloon. F/F, 1592cc (S4 OHV). Max speed 101mph, 0-60mph 14.6sec. The names were dragged from the Rootes Group files and dusted down to disguise the final two years' production of the Alpine and Solara. Both used the 1.6 engine, with no automatic option. The Rapier ran to remote-control door mirrors, metallic paint and a rev counter – exciting stuff. The Peugeot revolution was just round the corner...

HORIZON. 1977-85 (prod: 51,320 in UK). 5-door 4-seater hatchback. F/F, 1118/1294/1442/1592cc (S4 OHV), 1905cc diesel (S4 OC). Max speed

97mph, 0-60mph 12.3sec. Practical design using the smaller-capacity Alpine front-drive powertrain and suspension layout in a more compact five-door hatchback body, with 2.4in shorter wheelbase. Never sold in the UK with 1.6 petrol or 1.9 diesel engines. Even though the suspension was similar to the Alpine's, the handling was very much crisper. Considered good enough at launch to win 'Car of the Year' award, but dated very quickly. Another model where rust has despatched most to the scrapyard.

RANCHO. 1977-84 (prod: n/a). 3-door 5-seater estate. F/F, 1442cc (S4 OHV). Max speed 89mph, 0-60mph 14.9sec. Beneath that rugged – and mainly glass-fibre – Matra-built bodywork lurked nothing more than what was basically a Simca 1100 floorpan, with the 1.4/80bhp engine driving just the front wheels. Even with knobbly tyres and increased ground clearance, off-road abilities did not match the looks – as several owners found to their cost! But with today's boom in 'off-roaders', the Rancho suddenly looks like it was years ahead of its time.

TAGORA. 1981-84 (prod: 23,400). 4-door 5-seater saloon. F/R, 2165cc (S4 OC), 2664cc (V6 OC). Max speed 106mph, 0-60mph 11.3sec. Designed as an alternative to the hugely successful Peugeot 505, but lack of development and programme rationalisation meant that this ungainly saloon was shelved after just three years. Peugeot 2.2 in-line four and 2.7 V6 engines, with Peugeot transmissions, provided the power. The too-soft ride upset what was basically sound handling. Few and far between in the UK.

SAMBA. 1982-86 (prod: 198,470). 3-door 4-seater hatchback, 2-door 4-seater cabriolet. F/F, 954/1124/1360cc (S4 OHV). Max speed 93mph, 0-60mph 12.5sec. French-style badge-engineering, because the Samba was nothing more than a dressed-up three-door Peugeot 104. Four-bar grille, plain black bumpers and window surrounds, plus rubbing strips, made the difference, although the interior had the same stark 104 appearance. With largest 1360cc/71bhp engine and five-speed gearbox, performance was good and, as befitting a Peugeot, handling was neat.

TOYOTA (GB)

It was in 1965 that Coronas and Corollas started to arrive in the UK, the first proper Japanese car imports. But with its 'pile 'em high, sell 'em cheap' policy, Nissan was ahead in sheer volume by the mid-1970s. Toyota gave the public what it had been waiting for - cars which were sensibly priced, utterly reliable and easy to drive. But while the smaller cars were winners, some of the top-end models showed that Europe could still teach Japan a thing or two.

CARINA. 1977-84 (prod: 1,927,000). 2/4-door 5-seater saloon/estate; 2-door 4-seater coupé. F/R, 1588/1770cc (S4 OHV), 1588cc (S4 DOC). Max speed 94mph, 0-60mph 12.1sec. Conservative to the last, but with a longish front-engined, rear-drive range. Longer 98.5in wheelbase gave more interior space than previous models. Looks were about as adventurous as what lay underneath the ordinary bodies. Neither the twin-cam engine nor the coupé ever went on sale in the UK.

CARINA. 1984-88 (prod: 2,470,000). 4/5-door 5-seater saloon/hatchback. F/F, 1588cc (S4 OHV), 1770cc (S4 OC), 1974cc diesel (S4 OC). Max speed 101mph, 0-60mph 12.6sec. Totally new floorpan to accommodate front-drive, although 98.4in wheelbase was virtually the same as previous model. The 1.6/67bhp overhead valve engine was turned through 90 degrees to sit transversely, while the overhead cam 1.8 petrol and 2.0 diesel were new for the Carina. Conventional saloon was joined by a five-door hatchback, which Toyota called a Liftback. Struts at the front, a well-located dead axle at the rear and front-drive finally put some life into the handling.

CARINA. 1988-92 (prod: 2,617,000). 4/5-door 5-seater saloon/hatchback/estate. F/F, 1587/1988cc (S4 DOC), 1998cc diesel (S4 OC). Max speed 121mph, 0-60mph 8.7sec. Second-generation front-drive Carina, with saloon and hatchback rejoined by useful estate. Mainstream models used advanced 1.6/94bhp twin-cam 16-valve engines, while Executive hatchback – no estate, and saloon did not arrive until 1990 – had 126bhp version. Power steering standard across the range, and part of a generally good equipment list. The next model was to be the built-in-Britain Carina E.

CRESSIDA. 1977-80 (prod: 742,650). 4-door 5-seater saloon/estate; 2-door 5-seater coupé. F/F, 1808/1968cc (S4 OC), 1968cc (S4 DOC), 1988/2563cc (S6 OC). Max speed 106mph, 0-60mph 11.3sec. Replacement for the Corona, which was the very first car Toyota sold in the UK. Mid-Atlantic styling was on 97in wheelbase, with all cars sold in the UK using 2.0/90bhp engine. Suspension was uninspired, with struts at the front, live axle riding on coils at the rear, located by too-short Panhard rod which piled on the understeer. Rust claimed the majority.

CELICA. 1977-82 (prod: 1,399,520). 2/3-door 4-seater coupé/hatchback coupé. F/R, 1599cc (S4 DOC), 1968cc (S4 OC/DOC), 1988/2564cc (S6 OC). Max speed 111mph, 0-60mph 8.8sec. Using the Carina floorpan and, for majority of UK sales, 2.0 engine, the Celica added a sporty element to an otherwise conservative line-up. Long, sloping back and rather cluttered four (rectangular) headlamp grille added to go-faster appearance. Although only a two-door, the Celica had room, at a pinch, for four. Live axle rear end gave typically wayward handling.

CELICA ST/XT. 1983-85 (prod: 1,794,000). 2-door 2+2-seater coupé. F/R, 1972cc (S4 OC). Max speed 109mph, 0-60mph 10.5sec. New looks, with old fastback replaced by neat notchback two-door body on Carina floorpan. But with 2.0 engine giving just 103bhp, performance did not quite live up to looks. After just 12 months, XT replaced the ST, with same power but with new grille, plus covers over pop-up headlamps. Well-equipped, even running to air conditioning.

CELICA GT. 1985-90 (prod: 1,980,000). 3-door 2-seater hatchback coupé. F/F, 1998cc (S4 DOC). Max speed 130mph, 0-60mph 8.3sec. Overnight Toyota got serious about the Celica. Smooth, sweet-revving twin-cam 16-valve 2.0 litre engine put 147bhp very competently through the front wheels. This, plus the outstandingly good looks, superbly balanced handling and taut ride, suddenly set new standards. A few were sold with automatics, so halving enjoyment. Well-equipped too, with original air conditioning being dropped in autumn 1988 in favour of anti-lock brakes.

CELICA CABRIOLET. 1987-88 (prod: 72,500). 2-door 2-seater cabriolet. F/F, 1998cc (S4 DOC). Max speed 130mph, 0-60mph 8.3sec. In what must have been a misguided moment, Toyota gave the go-ahead for the soft-top Celica project from American Sunhood Co. With the hood up, the result looked like a badly-erected tent sitting on the beheaded remains of a gorgeous body. Scuttle shake managed to complete what was a rather unhappy picture. Thankfully, the idea was dropped after 18 months.

CELICA GT-FOUR. 1988-90 (prod: 26,350). 3-door 2-seater hatchback coupé. F/4×4, 1998cc (S4 DOC). Max speed 138mph, 0-60mph 7.7sec. Designed very much with World Rally Championship contention in mind, so a turbo was added to push power to 182bhp, along with full-time 4wd system. Already good handling was bettered with 6in wheel rims and improved aerodynamics. Successful at the job it was designed for, but for many the extra performance and even more memorable handling did not really justify the price hike.

CELICA SUPRA. 1982-85 (prod: 863,700). 3-door 2+2-seater coupé. F/R, 2795cc (S6 OC). Max speed 126mph, 0-60mph 8.1sec. Clean-cut coupé body, very different from smaller Celica, on 102in wheelbase. Fuel injection on 2.8 'six' produced a healthy 168bhp and performance to match. Semi-trailing arm rear suspension, with Panhard rod, kept rear wheels well located to put power onto the road. Well-equipped, although the later – and then-fashionable – electronic facia was a mess.

SUPRA. 1986-93 (prod: 970,000). 3-door 2+2-seater hatchback coupé. F/R, 2954cc (S6 OC). Max speed 136mph, 0-60mph 7.5sec. Classic front-engined, rear-drive layout retained, with fuel-injected 24-valve (but single overhead cam) six-cylinder 3.0 engine developing 201bhp. All-round independent suspension, with anti-lock brakes and power steering, gave easy handling but harsh ride. Equipment endless with power assistance for practically everything. Attractive but bulky shape had great presence.

SUPRA TURBO. 1989-92 (prod: 407,950). 3-door 2+2-seater hatchback coupé. F/R, 2954cc (S6 OC). Max speed 142mph, 0-60mph 6.1sec. With turbocharging boosting power of the 24-valve 3.0 'six' to 234bhp, the Supra qualified for supercar status. Massive torque gave outstanding flexibility, while straight-line acceleration was impressive. Handling, however, was being left behind by rivals such as the Nissan 300ZX and Honda NSX, while over-firm ride was mistaken for sporting character.

STARLET. 1978-84 (prod: 950,691). 3/5-door 4-seater hatchback. F/R, 993/1166/1290cc (S4 OHV). Max speed 83mph, 0-60mph 14.9sec. Compact looks might have said front-drive, but underneath was a front-engined, rear-drive layout. Reliable if rather unambitious overhead valve engines, with 1.3 not coming to UK until 1982, but most with five-speed gearboxes. Neat styling, appealing to undiscerning supermini buyers who wanted something different from run-of-the-mill Metros and Chevettes.

STARLET. 1984-90 (prod: 1,094,900). 3/5-door 4-seater hatchback. F/F, 999cc (S4 OC). Max speed 89mph, 0-60mph 15.3sec. Small cars equal small profits, so, with import restrictions, the new front-drive, transverse-engined Starlet was kept to just a single model in the UK. New 999cc 12-valve engine was aimed more at economy than performance, with light, slick five-speed gearbox. Main attractions were compact size – an inch over 12ft long – and complete ease of driving. Continued essentially unchanged until replaced in 1990 by what seemed to be exactly the same car...

COROLLA. 1980-87 (prod: 4,720,790). 3-door 4-seater hatchback; 4/5-door 4-seater saloon/estate. F/R, 1290/1588cc (S4 OC). Max speed 87mph, 0-60mph 17.6sec. Best-selling model name, although the product was changing rapidly. This was to be the last front-engined, rear-drive version, with saloon and estate using 1.3/59bhp pushrod engine, while the short-lived XE coupé had the 71bhp 1.6. Strut front suspension and well-located live rear axle gave predictable, safe handling, but the car itself was more worthy than remarkable.

COROLLA. 1983-87 (prod: 3,270,000). 3/5-door 4-seater hatchback; 3-door 4-seater coupé; 4-door 4-seater saloon/estate. F/F, 1290/1295cc (S4 OC). Max speed 118mph, 0-60mph 8.9sec. Toyota was one of the last majors to switch its best-selling model to front-drive, although rear-drive estate plodded on until 1987. All front-drive versions were on the same 95.7in wheelbase, with McPherson strut independent suspension front and rear. Engine was 12-valve 1.3/74bhp in 'cooking' models from 1985, while quick GT Liftback had twin-cam 16-valve 1.6 with 119bhp.

COROLLA GT. 1984-87 (prod: 958,760). 2/3-door 4-seater coupé. F/R, 1587cc (S4 DOC). Max speed 120mph, 0-60mph 8.5sec. While mainstream Corollas switched to front-drive, the fierce little GT coupé stayed resolutely with rear-drive. Twin-cam 16-valve 1.6 engine produced 124bhp, with vivid performance. Well-located live rear axle helped put power down to road without too much fuss, making it huge fun to drive. Needed care at the limit, while the ride was jarring. Well-equipped, but overtaken by more refined front-drive hot hatches.

COROLLA. 1987 to date (prod: 4,729,000). 3/5-door 4-seater hatchback; 4-door 4-seater saloon/estate. F/F or F/4×4, 1295cc (S4 OC), 1587cc (S4 DOC). Max speed 119mph, 0-60mph 8.0sec. Well-planned range, with hatchbacks, saloons and estates to span market. Mainstream versions stayed with 1.3/74bhp engine, with 'tamed' 94bhp version of the 16-valve twin-cam 1.6 for the five-door liftback and rare 4wd estate. GTi-16 squeezed 123bhp from the same engine, growing to 129bhp in 1989. Easy to drive and live with, although ride still too firm.

CROWN. 1980-83 (prod: 823,000). 4-door 5-seater saloon. F/R, 2759cc (S6 OC). Max speed 113mph, 0-60mph 10.4sec. Toyota's idea of a luxury car certainly was not Europe's. Massive US influence, even down to perimeter frame chassis. Wishbone front suspension with live axle at the rear, plus boulevard spring and damper settings, led to pudding-like handling. Six-cylinder 2.8 managed 145bhp, driving through a three-speed autobox. At close to 16ft long, it had everything in the way of equipment – including an air-conditioned rear shelf drinks cooler!

TERCEL. 1982-85 (prod: 1,073,720). 3/5-door 4-seater hatchback. F/F, 1295cc (S4 OC). Max speed 94mph, 0-60mph 13.5sec. Just one of Toyota's almost endless variations on the Corolla 95.7in wheelbase theme. Sharp-edged six-light styling, with 1.3/65bhp engine driving front wheels. Strut front suspension, with trailing arms at rear, gave secure handling. Practical enough, but it sat rather unhappily among the high-volume Corolla cars, with no real purpose in life.

TERCEL 4WD. 1983-88 (prod: see above). 5-door, 4-seater estate. F/4×4, 1452cc (S4 OC). Max speed 92mph, 0-60mph 14.9sec. Forerunner of the rugged 'leisure' 4wd off-roaders, and in Japan called the Sprinter Carib. Roomy estate car, with transverse 1.5/70bhp engine giving reasonable performance. A good load carrier, and with the add-in 4wd system the Tercel would keep going right through the worst weather and over fairly rough terrain. New looks early in 1985, with low-ratio transfer box and engine tweaks designed to improve torque. Indifferent dry-road handling, with live rear axle, was typically Toyota, as was the lavish equipment. But this was a generally good 4wd compromise, giving decent on-road refinement.

CAMRY. 1986-91 (prod: 1,002,400). 4-door 5-seater saloon; 5-door 5-seater estate. F/F or F/4×4, 1972cc (S4 OC), 1998cc (S4 DOC), 1839/1974cc turbo diesel (S4 OC). Max speed 114mph, 0-60mph 9.0sec. Toyota was still playing the conservative card in looks, but the engineering was progressing fast. The single-cam 2.0/106bhp engine was replaced in 1987 with a softer 126bhp version of Celica twin-cam 16-valve unit, giving smooth and flexible performance. New were the quickish turbo diesels, with 2.0 giving 83bhp. Chassis much as before, with refined handling, although ride was less so. All models had lavish equipment, with GLi Executive version adding air conditioning and cruise control. Four-wheel drive made a fleeting appearance in mid-1988.

CAMRY. 1983-86 (prod: 1,430,000). 4-door 5-seater saloon. F/F, 1832/1995cc (S4 OC), 1839cc turbo diesel (S4 OC). Max speed 116mph, 0-60mph 10.5sec. Nothing special to look at, with classic three-box saloon body on a 102in wheelbase, which gave reasonable interior room, but this was Toyota's first model to adopt a transverse engine with front-drive. The free-revving, if rather noisy, 1.8/90bhp engine gave surprisingly smart performance. Strut front suspension, with trailing arms and wishbones at the rear added up to predictable, safe handling. Lexus was then nothing more than a twinkle in Toyota's eye, but the build quality was already showing well enough to make the Camry Toyota's second best export model.

CAMRY V6. 1989-91 (prod: 457,900). 4-door 5-seater saloon. F/F, 2507cc (V6 DOC). Max speed 124mph, 0-60mph 9.8sec. The bland shape might not turn many heads, but the transverse 2.5 V6 four-cam 24-valve engine, a remarkably sophisticated unit matched to a silky-smooth four-speed automatic, gave easy, whisper-quiet performance, even if outright urge was a little stilted. Suspension was nothing special – and it showed against the mechanical refinement. With air conditioning, anti-lock brakes, cruise control and latterly leather upholstery, not a lot was lacking – except that the Camry was as anaesthetised in character as in looks. Build quality was outstanding, and Lexus was on the horizon...

MR-2. 1984-89 (prod: 166,104). 2-door, 2-seater sports coupé. M/R, 1587cc (S4 DOC). Max speed 120mph, 0-60mph 7.6sec. M for mid-engine, R for recreational, 2 for the number of seats. Mixed feelings over sharp-edged looks, but none about the way the 1.6/122bhp 16-valve twin-cam engine provided sweet, supple performance. McPherson struts front and rear, plus all-round disc brakes, made handling precise and safe. T-bar roof from autumn 1986. Main problem, despite the well-planned layout, was a shortage of cockpit space. But a great success in the UK.

MR-2. 1989 to date (prod: 189,720). 2-door 2-seater sports coupé. M/R, 1998cc (S4 DOC). Max speed 137mph, 0-60mph 7.6sec. No need to change the formula, but with the new, smoother-looking, lower, longer (by 9in) MR-2, there was now a choice of power. The same basic 2.0 16-valve twin-cam Camry/Celica unit was used, with the base version having 119bhp, the GT 158bhp. Great handling and grip except for sudden breakaway at the limit on early models – but the problem was soon resolved. Luggage space remained minimal, but not many buyers cared.

SPACE CRUISER. 1983-90 (prod: 225,700). 3-door 7-seater people carrier. F/R, 1812/1998cc (S4 OC). Max speed 91mph, 0-60mph 16.2sec. Not much imagination is needed to detect the Space Cruiser's forward control delivery van origins, but it was no conversion – a total reworking, with seating for seven plus reasonable equipment. Initial 1.8/75bhp replaced by 2.0/87bhp version. But no amount of disguise could hide the top-heavy handling and over-soft, pitchy ride. But as kids-to-school transport, unbeatable. The Previa which succeeded it in 1990 was far more radical.

LAND CRUISER. 1978-80 (prod: 173,850). 5-door 6-seater off-roader. F/4×4, 3878/4230cc (S6 OHV). Max speed 84mph, 0-60mph 23.1sec. Not so much an off-roader as a rough-roader. Indestructible separate chassis, with live axles carried on semi-elliptic springs. Relatively short wheel travel meant limited off-road abilities, but it was unbreakable when pounding down unmade roads. Easily maintained six-cylinder petrol engines were as tough as the rest of the car. But a rival to the Land Rover or Range Rover? Not with that on-road handling and ride!

LAND CRUISER. 1981-87 (prod: 198,350). 5-door 5-seater off-roader. F/4×4, 3980cc diesel (S6 OHV). Max speed 95mph, 0-60mph 19.3sec. Rugged as ever, and now with a distinctly mid-Pacific look, with rather too much chromium plating for European eyes. Still with semi-elliptic suspension, but now with 4.0 diesel thumping out 99bhp, increasing to 101bhp just before new model. Off-road abilities still restricted by suspension, while brick-like aerodynamics did nothing to help fuel consumption. Well equipped, but very expensive.

LAND CRUISER. 1987-90 (prod: 272,800). 5-door 5-seater off-roader. F/4×4, 3980cc diesel (S6 OHV). Max speed 87mph, 0-60mph 17.9sec. Gradually the Land Cruiser was being moved upmarket – shiny chromium-plated wheels, electric windows, central locking. With new injection system, power of the 4.0 diesel went a little higher, while a five-speed gearbox helped flexibility. But nothing could conceal that essentially simple – in every sense – chassis. Handling was in the same rugged category. Sold in the UK only as a five-seater estate, but available elsewhere in soft-top, pick-up and van versions – all of which helped it to outsell the Land Rover worldwide. But it was a flop here...

LAND CRUISER II. 1988-92 (prod: 342,190). 3-door 5-seater off-roader. F/4×4, 2446cc diesel (S4 OC). Max speed 81mph, 0-60mph 23.8sec. A move down towards the 'leisure' end of the 4wd market, with short 90in wheelbase and just three doors. There were still live axles below, but now on long-travel coil springs, giving far better off-road abilities, helped by limited slip diff. Turbo diesel 2.5 was smooth, with plenty of low-speed torque, but performance was hardly impressive. Well-equipped, even down to ridiculous gimmicks like an altimeter and turn-and-bank indicator on top of the dashboard! Better than before, but still no Land Rover.

TRIUMPH (GB)

After going into receivership in 1939, Triumph was bought by Standard in 1944. Nine years on came the hugely successful TR series, to be followed by the Herald/Vitesse models, as well as the Spitfire, GT6 and Stag. The big 2000 and 2500 saloons were rivals to Rover's 2000/3500 models. During the 1960s, Triumph was swallowed by Leyland, which became British Leyland in 1968.

DOLOMITE 1300/1500/1500HL. 1976-80 (prod: 75,286). 4-door 4-seater saloon. F/R, 1296/1493cc (S4 OHV). Max speed 89mph, 0-60mph 13.8sec. After the technically innovative front-drive 1500, Triumph backed down to produce the utterly conventional 1300/1500. Based on the rear-drive Toledo, but now with four doors, better trim and wider wheels. The 1300 and base 1500 stayed with piggy rectangular headlamps, while the twin-carb HL rated a new four headlamp front, with better instruments and improved performance. The engines were straightforward overhead valve units, with four-speed transmissions.

DOLOMITE 11850. 1976-88 (prod: 79,010). 4-door 4-seater saloon. F/R, 1854cc (S4 OC). Max speed 103mph, 0-60mph 10.9sec. If most of the 1850 had come from the Triumph parts store, at least the engine was new. The slanted four-cylinder unit, with a single overhead camshaft, was based on the larger unit developed for the Dolomite Sprint, but with just two valves per cylinder and a more modest 91bhp. New too was the all-synchromesh gearbox, with overdrive an option. The 1500 body was used, with a Toledo/1500 floorpan, with the four-headlamp grille and vinyl-trimmed C-posts. A comfortable, well-balanced car which thankfully had been throughly sorted before production started.

DOLOMITE SPRINT. 1973-80 (prod: 22,941). 4-door 4-seater saloon. F/R, 1998cc (S4 OC). Max speed 115mph, 0-60mph 8.7sec. At a time when four valves per cylinder were still spoken of in awe, Triumph developed a new cylinder head for the enlarged 1850 engine, with all 16 valves working from a single camshaft. With twin carbs, the result was a lively 127bhp. With a stronger overdrive gearbox, but still keeping the live rear axle (but with stiffened suspension, alloy wheels and wider tyres), the Sprint could show a clean pair of tail lights to many rivals. Despite some racing successes, the rather simple chassis was starting to be pushed its limits. The 2.0 16V engine never officially made it into the TR7, much to the disappointment of loyal Triumph followers.

SPITFIRE 1500. 1970-80 (prod: 95,829). 2-door 2-seater convertible. F/R, 1493cc (S4 OHV). Max speed 101mph, 0-60mph 10.1sec. Last of the line for the separate-chassis Triumphs, now with the 71bhp version of the 1.5 overhead valve engine, with the option of an overdrive on the four-speed gearbox. The revised rear suspension, dating back to the Herald/Vitesse era, tamed the rather wayward handling of the original, but performance was not exactly in line with the sporty looks.

TR7. 1975-81 (prod: 112,368 all models). 2-door 2-seater sports coupé. F/R, 1998cc (S4 OC). Max speed 110mph, 0-60mph 9.1sec. After the rorty, fuel-injected TR6, the awkward-looking, underpowered TR7 was hardly a worthy successor. McPherson struts at the front and live axle behind gave reasonable handling, but the slant-four 2.0 version of the overhead-cam engine designed for the Dolomite managed just 105bhp. A version with the 16-valve Dolomite Sprint engine, which buyers clamoured for, never materialised. Build quality problems had just about been solved when the TR7 was dropped.

TR7 CONVERTIBLE. 1979-81 (prod: see above). 2-door 2-seater convertible. F/R, 1998cc (S4 OC). Max speed 110mph, 0-60mph 9.1sec. Too late to do much for the TR7's reputation, the open version arrived in 1979, along with a standard five-speed gearbox, previously an option. With the hood down, the TR7 convertible managed to look far better than the quirkily-styled tin-top. Unfortunately, hoods seemed to last even less well than the rest of the car.

TR8. 1980-81 (prod: 2497). 2-door 2-seater coupé/convertible. F/R, 3528cc (V8 OHV). Max speed 135mph, 0-60mph 8.5sec. Just a few genuine right-hand drive TR8s survive, with virtually all production heading across the Atlantic. This was what the TR7 should have been from day one, with the 3.5 Rover V8 engine, developing 133bhp even in US de-toxed form, providing much-needed punch. Power steering was standard and automatic an option, while the main chassis shortcoming was in the braking. Many TR7s were re-engined to become phoney TR8s, so beware.

ACCLAIM. 1981-84 (prod: n/a). 4-door 5-seater saloon. F/F, 1335cc (S4 OC). Max speed 97mph, 0-60mph 11.7sec. With the Rover 200 still three years away and Dolomite sales sliding, desperate measures were called for. The quick answer was for the Honda Ballade to be assembled in what was originally a 'box of bits' operation in the UK, and called the Triumph Acclaim. If the styling was a little dated, the public quickly came to appreciate the lively 70bhp overhead-cam engine and slick(ish) five-speed gearbox. And there was something new from BL – build quality and reliability. With hindsight, a landmark as the start of a fruitful relationship between Honda and BL/ARG/Rover.

TVR (GB)

Among the smaller makers, Blackpool-based TVR ploughs it own unique furrow. Development costs kept down by sticking to a straightforward tubular chassis and, until more recently, closed two-seater coupé styling in glass-fibre which got round body rigidity problems. Increasingly bigger engines and more power, plus unyielding suspension, put later cars in the heroic category.

TASMIN. 1980-84 (prod: n/a). 2-door 2-seater coupé; 2-door 2+2-seater coupé/convertible. F/R, 1993cc (S4 OHV), 2792cc (V6 OHV), 3528cc (V8 OHV). Max speed 130mph, 0-60mph 6.3sec. TVR finally dropped its familiar, curvy 'Grantura' look which its cars had followed since the 1950s, adopting a wedge style penned by Oliver Winterbottom, who was responsible for the similar-looking 1970s Lotus Elite/Eclat. But the new Tasmin retained the previous M-series chassis, extended by 4in, with independent rear suspension, using Jaguar parts. Launched as a two-seater coupé, joined in 1981 by a 2+2 coupé and convertible. Ford 2.8 V6 power at first, then Ford 2.0 'four' and, after take-over by Peter Wheeler, Rover 3.5 V8.

280i. 1984-87 (prod: n/a). 2-door 2-seater coupé/convertible. F/R, 2792cc (V6 OHV). Max speed 128mph, 0-60mph 7.8sec. Although the

Tasmin name was dropped, the model range went on essentially as before. The 280i stayed with Ford V6 power and the rugged tubular backbone chassis clad in good-looking glass-fibre bodywork, with big, faired-in, retractable headlamps and a neat front spoiler. Handling was basically good, even if its oversteer tendencies could approach the 'white-knuckle' stage at times.

350i/390i. 1984-89 (prod: n/a). 2-door 2-seater convertible/coupé. F/R, 3528/3943cc (V8 OHV). Max speed 143mph, 0-60mph 5.7sec. TVR dropped the Ford V6 engine in 1987, settling exclusively for the Rover V8 power that had been introduced three years earlier. With its light-alloy block, the V8 was not only lighter, but also had far more scope for capacity expansion. The first move was from 3.5/190bhp to 3.9/268bhp. Five-speed Rover gearboxes were normally used, although a few cars were built with three-speed automatics. TVR's muscular image was growing fast.

400/420/450SEAC. 1986-91 (prod: n/a). 2-door 2-seater convertible. F/R, 3943/4228/4441cc (V8 OHV). Max speed 155mph, 0-60mph 4.5sec. The capacity of the Rover V8 engine appeared to be infinitely elastic, with TVR pushing it through the 4.0 mark to 4.2 and then 4.4. To exploit this extra power, the SEAC was created. The initials were for Special Equipment Aramid Composite, which indicated that both carbon-fibre and Kevlar were being used in the body. The result? The fastest TVR yet, with Countach-rivalling acceleration.

400/450SE. 1988-91 (prod: n/a). 2-door 2-seater convertible. F/R, 3943/4441cc (V8 OHV). Max speed 155mph, 0-60mph 4.7sec. The 'standard' range was revised to the new-look 400SE and 450SE models, which had a deeper front spoiler (with driving lamps) and prominent side skirts. The 3943cc engine was still giving 268bhp while the 4441cc unit – should the car have been called the 440SE? – ran at 319bhp, with performance and heroic handling to match.

S/S2/S3. 1986-92 (prod: n/a). 2-door 2-seater convertible. F/R, 2792/2922cc (V6 OHV). Max speed 141mph, 0-60mph 6.8sec. With the 400 range putting TVR ownership beyond many pockets, the retro-look S was created to fill the gap lower down the market. The chassis was based on the Tasmin's, but with trailing arm rear suspension. The 2.8 Ford V6 and transmission provided plenty of reliable power, with the new 2.9 going into the S2 in 1988. The S3, with longer doors and a slightly changed front, came in 1990. This was very much a driver's car, with wonderful performance and rewarding – and unforgettable – handling. The car which made TVR, uniquely in the UK, a recession-beating manufacturer, with escalating sales through the early 1990s.

TUSCAN. 1988-92 (prod: n/a). 2-door 2-seater convertible. F/R, 4441cc (V8 OHV). Max speed 165mph, 0-60mph 3.7sec. The original plan was for the Tuscan to be a road car, but in the end TVR decided that it should be used for racing only, so no Type Approval was obtained. That did not prevent, however, some appearing on the road. Same tubular chassis, but this time with double wishbone suspension front and rear, and the 4.4 V8 pumping out over 400bhp. The race series produced some memorable and sensational driving. From these roots grew the sensational Griffith of the early 1990s.

VANDEN PLAS (GB)

Once a well-known coachbuilder (many 'WO' Bentleys wore VDP bodies), the company became part of BMC during the late 1950s. The name was used as a marque in its own right from the 1960s to distinguish up-market versions of very ordinary cars, with leather, thick carpets and some veneer hopefully transforming mundane models like the Allegro. Sights were later lowered, when VDP was simply used to define the top trim level.

PRINCESS 1500/1750. 1977-80 (prod: 11,842). 4-door 4-seater saloon. F/F, 1485/1748cc (S4 OC). No one could ever call the Allegro graceful, but what BL did to it in the cause of boosting sales was little short of cruel. The inflated bonnet and out-of-proportion VDP grille did nothing for the dumpy lines. Nor could leather, quality carpets and walnut conceal the fact that underneath the Princess was nothing more than an Allegro. All were powered by E-series Maxi engines, with five-speed gearboxes. In the final months, production was moved from London to the doomed MG plant at Abingdon.

VAUXHALL (GB)

Absorbed into General Motors in 1925, Vauxhall pursued its own design line until the 1970s, when ideas seemed to stagnate. Over the next few years, Vauxhall came to depend more and more on designs from Opel, a branch of the family it had for so long ignored. The Astra (*née* Kadett) of 1980 was the start of Vauxhall's move from classic longitudinal-engined, rear-drive layouts to modern transverse-engined front-drive thinking.

CHEVETTE. 1975-84 (prod: 415,608). 2/3/4/5-door 4-seater saloon/hatchback/estate. F/R, 1256cc (S4 OHV). Max speed 92mph, 0-60mph 14.5sec. As Detroit started to hand over European design and engineering to Opel, the Chevette became a final fling for Vauxhall. Into what was a topped-and-tailed Opel Kadett went the Viva 1.3 engine and four-speed gearbox, driving to a Kadett torque tube rear axle layout. The result was surprisingly capable, with reasonable performance, good economy and sound handling.

CHEVETTE HSR. 1979-80 (prod: 50). 3-door 4-seater hatchback. F/R, 2279cc (S4 DOC). Max speed n/a, 0-60mph n/a. Fierce, rackety and successful 'evolution' development of the 500-off HS. Vauxhall-developed 16-valve twin-cam head on 2.3 VX4/90 bottom end finally produced 150bhp. With Getrag five-speed gearbox and twin-plate clutch, plus properly-located rear axle and wider wheels, the HSR became a rough, tough rally winner and an exciting road car.

CAVALIER. 1975-81 (prod: 238,980 all types). 2/4-door 5-seater saloon. F/R, 1256/1584/1897/1979cc (S4 OHV). Max speed 111mph, 0-60mph 9.2sec. Faced with soaring Cortina sales, Vauxhall's FE range was fading fast, so the unheard-of front-engined, rear-drive Opel Ascona was given a smooth new nose, Vauxhall badges and a new name – Cavalier. Until FE production was finally wound down at Luton, the new model was built at GM's Antwerp plant. Viva-engined version was added to Opel's cam-in-head range in 1977. If not hugely exciting to drive, they at least provided Vauxhall dealers with something for the fleet managers.

CAVALIER GLS/SPORTHATCH. 1975-81 (prod: see above). 2/3-door 4-seater coupé/hatchback. F/R, 1584/1897/1979cc (S4 OHV). Max speed 109mph, 0-60mph 10.4sec. Straight-forward badge engineering job on the Opel Manta. Initially marketed as a notchback coupé, with smaller cam-in-head Opel engines. The hatchback 2.0 Sporthatch, the best of the range, was launched in 1978. It scored heavily over the Ford Capri, with a better image, more room and nicer handling.

CARLTON. 1978-86 (prod: 80,000). 4/5-door 5-seater saloon/estate. F/R, 1979/2197cc (S4 OHV), 1796cc (S4 OC), 2260cc diesel (S4 OC). Max speed 108mph, 0-60mph 11.2sec. Another piece of essential badge-engineering, this time the Opel Rekord becoming the Vauxhall replacement for the Luton-designed fading stars, the VX1800 and 2300. Utterly conventional, with diesel 2.3 and Family II 1.8 engine added in 1983, the 2.2 a couple of years later. In the hard-fought Granada class, never quite a major challenger. Stodgy, but worthy.

ROYALE SALOON/COUPÉ. 1978-82 (prod: 7119). 4-door 5-seater saloon; 3-door 5-seater coupé. F/R, 2784/2986cc (S6 OHV). Max speed 115mph, 0-60mph 12.1sec. Personality problems were about to afflict the new big Vauxhalls. Once more the stock of Griffin badges was raided, this time to stick on Royale versions of Opel's Senator saloon and Monza coupé. Later they were to become Opels – and then Vauxhalls once more. Fuel-injected 180bhp 3.0 engine came in 1980. All-round independent suspension gave fine handling, while equipment levels improved further with time.

ASTRA MKI. 1980-84 (prod: 1,117,662). 3/5-door 4-seater hatchback/estate. F/F, 1297/1598/1796cc (S4 OC), 1598cc diesel (S4 OC). Max speed

110mph, 0-60mph 9.8sec. Luton finally surrendered all design to Opel, with the new model initially being sold in the UK as a Kadett until Chevette production could be run out. First front-drive design, in neat, sharp-edged hatchback and estate bodies. All-new Family-series single overhead cam engines made most rivals seem very dated, and gave lively performance. The diesel followed on VW's heels for response and economy. Neat, agile handling and firm ride gave a whole new look to the Vauxhall image.

ASTRA MKII. 1984-91 (prod: see above). 3/5-door 4-seater hatchback/estate. F/F, 1196cc (S4 OHV), 1297/1389/1598/1796cc (S4 OC), 1598/1699cc diesel (S4 OC). Max speed 123mph, 0-60mph 8.6sec. After the clean-cut shape of the original Astra, the swooping, curved lines of the second took time to accept. Chassis was revised, rather than transformed, with McPherson struts at the front, torsion beam axle at the rear. The 1.3 engine was replaced by 1.4 in 1989, with same power (75bhp) but better torque. GTE went from 1.8/112bhp to 2.0/124bhp in spring 1987. Lines may have been aerodynamic, but the high tail made the interior gloomy.

ASTRA GTE 16V. 1988-91 (prod: see above). 3-door 4-seater hatchback. F/F, 1998cc (S4 DOC). Max speed 134mph, 0-60mph 7.7sec. With a new double overhead cam cylinder head and four valves per cylinder, power of the 2.0 injection engine was pushed to 156bhp. With the slippery body shape, the 134mph maximum made this the fastest of all the hot hatches. Power steering was standard, but both handling and ride were never in the same class as the performance. However, the 16V GTE became a much sought-after prize among fleet users.

ASTRA CONVERTIBLE. 1987-91 (prod: 6764). 2-door 4-seater convertible. F/F, 1586/1998cc (S4 OC). Max speed 120mph, 0-60mph 8.8sec. The soft-top version was planned at the hatchback's drawing board stage, so the execution was neat. Semi-complete two-door 1.6/82bhp and 2.0/115bhp hatchbacks were sent to Italian coachbuilder Bertone for conversion, with ready-for-sale cars being returned, 2.0 versions being available with power hoods and electric front windows. Clever stiffening across bulkheads and along sills resulted in a rigid, shake-free shell. One of the best-looking soft-tops, although the handling was not improved.

BELMONT. 1986-91 (prod: see above). 4-door 4-seater saloon. F/F, 1297/1389/1598/1796cc (S4 OC), 1598/1699cc diesels (S4 OC). Max speed 124mph, 0-60mph 9.0sec. 'It's not just a booted Astra' was the party line at the beginning, but by the time the end was in sight the struggling Belmont had been renamed the Astra Belmont. The same petrol engine range up to 1.8/112bhp as the hatchback, and the diesels too. What the powerful versions had in performance they lacked in appeal, with roomy boot sitting unhappily on the otherwise aerodynamic lines. From day one, the Belmont was somehow an old man's car. Lower window line at rear gave rear seat passengers more light than in the Astra, but little more space.

NOVA. 1983-92 (prod: 446,462). 2/4-door 4-seater saloon, 3/5-door 4-seater hatchback. F/F, 993cc (S4 OHV), 1196/1297/1389/1598cc (S4 OC). Max speed 114mph, 0-60mph 9.1sec. Like Ford with the Fiesta seven years earlier, GM Europe broke new ground with its new supermini being built in Spain. Known in the rest of Europe as the Opel Corsa, but badged as the Nova in the UK. Pushrod 1.0/45bhp engine was carried over from the rear-drive Kadett, but remainder were all Family I/II overhead cam units. Quickest was the 1.6/100bhp GTE, but it was never sparkling. Dull looks and handling, while interiors were hardly award winners.

CAVALIER. 1981-89 (prod: 806,359). 4/5-door 5-seater saloon/hatchback. F/F, 1297/1598/1796/1998cc (S4 OC), 1598cc diesel (S4 OC). Max speed 110mph, 0-60mph 8.7sec. GM got the drop on Ford, with the new front-drive Cavalier launched just months ahead of the Sierra. Unlike the Ford, available as saloon or hatchback from the start. Family I and II engines initially with complex Varajet II carburettor, injection coming in 1985 with 1.8/115bhp models. MacPherson strut front suspension with torsion beam at the rear meant good handling, with only the well-equipped CDi getting power steering as standard.

CAVALIER SRi 130. 1987-88 (prod: see above). 4/5-door 5-seater saloon/hatchback. F/F, 1998cc (S4 OC). Max speed 120mph, 0-60mph 8.7sec. Top Cavalier power output until this model had been the 2.0/115bhp version of the Family II engine. With different camshaft and revised engine management, power for the 2.0i SRi 130 was lifted to 130bhp, backed by a close-ratio gearbox, with no auto option. Modified suspension and deeper front spoiler helped high-speed handling, although it still was not that great.

CAVALIER ESTATE. 1983-88 (prod: see above). 5-door 5-seater estate. F/F, 1598cc (S4 OC), 1598cc diesel (S4 OC). Max speed 103mph, 0-60mph 10.9sec. Two years after launch, Vauxhall rather tentatively unveiled the estate. But this was an Australian rather than European production, and limited to just the 1.6 90bhp petrol and 54bhp diesel engines. Same 101in wheelbase as rest of range, but 2in longer overall. Clever sheer-faced tail design incorporated a deflector across the top to keep the glass clear, and the bumper was integral with the tailgate to give a very low sill. The estate was not carried over to the new Cavalier range.

CAVALIER CONVERTIBLE. 1986-88 (prod: 1265). 2-door 4-seater convertible. F/F, 1796cc (S4 OC). Max speed 114mph, 0-60mph 9.3sec. By now planning for the new Cavalier was well under way, but GM wanted to cash in on the booming demand for soft-tops. German coachbuilders Hammond and Thiede were commissioned to carry out conversions on the two-door saloon, which had never been sold as a Vauxhall model. Only made with the 1.8/115bhp injection engine. Hood folded into a structural box behind the rear seat, in turn cutting down boot space.

CAVALIER. 1988 to date (prod: 642,866). 4/5-door 5-seater saloon/hatchback. F/F, 1389/1598/1796/ 1998cc (S4 OC), 1699cc diesel (S4 OC). Max speed 128mph, 0-60mph 9.5sec. With such an excellent engine range, the designers were able to make the new Cavalier even better. Five-speed gearboxes became standard, plus option of new four-speed auto. No major change in size, but appeal was widened with more high-performance versions. Although there were no major chassis changes, handling was improved – but it still did not sparkle.

CAVALIER 4WD. 1988 to date (prod: 6022). 4-door 5-seater saloon. F/4×4, 1998cc (S4 OC). Max speed 123mph, 0-60mph 8.6sec. The 4wd system used in the production cars had little to do with that developed for the rally Kadett. New semi-trailing arm rear suspension had to be developed, as well as a revised boot floor pressing to accommodate the rear differential. Front-to-rear torque split was adjusted using a viscous coupling. Made in only limited numbers and only as a saloon, and, unusually, in just the basic L trim at first.

CAVALIER 16V. 1989 to date (prod: 11,054). 4-door 5-seater saloon. F/F or F/4×4, 1998cc (S4 DOC). Max speed 137mph, 0-60mph 7.5sec. This is where the four-wheel drive system really paid off, because putting all 150bhp through the front wheels alone meant furious wheelspin. Despite the lower look, alloy wheels and undoubted performance, the 16-valve Cavalier never achieved the status of Ford's Cosworth models – but the deadlock security system improved the chances of it remaining where you parked it.

CALIBRA. 1989 to date (prod: 24,385). 2-door 4-seater coupé. F/F, 1998cc (S4 OC). Max speed 127mph, 0-60mph 10.0sec. Brilliant marketing move, with the rather ordinary Cavalier chassis and 2.0/115bhp engine given a head-turning coupé body. A major bonus was that four people really could be accommodated and there was reasonable space for luggage. The pity was that the rather ordinary handling and dull ride, plus mediocre performance, did not quite match the sensational looks. However, Vauxhall had the 150bhp 16V, 201bhp 4wd turbo and eventually 170bhp V6 versions hiding round the back for the 1990s.

CARLTON. 1986-94 (prod: 241,051). 4/5-door 5-seater saloon/estate. F/R, 1796/1998cc (S4 OC), 2594/2969cc (S6 OC), 2260cc diesel (S4 OC). Max speed 129mph, 0-60mph 10.5sec. Known in the rest of Europe as the Opel Rekord. Under the rather conservative, but aerodynamic, shape was an eminently sensible car. The 1.8/90bhp carburettor engine gave moderate performance, improved with the 115bhp injection version. The big cam-in-head sixes continued, the Dual Ram 2.5 version giving 150bhp. Diesel power was limited to the basic 2.3/73bhp unit during the 1980s, the 100bhp turbo version not arriving until 1991. If the looks were not that arresting, the fine rear-drive handling was another matter.

CARLTON GSI 3000 24V. 1987-94 (prod: 1463). 4/5-door 5-seater saloon/estate. F/R, 2969cc (S6 OC). Max speed 147mph, 0-60mph 6.3sec. The 12-valve 177bhp version of the GSi was a surprising Carlton model, so the 204bhp 24-valve version was amazing, especially in that rather bland body. With wider wheels and revised spring/damper settings, the chassis proved easily able to handle the extra power, making this a driver's car *par excellence.* The four-speed automatic option simply added refinement. At the price the equipment spec had to be the best around. Something of a wolf in sheep's clothing, with abilities close to those of the lauded BMW M5. Diamond estate version sold only 90.

LOTUS CARLTON. 1980-92 (prod: 440). 4-door 5-seater saloon. F/R, 3615cc (S6 DOC). Max speed 175mph, 0-60mph 5.2sec. Having acquired Lotus, GM seemed duty-bound to do something with its special abilities. With a new twin-cam cylinder head, capacity raised to 3.6 and boosted with twin intercooled turbos, power was pushed to an awesome 377bhp. Suspension and massive brakes were straight from the race track, as was the six-speed gearbox – and even the looks suggested automotive use of steroids. At launch, busybody hands were thrown up in horror when the 175mph top speed was revealed. But in practice, it was a delight to drive, with outstandingly safe, accurate handling – but the recession scuppered hopes of an immediate sell-out. Likely to go down in history as the fastest road-going five-seater ever made.

SENATOR. 1984-87 (prod: 33125). 4-door 5-seater saloon. F/R, 2490/2968cc (S6 OC). Max speed 128mph, 0-60mph 8.8sec. There was a hiatus while marketing departments made up their minds. Until autumn 1984, the new Senator wore Opel badges, but from that date became a Vauxhall, although it was never built in the UK. A real – and better – Granada rival, with a roomy saloon body, independent suspension (struts at the front, trailing arms at the rear), and either the 140bhp 2.5 or 180bhp 3.0 cam-in-head engines. Excellent handling and nice ride – but many succumbed to rust too early.

SENATOR. 1987-93 (prod: see above). 4-door 5-seater saloon. F/R, 2490/2969cc (S6 OC). Max speed 143mph, 0-60mph 8.3sec. Despite being based on the Carlton, clever cosmetics – with a 'chip-cutter' grille and revised rear end – managed to make the Senator feel a far larger car. The cam-in-head 2.5 and 3.0 engines were kept, joined in late 1987 by a 204bhp 24-valve version of the 3.0. Dual-range four-speed automatic was outstanding, so few were sold with the clunky-change manual 'box. Suspension was similar to the Carlton's, which meant fine handling and good ride. Despite terrific equipment and plush trim, lack of glamour meant that the Senator was never a real BMW rival. But this was an unsung hero: durability to 200,000-plus mileage was proved by extensive police use.

VOLKSWAGEN (D)

Like Ford, the success of Volkswagen depended for almost too long on a single model. The Beetle made VW - and very nearly broke it. Various air-cooled replacements failed to impress buyers, but in 1974 the launch of the Golf ensured the company's future. In Germany VW acquired NSU and Audi, while at the turn of the 1980s/90s it moved further into Europe to take over Seat in Spain and Skoda in Czechoslovakia.

PASSAT. 1973-80 (prod: 1,769,700). 2/3/4/5-door 5-seater saloon/hatchback/estate. F/F, 1297/1470/1588cc (S4 OC), 1470cc diesel (S4 OC). Max speed 103mph, 0-60mph 11.2sec. After various attempts to find successors to the Beetle, Volkswagen finally arrived at the right formula with the Golf – and with the Passat. Plenty of Audi underneath, with north-south water-cooled engine and front-drive, and roomy saloon, hatchback and estate bodies styled by ItalDesign. Smallest-engined version, built mainly as a European tax-beater, was never sold in the UK market. Diesel, based on petrol engine, from 1979.

PASSAT. 1980-88 (prod: 1,978,200). 4/5-door 5-seater saloon/hatchback/estate. F/F, 1595/1781cc (S4 OC), 1921/1994cc (S5 OC), 1599cc diesel (S4 OC). Max speed 105mph, 0-60mph 10.5sec. With Polo and Golf now established at the lower end of the market, VW was able to set its sights rather higher with the new Passat. Bigger than before – estates were close to 15ft long – with engines still north-south. At start of 1983, Audi five-cylinder 1921cc/112bhp carburettor engine was added, replaced in autumn by new larger-capacity 1994cc/115bhp injection version. Turbo version of 54bhp diesel, with 70bhp, arrived in 1985. Secure handling, good ride and superb build quality were hallmarks.

SANTANA. 1983-85 (prod: 193,540). 4-door 5-seater saloon. F/F, 1595/1781cc (S4 OC), 1921/1994cc (S5 OC). Max speed 104mph, 0-60mph 11.0sec. A piece of marketing theory that did not quite work. The MkII Passat was launched in hatchback and estate form only, the saloons wearing Santana badges. But to most people they were just Passat saloons, and at the beginning of 1985 Volkswagen abandoned the pretence of the Santana name and relaunched the models as the Passats.

PASSAT. 1988 to date (prod: 1,988,650). 4/5-door 5-seater saloon/estate. 1781/1984cc (S4 OC), 1588cc diesel (S4 OC). Max speed 128mph, 0-60mph 10.2sec. New, more rounded look, with the popular hatchback version now mysteriously abandoned. And the new transverse engine location meant there was no longer space for the five-cylinder units. Rather 'sensible' image was improved with 16-valve twin-cam 1.8 engine from Golf GTi, with 136bhp. Super-safe handling and good ride – but one result of those good aerodynamics was indifferent ventilation.

GOLF. 1974-83 (prod: 10,000,000 all types). 3/5-door 4-seater hatchback. F/F, 1093/1271/1457/1470/1588cc (S4 OC), 1470/1588cc diesels (S4 OC). Max speed 99mph, 0-60mph 11.4sec. Since the Beetle, VW had been desperately searching for a replacement. Huge sums were invested in the Golf project – and the rest we all know. Transverse, water-cooled engines driving the front wheels, neat and sharply-styled Giugiaro hatchback body, tidy and safe handling – it was a transformation. The small, high-speed diesel, based on the new single-cam petrol engine, started a revolution which was to change the face of motoring.

GOLF CABRIOLET. 1980-93 (prod: 400,871). 3-door 4-seater cabriolet. F/F, 1457/1585/1781cc (S4 OC). Max speed 116mph, 0-60mph 9.1sec. Not content with creating the hot hatch, VW followed by re-introducing the cabriolet. Karmann at Osnabrück, in north-west Germany, engineered and carried out the conversions, initially using the 1.8/112bhp GLi three-door as the basis. Over the next 13 years, and still using the MkI bodyshell, innumerable variations on the cabriolet theme were built – and buyers did not seem to mind the old-fashioned looks, cramped rear seats and awkwardly-folding hood. Eventually replaced in 1993 by MkIII cabriolet.

GOLF GTI. 1975-83 (prod: 600,000). 3/5-door 4-seater hatchback. F/F, 1588/1781cc (S4 OC). Max speed 113mph, 0-60mph 8.9sec. Just who invented the phrase 'hot hatchback' is not recorded, but the car responsible has to be the Golf GTi. With Bosch injection, the 1.6 engine's power was pushed to 110bhp. For the final three months, with the 1.8, power was 112bhp. Above all, the handling was a perfect match for the extra urge, helped by wider alloy wheels and tuned suspension. The black grille, bumpers, rear window surround and wheelarch trims were all that was needed to say GTi.

GOLF II. 1984-91 (prod: 9,790,930 all types). 3/5-door 5-seater hatchback. F/F, 1043/1272/1595/1781cc (S4 OC), 1588cc diesel (S4 OC). Max speed 111mph, 0-60mph 9.8sec. Seven inches longer, a couple of inches wider, but essentially the same eminently practical hatchback. The underpowered 1.1/45bhp base version was quickly dropped. But the rest of the engine range was made even better with hydraulic tappets (no need for adjustment), and electronic ignition from late 1985. The diesel choice was enlivened with turbo version raising power from 54bhp to 70bhp, with later Umwelt (environment) version catalyst-equipped to set a new benchmark in low exhaust emissions. Handling and ride improved in line with the Golf's increased size.

GOLF GTI. 1984-91 (prod: see above). 3/5-door 4-seater hatchback. F/F, 1781cc (S4 OC). Max speed 116mph, 0-60mph 8.7sec. Even with a whole host of GTi rivals, the Golf remained the one everyone was trying to match. Appeal was widened with the five-door from spring 1985. Apart from hydraulic tappet engine, the only changes VW needed to make were in mid-1987, when the wipers (on all models) were finally handed for RHD, the front quarterlights vanished and a new four-bar grille appeared. Even though prices rocketed and alloy wheels became extras, demand for the GTi did not slacken.

GOLF GTI 16V. 1986-91 (prod: see above). 3/5-door 4-seater hatchback. F/F, 1781cc (S4 DOC). Max speed 123mph, 0-60mph 8.0sec. Rather than following the perhaps too-obvious turbocharger route, Volkswagen improved the efficiency of the 1.8 GTi engine with a new cylinder head. Twin camshafts and four valves per cylinder, with revised engine management electronics, produced 139bhp. While the badges on the tailgate might have been impressive, the extra cost and peaky power delivery made the ordinary eight-valve GTi seem a better bet.

GOLF SYNCRO. 1988-91 (prod: n/a, UK sales: 678). 3/5-door 4-seater hatchback. F/4×4, 1781cc (S4 OC). Max speed 111mph, 0-60mph 10.3sec. The four-wheel drive system was developed not so much for sporting use, but to keep those who lived in snow-bound mountain regions moving through the winter – so sales in the UK were few and far between. The 4wd system used a viscous centre diff to split torque front to rear, a 1.8/90bhp engine providing the power. Traction was helped by 6in wheels and low-profile tyres, riding under neat black wheelarch extensions.

GOLF RALLYE G60. 1989 (prod: 9780). 3-door 4-seater hatchback. F/4×4, 1763cc (S4 DOC). Max speed 127mph, 0-60mph 8.7sec. Although Audi had swept the rallying scene with its quattros, Volkswagen took its own high-performance, four-wheel drive route. The Rallye was based on a three-door GTi, with the Syncro 4wd system. But by using the twin-cam, 16-valve head and G-lader supercharging system, power was pumped to 160bhp. Performance was impressive and the handling outstanding, but the Rallye G60 never featured on the rally scene, domestic or international.

SCIROCCO. 1974-82 (prod: 504,200). 3-door 4-seater hatchback coupé. F/F, 1457/1588cc (S4 OC). Max speed 114mph, 0-60mph 8.9sec. It was almost as if VW was scared of success, because the Scirocco was launched a few months before the new Golf. It used the Golf floorpan and powertrain, with neat, attractive coupé body designed by Giugiaro and built by Karmann. The 1.6/110bhp GTi version was made in LHD form only until 1979, when it became the RHD GLi. Handling was every bit as good as the Golf GTi's.

SCIROCCO. 1982-92 (prod: 340,700). 3-door 4-seater hatchback coupé. 1487/1588/1595/1781cc (S4 OC). Max speed 118mph, 0-60mph 8.3sec. A curious loss of direction for Volkswagen. Gone were the original Scirocco's clean-cut lines, and in their place was a bulky, softened look, with an odd split window in the tailgate. It was still based on Golf mechanicals, but both ride and handling were anaesthetised. The GTi, dropped in 1988, managed to retain some performance. The GT, however, did not with just 90bhp. Space, especially in the back, was too restricted for family use. In every way a dull car which soldiered on way past its sell-by date.

POLO. 1975-81 (prod: 768,200). 3-door 4-seater hatchback. F/F, 895/1093/1271cc (S4 OC). Max speed 85mph, 0-60mph 16.0sec. Volkswagen moved in at the supermini end of the market with what was in effect a downsized Golf. Just a single three-door hatchback body, powered by a new range of single-cam engines, with four-speed gearboxes. The 1.3 version was never sold in the UK. All-independent suspension, nice handling, slick styling and fairly roomy, if rather plain, interior gave it huge appeal.

POLO. 1981 to date (prod: 2,490,740). 3-door 4-seater hatchback/coupé. F/F, 895/1043/1272cc (S4 OC). Max speed 95mph, 0-60mph 13.8sec. The larger replacement Polo started life as a hatchback (with the vertical-tailgate looks of a small estate), with the coupé, in turn more like a conventional hatchback, arriving two years later. The 895cc engine was dropped, and, like the rest of the VW transverse engine range, hydraulic tappets were used from autumn 1985. The 1.1/50bhp Formel E (for economy) had three 'normal' gear ratios plus a very tall top – the idea was dropped in 1986. Despite a major facelift in 1990, the age of the design was starting to tell alongside better competitors, against which the Polo looked singularly unexciting.

DERBY. 1977-81 (prod: 303,900). 2-door 4-seater saloon. F/F, 895/1043/1272cc (S4 OC). Max speed 93mph, 0-60mph 13.6sec. Volkswagen was among the first to show that small saloons based on good-looking hatchbacks somehow achieve instant anonymity. Same wheelbase, suspension and engine range as the Polo, but with a huge (for size of car) boot which added a foot to the overall length. Even the name seemed rather unattractive.

CLASSIC. 1981-92 (prod: inc in Polo). 2-door 4-seater saloon. F/F, 1043/1272cc (S4 OC). Max speed 95mph, 0-60mph 13.2sec. Built on the same 91.3in wheelbase as the Polo, but 12.6in longer, the extra metal all in the boot overhang aft of the rear axle line. And again, the same engine and transmission range as the hatchback. The range started to be trimmed towards the end of the decade, and the saloons received a similar face-lift to the Polo in 1990.

JETTA. 1981-84 (prod: 1,700,000). 4-door 4-seater saloon. F/F, 1043/1272/1457/1588cc (S4 OC). Max speed 97mph, 0-60mph 13.0sec. As with the Polo and Derby/Classic relationship, the Jetta was a natural saloon progression from the Golf idea. The huge boot gave more load and passenger carrying ability, although performance was limited with the smaller engines. Same fore/aft dimensions inside, but rather better rear-seat headroom. Styling at the front differed too, with rectangular rather than round headlamps.

JETTA. 1984-92 (prod: 4,390,790). 4-door 4-seater saloon. F/F, 1272/1595/1781cc (S4 OC), 1588cc diesel (S4 OC). Max speed 117mph, 0-60mph 9.0sec. The Golf had bags of image but the Jetta had none – although mechanically they were virtually identical. The extra 12in added weight, which made the Jetta marginally slower than hatchback equivalents. In return you got 23cu ft of boot space, against the Golf's 16.7. The 1.8/112bhp GTi was every bit as good to drive as the Golf, but miles behind when it came to showroom appeal.

JETTA 16V. 1987-91 (prod: see above). 4-door 4-seater saloon. F/F, 1781cc (S4 OC). Max speed 126mph, 0-60mph 7.9sec. Launched shortly after the Golf version, with the same 1.8 engine wearing a new twin-cam 16-valve cylinder head and producing 139bhp. With rather more evenly distributed weight, thanks to boot overhang, experts argued that the handling was marginally better than the hatchback's. Clever used car buyers went for the Jetta 16V, where lack of kudos was reflected in lower prices. But like all its ilk, build quality was unbeatable.

CORRADO. 1989 to date (prod: 459,890). 3-door 4-seater hatchback coupé. F/F, 1781cc (S4 OC). Max speed 140mph, 0-60mph 8.1sec. From the start it was made clear that the Corrado was never intended to be a replacement for the Scirocco – it was far too good for that. The smooth good looks concealed an outstanding chassis which proved itself able to handle more and more power with ease. Launched with the 1.8/136bhp 16-valve twin-cam engine, or 160bhp in supercharged G60 LHD form. But it was Volkswagen's 2.8/190bhp VR6 engine, launched in 1992, which was to prove just how good the Corrado chassis could be.

VOLVO (S)

Although founded in 1926, Volvo was virtually unknown in the UK until the 1960s, when imports of the 122 Amazon started. Until the front-drive 800-series models in the 1990s, the Volvo dictum was one of conservative front-engined, rear-drive engineering. It bought into Daf in 1975 to give it a small-car capacity with the 300 series. Safety has always featured heavily in Volvo's marketing image - along with green wellies and Labrador dogs.

66. 1975-80 (prod: 106,137). 2/3-door 4-seater saloon/estate. F/R, 1108/1289cc (S4 OHV). Max speed 86mph, 0-60mph 17.4sec. With just a few engineering changes and new badges, the Daf 66 almost overnight became the Volvo 66, the immediate result of the Swedish company buying into the Dutch vehicle maker. The Renault engine (1.3/57bhp for the UK) and Variomatic stepless transmission were retained, with de Dion rear suspension geometry. Lack of performance meant that indifferent handling did not matter, while ease of driving gave it pensioner appeal.

240 SALOON. 1978-92 (prod: 1,483,351). 4-door 5-seater saloon. F/R, 1986/2127/2316cc (S4 OC), 2383cc diesel (S4 OC). Max speed 111mph, 0-60mph 9.7sec. The tank-like car which really put Volvo on the motoring map in the UK. Plenty of the previous 140 model was still there, but the overhead-cam engines were new. Power ranged from 2.0/113bhp, through 2.1/107bhp to 2.3/136bhp, the last with injection in the GLT. The later turbocharged 2.3 reached 155bhp. Some versions had a four-speed gearbox with Laycock overdrive. McPherson strut front suspension and live axle at the rear meant utterly predictable handling but less than average ride.

240 ESTATE. 1978-93 (prod: 959,044). 5-door 5-seater estate. F/R, 1986/2127/2316cc (S4 OC), 2383cc diesel (S4 OC). Max speed 114mph, 0-60mph 10.1sec. This was to become one of the most familiar estate shapes of the 1980s, easily outselling all other large-load carriers. Robust build, traditional character and square-back practicality (with near-vertical tailgate) made it the antique dealers' favourite. Engine line-up was the same as the saloon, with the diesel – VW sourced – never available in the UK. Even neglected, they seem to last for ever.

264. 1974-85 (prod: 169,127). 4/5-door 5-seater saloon/estate. F/R, 2664/2849cc (V6 OC). Max speed 111mph, 0-60mph 10.8sec. The thinking seemed right, with the then-new V6 engine (developed with Peugeot and Renault) in the 240 saloon/estate body. But it was too expensive and thirsty. Engine size went up to 2.85/155bhp in 1982, when it was sold in the UK only in estate form. Separate Laycock overdrive was used with the manual four-speed gearbox. The extra engine weight over the front wheels made handling ponderous, despite power steering.

262. 1977-81 (prod: 9951). 2-door 5-seater coupé. F/R, 2664/2864cc (V6 OC). Max speed 120mph, 0-60mph 10.1sec. Volvo's uncompromisingly rugged, angular lines presented Italian coachbuilder Bertone with something of a challenge. The 262 was the unhappy – almost sinister-looking – result, with too-small cabin perched atop a block-like body. But it was quick, with 120mph plus top speed, and the standard of trim was a good example of Bertone's skills. Only a few came to the UK, with the majority heading for the US market.

340/360. 1976-91 (prod: 1,086,405). 3/5-door 4-seater hatchback; 4-door 4-seater saloon. F/R, 1397cc (S4 OHV), 1721/1986cc (S4 OC). Max speed 116mph, 0-60mph 8.9sec. This model had started life on the Daf drawing board, but was overtaken by the Volvo acquisition. The 340 began as a hatchback, with saloon added in 1983. Renault engines again, with 340s having 1.4/70-72bhp, and 1.7/80bhp. The 360s had 2.0 engines in 92-115bhp guise, all matched to five-speed manual gearboxes. De Dion layout at the rear. Worthy successor to the 66, with the same 'old fogey' image, and remarkably popular in the UK – but still one of the dullest cars of the decade.

700. 1984-91 (prod: 1,237,200). 4/5-door 5-seater saloon/estate. F/R, 1986/2316cc (S4 OC), 2849cc (V6 OC), 2383cc diesel (S4 OC). Max speed 120mph, 0-60mph 9.5sec. Short-lived (by Volvo standard) big saloon and estates, with near-vertical rear window and chrome embellishment giving distinctly trans-Atlantic look. Engine range was expanded with 16-valve version of 2.3 with 155bhp, plus turbo version of eight-valve 2.3 with 182bhp. Turbo diesel, with 109bhp, was surprisingly quick. Estates were of stately home size, but the suspension, with McPherson struts at the front and live axle at the rear, was responsible for rather sluggish handling. Restyling in 1987 softened the angular lines and improved the interior. A great success in the UK.

480. 1987 to date (prod: 72,304). 2-door 2+2-seater coupé. F/F, 1721cc (S4 OC). Max speed 122mph, 0-60mph 9.6sec. Staid Volvo revived the P1800 idea with the 480 coupé – and produced its best-looking car. Renault 1.7 engine, with S (102bhp), ES (109bhp) and Turbo (120bhp) versions, driving through the front wheels for the first time. Handling did not quite match the sporting appearance, but it was good enough. Unusual facia design, but the whole interior had a rather gloomy feel. Rumours of a convertible version were repeatedly denied by Volvo and never materialised, despite concept versions appearing at some shows.

440. 1989 to date (prod: 337,240). 4-door 4-seater saloon. F/F, 1721cc (S4 OC). Max speed 122mph, 0-60mph 9.6sec. With the ageing 300-series being pruned back, the 440 was the replacement as a four-door saloon, again built in the Netherlands. Just one engine, the Renault-built 1.7, was used, with power ranging from 90bhp on carburettors to 109bhp with injection, to 120bhp with turbocharging. Non-turbo capacity went to 1794cc in 1991. Basically sound handling, but the design was rapidly overtaken by most European rivals.

WESTFIELD (GB)

It's always dangerous ground when manufacturers sail too close to others' designs, as Westfield found out. Caterham Cars took legal action when the Westfield Seven 'lookalike' of its own Seven appeared in 1984 - and won its case. The Westfield design was altered to satisfy Caterham, but there's no mistaking the origins.

SE. 1988 to date (prod: 350). 2-seater convertible. F/R, 1596cc (S4 OC). Max speed n/a, 0-60mph n/a. In the wake of legal action, Westfield replaced its Seven model with the SE. If the looks were rather similar to Caterham's genuine article, they were sufficiently different not to cause repeated legal problems – and these glass-fibre cars were rather cheaper, invariably sold in component form. A variety of engines could be used, but most were made with the 1.6 Ford overhead-cam unit. The ultimate SE had the Rover V8 shoehorned – just – under its bonnet.

ZASTAVA (YU)

As Yugoslavia tore itself to pieces in the early 1990s, Zastava's future seemed uncertain. The factory, located in Serbia, was part owned by Fiat, for whom it assembled a variety of entry-level models, mainly for sale in Italy, as well as its own Yugo-badged cars. During the late 1980s, A-suffix models were made for the US market, but even rock bottom pricing could not save the project.

45/55/65. 1983-91 (prod: n/a). 3-door 4-seater hatchback. F/F, 903cc (S4 OHV), 1116/1301cc (S4 OC). Max speed 87mph, 0-60mph 15.7sec. Underneath it was pure Fiat 127, complete with the same clattery pushrod engines and single-cam larger ones. Zastava's own three-door hatchback body was hardly memorable, with an over-high hatchback sill and cramped rear seat space. Clumsy 'go faster' body kits did absolutely nothing for what little image these cars had. Bargain-basement pricing reflected the atrocious build quality.

3/4/5 SERIES. 1983-90 (prod: n/a). 3-door 4-seater hatchback. F/F, 1116/1301cc (S4 OC). Max speed 86mph, 0-60mph 13.8sec. Fiat's own 128 was a good car, but by the time Zastava had finished with it, its own mother would not have recognised it. The hatchback grafted onto the back did make it a shade more practical than the original, but not even the pricing could make up for shoddy manufacture. Front-drive handling was predictable enough, but the choppy ride and noisy engines must have made buyers wonder if they had spent their money wisely. They may have been cheap, but depreciation was horrendous.

SANA. 1989-92 (prod: n/a). 5-door 4-seater hatchback. F/F, 1372cc (S4 OC). Max speed 93mph, 0-60mph 15.3sec. On paper it seemed that Zastava had finally got it right. Off-the-shelf ItalDesign body had Tipo overtones, while underneath there was the usual assembly of ageing Fiat components, including engine, gearbox and suspension. In practice, the lack of attention to detail and the way the Sana was put together shattered virtually every illusion buyers might have had.

Picture Acknowledgements

The author and publisher are grateful to all the motor manufacturers who supplied photographs of their models for use in this book. In addition they would like to thank the Haymarket Publishing Motoring Photolibrary, David Hodges and B.J.Priestman of the Crayford Convertible Car Club.